The Unchanging Truth of God?

The Unchanging Truth of God?
Crucial Philosophical Issues for Theology

Thomas G. Guarino

The Catholic University of America Press
Washington, D.C.

Library of Congress Cataloging-in-Publication Data

Names: Guarino, Thomas G., author.
Title: The unchanging truth of God? : crucial philosophical issues for
    theology / Thomas G. Guarino.
Description: Washington, D.C. : The Catholic University of America Press,
    2022. | Includes bibliographical references and index.
Identifiers: LCCN 2021056200 (print) | LCCN 2021056201 (ebook) | ISBN
    9780813234717 (paperback) | ISBN 9780813234724 (ebook)
Subjects: LCSH: Catholic Church and philosophy.
Classification: LCC BX1795.P47 G83 2022 (print) | LCC BX1795.P47 (ebook)
    | DDC 282.01—dc23/eng/20220111
LC record available at https://lccn.loc.gov/2021056200
LC ebook record available at https://lccn.loc.gov/2021056201

Table of Contents

Acknowledgments

I would like to express my gratitude to the many people who have aided the research for this volume. These include the Rev. Dr. Joseph Reilly, dean of the School of Theology of Seton Hall University, for his generous support; Dr. John Buschman, dean of Seton Hall University libraries, for kindly providing a suitable area for research and writing; the faculty and staff of Seton Hall libraries, especially Stella Wilkins, Andrew Brenycz, and Mabel Wong, for their friendly and competent assistance; and, finally, Theresa Miller, for her unfailing help with many book-related tasks.

General Introduction

W hy a book examining the philosophical issues central to theology? Does not theology stand on its own, clearly mediating the truth of divine revelation? And isn't philosophy—at least often enough—an alien counter-narrative, a discordant competitor to theology's claims? Haven't distinguished theologians argued through the centuries that philosophy serves only to deface and deform biblical and theological purity?

In truth, proper philosophical reasoning is essential to theology, supporting in the natural order the intelligibility of the doctrinal claims asserted by the Christian faith. And those claims are considerable. For Catholic teaching insists that it mediates states of affairs that are universally, trans-temporally and trans-culturally true. This robust insistence on the universal and perduring truth of divine revelation entails, by necessity, strong philosophical claims as well—both epistemological and metaphysical—which must themselves be defended.

All of the essays in this volume reflect, from different perspectives, on what it means to speak of truth that is perpetual, universal, and materially identical over time. How, in a postmodern epoch, can we assert such truth, which appears to glide over vast socio-cultural-linguistic differences—to regard them as merely "accidental"—at the very time when contemporary philosophy is celebrating otherness, "*différance*," and the heteromorphous nature of reality?

At issue is the need for Catholic philosophers and theologians to offer a theoretical defense for the doctrinal claims of the Christian faith. Can one defend the *very possibility* of trans-cultural and trans-temporal truth? Can one defend the very possibility of the material continuity of textual meaning (e.g. of the Creed) over time? Can one defend the very possibility of predicating finite names formally and substantially of the infinite Godhead?

It is not enough to insist, as some do, that Scripture and the Church teach clearly on such matters. There must also be a theoretical defense—part of the *intellectus fidei*—so that the legitimate claims of reason are satisfied. It is one thing to say that there exist biblical warrants for perduring truth over time. It is another to ensure that such claims can also be philosophically defended. Precisely for this reason Pope John Paul II insisted in

1

his 1998 encyclical *Fides et ratio*, that theology needs philosophy "to confirm the intelligibility and universal truth of its claims"[1] Catholicism has always looked for philosophical forms that are adequate to the content of the Christian faith. Which kind of philosophy, John Paul II asked, can fulfill the "*officium congruum*" or appropriate office of supporting the truth of divine revelation? In fact, the pope argues that philosophies with a "metaphysical horizon" are essential for theology.[2] He further asserts that "a philosophy which shuns metaphysics would be radically unsuited to the task of mediation in the understanding of Revelation."[3] Why this insistence on some form of metaphysics? Because such philosophies are robustly supportive of the continuity, universality, and material identity of doctrinal claims over time.

Given the clear logic that animates this magisterial endorsement, one might think that theology would welcome those philosophies, particularly metaphysics, which are capable of supporting Christianity's doctrinal claims. But this is often not the case. Such philosophies have been resisted, even strenuously so, in certain sectors of Catholic theology. Why has this been so?

ANTI-METAPHYSICAL THOUGHT

Concerns about philosophical intrusion on divine revelation go back to the ancient world, with deep uneasiness expressed about the intermingling of philosophy and theology in authors such as Tertullian and Jacopone da Todi. This lingering apprehension reached a crescendo in the work of Martin Luther who did not hesitate to say that "Whoever wishes to be a Christian must be intent on silencing the voice of reason."[4] The legitimate evangelical concern of Luther and others is that theology will establish a conceptual basis for faith outside of faith—that is to say, philosophical reasoning will take the place of, or will need to "authorize" biblical claims. This was the basis of Luther's polemic against Pseudo-Dionysius' Platonism and, especially, against Scholastic metaphysics: they allegedly sought to provide

---

1 John Paul II, Encyclical Letter *Fides et ratio* (September 14, 1998), no. 77.

2 *Fides et ratio*, no. 83.

3 *Fides et ratio*, no. 83.

4 Jaroslav Pelikan and Helmut T. Lehmann, eds., *Luther's Works* (St. Louis: Concordia, 1959), vol. 23, 99. A more fully rounded treatment of Luther's thought may be found in the first essay in this volume.

a foundation for theology apart from biblical truth. Luther's fears about philosophy's attempts to colonize and domesticate theology continue to inform a significant strand of Protestant thought. Since I examine several of these authors at length in the first chapter of this volume, I will only discuss here more recent manifestations of anti-metaphysical thinking.

BARTHIAN FIDEISM

Karl Barth, the great Reformed theologian, was deeply concerned about Catholicism's reliance on metaphysics, as is clear from his *Church Dogmatics*. From Barth's perspective, the fight for the purity of biblical truth had to be fought on two fronts. On the one hand, he feared liberal Protestantism—particularly the Schleiermacher-Ritschl-Hermann school of thought—which appeared to sanction theological truth only if it had some palpable touchstone in human experience. On the other hand, he shunned Catholicism, which relied on the metaphysical *analogia entis* and its linguistic correlate, the analogical predication of names to God. Both of these approaches, Barth insisted, sought to justify theological claims on the basis of human insights rather than on the basis of biblical revelation. A general anthropology or philosophy was first developed, only secondarily making room for revealed truth. The result was that historically specific biblical events—God's concrete actions in salvation history—needed to find some foundation in the ahistorical generalities of philosophy. As Barth states it: at issue is "whether there really is an essence-context superior to the essence of the church."[5] Precisely this fear of other contexts or "other faiths" superior to the Gospel gave rise to Barth's well-known sentence, "I regard the *analogia entis* as the invention of the Antichrist, and think that because of it one cannot become Catholic."[6] In other words, metaphysics—an alien religion— was allegedly given pride of place in theological thinking. An "essence-context" had been established that was superior to the Church and so superior to divine revelation itself.

There was a vigorous Catholic response to what was often called Barthian fideism—a response, however, that did not overlook Barth's legitimate concerns. Theologians such as Hans Urs von Balthasar and Henri Bouillard ardently defended the need for metaphysics in theology, but each sought a via media between dogmatic fideism (Barth) and what was regarded as neo-

---

5 Karl Barth, *Church Dogmatics* I/1, trans. G. T. Thomson (Edinburgh: T&T Clark, 1949), 40.
6 Barth, *Church Dogmatics* I/1, x.

Scholastic rationalism. Both theologians agreed with Barth that a certain kind of Catholic theology, eager to answer Enlightenment objections against the very idea of divine revelation, veered towards rationalism in its rejoinder. Under the influence of modernity, neo-scholasticism failed to defend clearly an essential point: the *analogia entis* is always inscribed within the *analogia gratiae* since creation (the root of the ontological bond between God and humanity) is first and foremost grace.

Balthasar and Bouillard further insisted that the Church's invocation of philosophy in general, and metaphysics in particular, takes place only within the *unicus ordo supernaturalis*—the order of grace. At the same time, however, the natural, philosophical order could not be compromised or overthrown since the created estate possessed an inner identity and stability, an inherent structure with its own capacities and power, even "apart" from the further molding that is bestowed by revelation and grace.[7] For this reason, in their reply to Barth's well-known judgment on Anselm's ontological argument—that it was intended to convince only those who already shared Anselm's Christian faith—Bouillard and Balthasar insist that the Reformed theologian was in error. The monk of Bec clearly intended, as he makes clear also in his *Monologion*, to convince unbelievers. Nonetheless, they agree, Barth was correct in insisting that the "full realization of the philosophical act" only takes place in Revelation.[8]

HERMENEUTICS AND POSTMODERN PHILOSOPHY

Barth's dogmatic fideism is only one enemy of metaphysical thinking within theology. A more powerful opponent today—one in hegemony in several quarters of Christian thought—is philosophical hermeneutics.

Under intense pressure from the contemporary emphasis on human historicity, cultural-linguistic specificity, and paradigm-bound rationality, Catholic theology started to question its earlier reliance on metaphysics to support its universal truth-claims. Sensitive to these newly-presenced horizons, historically conscious theologians such as Karl Rahner and Bernard Lonergan increasingly sought to incorporate these dimensions into their theological thinking—although neither abandoned (transcendental) meta-

---

7 The "stability" of the natural order is discussed at length in essay three, "Contemporary Lessons from the *Proslogion*."

8 See Hans Urs von Balthasar, *The Glory of the Lord*, vol. 2, trans. Andrew Louth, et al. (San Francisco: Ignatius Press, 1984), 233.

physics and its attendant characteristics. But it was precisely this preservation of the transcendental subject—regarded by many as little more than a vestigial inheritance from Kant—that was challenged by a number of influential thinkers who argued that transcendental theology, ultimately captive to the metaphysics of modernity, did not adequately deal with the overarching perspectives of socio-cultural-historical particularity.

The true challenge for theological thinking, it has been argued, is to take full account of the ontological and epistemological dimensions unveiled by contemporary philosophy: Heidegger's primordial notion of historicity; Wittgenstein's cultural-linguistic web of experience; Gadamer's *phronēsis*-based rationality; and Habermas' neo-pragmatic communicative theory. Each of these thinkers opposed universal metaphysical systems— the kind of totalizing thinking that ignored and devalued the enveloping horizons of history and culture. The influence of these philosophers—particularly Heidegger's and Gadamer's unrelenting attacks on metaphysical thought—fueled the Catholic turn toward hermeneutics.[9]

Of course, questions about the relationship among history, truth, and Christian doctrine have been pervasive since the Modernist crisis at the turn of the twentieth century. But these questions have become increasingly persistent and unremitting: How does the socio-cultural embeddedness of all thinking affect the claim of doctrine to be universally, trans-culturally, and trans-temporally true? Do not the traditional characteristics associated with doctrine—its perpetuity, universality, and material identity over time—seem naïve given the profound effects of historicity? Are not cultural-linguistic boundaries determinative of all truth-claims, including doctrinal ones?

Martin Heidegger argued that the Western metaphysical tradition from Plato onwards had buried historical thinking in its search for immutable anthropological and cosmological structures—for the underlying architecture of humanity and the world. Following Heidegger's (and Gadamer's) lead, hermeneutical theology, to the contrary, has placed its accent on the historicity constitutive of human life and thought, even insisting that the ascent of hermeneutics has meant the death of metaphysics. As John Caputo has argued, one cannot "freeze the [historical] flux" with *eidos, ousia, esse,*

---

9 Hermeneutical thought can also be called "postmodern" since it calls into question Kantian and Enlightenment thinking. But hermeneutics is best described as "moderate postmodernism," at a remove from more radical thinkers such as Nietzsche, Derrida, and Vattimo. I have discussed the distinction between moderate and "strong" postmodernism in essay four, "Postmodernity and Five Fundamental Theological Issues."

essentia, actualitas, res cogitans, the transcendental ego, or any other foundation. The event character of Being is such that it is given differently in each epoch. The Heideggerian *es gibt* confounds every metaphysical attempt to "outflux the flux."[10]

This kind of anti-metaphysical thinking, characteristic of Heidegger and his philosophical allies, is already visible in the nineteenth century—in Wilhelm Dilthey's *Introduction to the Human Sciences* of 1833. Dilthey argues that, beginning with St. Augustine, a new form of reasoning was initiated. Augustine was less interested in the *logos*-structure of the world (and the participatory metaphysics which it engenders) than in the interior life. Crucial here is Augustine's famous line in the *Soliliquies*, "I wish to know God and the soul." When Reason asks, "nothing more?," Augustine responds, "nothing at all." Just here Dilthey detects a pronounced turn to self-consciousness and subjectivity, with a consequent loss of interest in the very structure of the world as mediative of God's presence.[11]

For Dilthey, the cosmic and metaphysical thinking endemic to Hellenism gradually recedes before the interiority characteristic of Christian life and thought. With its decided accent on the soul's relationship to God, Christian faith corrodes and dissolves metaphysics, a dissolution that results (happily for Dilthey) in the philosophical subjectivism of Immanuel Kant. *Kosmos* and *physis* are no longer significant purveyors of meaning, but rather only human self-consciousness. Given this perspective, it is unsurprising that Dilthey develops an antipodean Hebraic-Hellenic typology that will have a strong influence on Heidegger and on significant sectors (mostly Protestant but Catholic as well) of theological thought. As the young Heidegger writes in 1919, "Epistemological insights, extending as far as the theory of historical knowledge, have made the system of Catholicism problematic and unacceptable to me—but not Christianity and metaphysics (the latter, to be sure, in a new sense)."[12]

Two years later Heidegger gives us a clearer idea of why traditional metaphysics needs to be overcome and destroyed. He argues that the eschatological and apocalyptic language of the Pauline epistles—with their strong

---

10 John D. Caputo, *Radical Hermeneutics* (Bloomington: Indiana University Press, 1987), 257–64.

11 Wilhelm Dilthey, *Introduction to the Human Sciences*, trans. Ramon J. Betanzos (Detroit: Wayne State University Press, 1988), 231–39.

12 Cited by John Caputo, "Heidegger and Theology," in *The Cambridge Companion to Heidegger*, ed. C. Guignon (Cambridge: Cambridge University Press, 1993), 272.

sense of anxiety, judgment, and foreboding—gradually receded in Christian thought before the language of substance and being borrowed from Greek philosophy. Early in the Church's life, Heidegger concludes, the "[truly] Christian understanding is hidden behind a Greek view of reality."[13] Like Dilthey, Heidegger insists that Christian theology steadily turned away from a genuinely scriptural attitude toward the fixed, the immutable, and the substantial. Imported Hellenistic thinking buried the experience of authentic instability and eschatological expectation that boldly characterizes the New Testament. Theology gradually turned toward the "onto-theological"— toward a god who was understood within the parameters of Greek philosophy as *Ipsum Esse Subsistens*.

When he publishes *Being and Time* a few years later, Heidegger drops the explicitly religious language, although his fundamental thesis remains in place. The entire post-Socratic tradition of Western thought has been a "forgetting of Being." Philosophies of substance have led to objectification and reification, confusing one episodic "appearance" of being in history with Being itself. Under pernicious Hellenistic influences, Being is thought of as that which is perduringly ready-at-hand, rather than as that which is irruptive, illuminative, and temporally disclosive.

True philosophical thinking, Heidegger insists, asks about the *origin* of the "episodic appearances" of Being, not about the specific "sendings" that began with Anaximander. Traditional metaphysics, with its accent on essences, on the *actus essendi*, on the *logos*-structure of reality, names only *particular appearances* of being—and is therefore implicated in the forgetfulness of Being itself. This is why Heidegger is convinced that to speak of God as *Ipsum Esse Subsistens* is to name a god before whom one cannot dance or sing, a god of the philosophers, but not the Christian God. It is also why, for Heidegger, theology cannot be considered a primordial discipline—*because it does not think Being*.[14]

Why has this Heideggerian attack on traditional metaphysics—and its turn to deeply historicized thinking—been attractive to significant sectors of Catholic theology? Before answering that question, allow me to add a few words about Hans-Georg Gadamer, the philosopher who, building on

---

13 Martin Heidegger, *The Phenomenology of Religious Life*, trans. Matthias Fritsch and Jennifer Anna Gosetti-Ferencei (Bloomington: Indiana University Press, 2004), 67–82, at 73.

14 See *The Piety of Thinking*, trans. J. Hart and J. Maraldo (Bloomington: Indiana University Press, 1976), 6.

Heidegger's *Abbau* of Western philosophy, became the primary architect of contemporary hermeneutical theory.

Convinced that Heidegger had unmasked the errors within the philosophical tradition, Gadamer applies Heidegger's insights not only to interpretative theory but to the notion of truth itself. For Gadamer, the only truth that is available to us—that is, the only notion that takes full account of the encompassing horizons of history, culture, and language—is *phronēsis* or practical reason that generally follows Aristotle's account in book six of the *Ethics*. While Aristotle speaks of both *epistēmē* and *phronēsis*, Gadamer leaves *epistēmē* aside precisely because it deals with irreversible principles, matters that could not be otherwise. *Epistēmē* must be abandoned, Gadamer insists, because history and finitude have taught us that no such veridical irreversibility exists—or can exist. To assert such irreversibility would be to misunderstand entirely the penetrating and pervasive effects of temporality. *Phronēsis*, on the other hand, deals with *endechomena*: matters that could be otherwise. This is deeply appealing to Gadamer because, in a world profoundly marked by contingency and provisionality, this is the only notion of truth that is ontologically warranted.

This marked accent on contingency is why Gadamer also argues—and this constitutes a centerpiece of his hermeneutical theory—that one cannot make the traditional distinction between understanding and application. Why? Because there exists no ontological basis for such a distinction—a distinction requiring the notion of a common human nature as a philosophical foundation ensuring re-cognitive understanding across vast socio-cultural-temporal-linguistic differences.[15] It is unsurprising, therefore, that throughout his opus magnum, *Truth and Method*, Gadamer continually attacks the very notion of human nature as a remnant of metaphysical thinking.[16]

Gadamer fully recognizes that Heidegger's attack on metaphysics—and his own strong emphasis on *phronēsis* as the only possible notion of truth—cut to the heart of the Catholic dogmatic tradition. Gadamer himself makes two revelatory comments about just this point. Of Heidegger he says: All

---

15 I have treated the issue of re-cognitive or re-productive interpretation at length in *Foundations of Systematic Theology* (New York: T & T Clark, 2005), 169–208. This point of view argues that one can understand the meaning embedded in an historical text despite vast temporal, societal, and cultural differences. Even centuries later, an interpreter can recover and understand the spiritual endowment "affixed" within the written form.

16 Rather than speak of a stable human nature, postmodern thinkers (even moderate ones such as Gadamer) are much more likely to refer to a culturally constituted human rationality emerging from the tight web of history, society, and language.

of his efforts "were motivated by a desire to free himself from the dominating theology in which he had been raised [Catholicism]—so that he could be a Christian."[17] Gadamer here strikes a note reminiscent of both Luther and Dilthey. Only by excising the metaphysical tradition—a vestige of pagan, Hellenistic thought—can one finally discover biblical purity. Similarly, responding to the complaint of Leo Strauss that *Truth and Method* destroys the stability of textual meaning, Gadamer replies, "What I believe to have understood through Heidegger (and what I can testify to from my Protestant background) is, above all, that philosophy must learn to do without the idea of an infinite intellect. I have attempted to draw up a corresponding hermeneutics."[18] By Gadamer's reckoning, both hermeneutical phenomenology and the Reformation, with their marked accents on human finitude and epistemological limitations, have necessitated a new understanding of hermeneutics and of truth—one freed from the doctrinal tradition of the Church.[19] Insofar as Gadamer's interpretative theory is militantly non-metaphysical—and denies the material identity of truth-claims over time—one can conclude that for him the Christian faith is not about perduring cognitive affirmations, but concerns only, to use Heidegger's term, "faith-filled *Dasein*."

After this brief review, we can now return to our original question: What has been so attractive to Catholic theologians in this ardent rejection of metaphysical thinking, and in the concomitant turn toward a hermeneutical position deeply incongruent with the Christian dogmatic tradition? Why, in other words, have Heidegger and Gadamer been so influential in Catholic theology? Several reasons may be adduced. Soon after Vatican II ended, Catholic theologians sought philosophical forms that would help to explain the new conciliar emphases. As everyone knows, the council, without deviating from Catholic doctrine, also had a strongly pastoral character. Indeed, John XXIII in his opening speech, *Gaudet mater ecclesia*, mentioned

---

17 Hans-Georg Gadamer, *Heidegger's Ways* (Albany: SUNY Press, 1994), 170.

18 See Hans-Georg Gadamer, "Correspondence concerning *Wahrheit und Methode*," *Independent Journal of Philosophy* 2 (1978): 10. Of course, classical Protestantism also recognizes the Christian doctrinal tradition. As Geoffrey Wainwright avers, "For classical Protestants . . . the Apostles' Creed and the conciliar Creed of Nicea, Constantinople and Chalcedon—precisely, of course in their fidelity to Scripture—have always been taken as the irreversible deliverances and continuing guides of the Tradition." See *Is the Reformation Over?* (Milwaukee: Marquette University Press, 2000), 39.

19 See, for example, Gadamer's comments on finitude and knowing in *Truth and Method*, 2nd rev. ed., trans. J. Weinsheimer and D. G. Marshall (New York: Continuum, 1993), 357.

a teaching authority which is *"primarily pastoral in character"*—a phrase that was appealed to frequently by the conciliar bishops.[20] Even more important is the statement of Vatican II's Theological Commission which, in response to a question about the "theological qualification" attached to *Lumen gentium,* spoke of the "pastoral purpose of the present council."[21] This marked accent on the pastoral rather than the doctrinal led theologians in new directions—often with the sense that the kind of metaphysical language of the past was no longer appropriate for the current pastoral tasks.[22]

Another reason for the ascendency of hermeneutics in Catholic thought is the lively sense of "change" entertained by Vatican II. Words indicating some kind of variation—development, *ressourcement,* and *aggiornamento*—were regularly invoked by both the conciliar bishops and periti.[23] And thinkers such as John Henry Newman and Johann Adam Möhler, both of whom highlighted the importance of temporality and development in their writings, were lauded as innovative and transformative conciliar inspirations.[24]

Another factor contributing to the demise of metaphysics and the rise of hermeneutics was the strong sense that Vatican II had unlocked a new epoch for Catholicism, even asserting a tangible break with the past. Joseph Ratzinger, for example, soon after the council ended, stated that on the day *Dignitatis humanae* was formally promulgated by Paul VI (Dec. 7, 1965)—with the Declaration on Religious Freedom having been overwhelmingly approved by the bishops—"there was in St. Peter's the sense that here was the end of the Middle Ages, the end even of the Constantinian age."[25] There could hardly exist a stronger sense of epochal change and innovation than

---

20 See Jared Wicks, *Investigating Vatican II* (Washington, DC: The Catholic University of America Press, 2018), 27–29.

21 See *Acta synodalia sacrosancti concilii oecumenici Vaticani II,* III/8, 10 (March 6, 1964).

22 An example may be found in the comment of the Secretariat for Promoting Christian Unity which, in its *relatio* for the revised text of *De oecumenismo* (issued in September, 1964), stated that the decree has a "pastoral nature which generally does not admit the use of dogmatic, scholastic terminology [. . .] ." See *Acta synodalia,* III/2, 335.

23 For the precise meaning of these terms at Vatican II, see Thomas G. Guarino, *The Disputed Teachings of Vatican II: Continuity and Reversal in Catholic Doctrine* (Eerdmans Publishing, 2018), 55–72.

24 Pope Paul VI even spoke of Vatican II as "Newman's hour." See *L'Osservatore Romano* (Italian edition) (April 7–8, 1975), 1. Cited in Avery Dulles, *Newman* (London: Continuum, 2002), 151.

25 Joseph Ratzinger, *Theological Highlights of Vatican II,* trans. Henry Traub, Gerard C. Thormann, and Werner Barzel (Mahwah, NJ: Paulist Press, 2009), 144.

stating that one of Vatican II's documents brought an end to a tradition dating back to the fourth century.

Moreover, Ratzinger did not hesitate to speak of Vatican II's *Gaudium et spes* as a "countersyllabus," meaning by this that the Pastoral Constitution reversed the strong condemnations of modernity found in the Syllabus of Errors of 1864.[26] As Ratzinger would later say (as Pope Benedict XVI) in his 2005 Christmas speech, to counter the aggressive liberalism of the nineteenth century, Pius IX issued "a bitter and radical condemnation of this spirit of the modern age." In order to reestablish fruitful dialogue with society, "the Council had to determine in a new way the relationship between the Church and the modern era."[27] This reversal—at the very least in form and tone—indicated a new era of theological thinking was at hand.

All of these factors, with their strong accent on the need for theological and ecclesial changes in response to history, impelled theologians to retreat from metaphysical thinking and to embrace philosophies emphasizing the importance of evolution, mutability, and historicity. It is precisely these dimensions of life and thought that led theologians to Heidegger and Gadamer, with their stress on the constitutive role of temporality in human being and knowing.

Further endearing these thinkers to Catholic theologians was their unrelenting critique of rationalist modernity—and their attempt to offer a counternarrative to the exhausted ideas of modern philosophy. Heidegger and Gadamer not only helped Catholic theologians to overcome a stolid neo-scholasticism, but also to expose an outdated rationalism which failed to recognize the *weaknesses* of Enlightenment modernity: its attempt to pin down reason to the limited canons of empiricism and positivism; its devaluation of the role of tradition; and its attempt to reduce truth to methodology, particularly those methods and canons associated with scientific inquiry. Against these tendencies, Heidegger argued that modern rationalism reduced thinking—true philosophical wonder—to mere *techné*. Gadamer, for his part, spoke enthusiastically of the importance of tradition, arguing that modernity itself was tradition-bound—and so, on a superficial level, appeared to be endorsing a central tenet of Catholic theology. Their accent on historicity was also attractive to those seeking a more localized, contextual theology. For some, the end

---

26 Joseph Ratzinger, *Principles of Catholic Theology*, trans. Mary Frances McCarthy (San Francisco: Ignatius Press, 1987), 381–82.

27 *Christmas Address to the Roman Curia* (December 22, 2005).

of metaphysics inevitably meant the end of universal ecclesiology and of universal doctrine. Witness the barrage of arguments lodged by theologians ardently opposed to the promulgation of a comprehensive Catechism of the Catholic Church.[28] On what grounds could one speak of universal Christian doctrine given socio-cultural-linguistic specificity?

But the problems with adopting Heidegger and Gadamer as philosophical cicerones are legion—and discussed at length in the essays which follow. Neither thinker offers a philosophical "form" which can support the transcultural and transtemporal stability, universality, and material identity of Christian doctrine. In the language of *Fides et ratio*, neither thinker offers a philosophy which can fulfill the *"officium congruum"*—the suitable office subserving divine revelation. On the contrary, their thought profoundly undermines Catholic doctrinal claims.

A PRO-METAPHYSICAL RESPONSE

As earlier noted, for certain theologians—Protestant and Catholic alike— there exists the palpable concern that philosophy has domineering tendencies, that it represents an alien competitor to revelation's assertions about humanity and the world.[29] Today, this fear is often joined to the claim that theology must avoid "foundationalism"—that is, allowing some standard external to theology to be the criterion for theological truth and certainty.[30] This concern *would* be justified if Catholicism extended epistemic primacy to some particular philosophy, not disciplining it with the light of divine revelation. In fact, such disciplining has always been crucial to Catholic theology, as evidenced by the "spoils from Egypt" trope invoked by theologians from the third century onwards. In a tradition extending from Origen to Basil, from Augustine to Aquinas and Newman, the leading idea has been that theology can use philosophical wisdom, and indeed, secular wisdom of any kind, although always subject to biblical truth.

---

28 Avery Dulles outlines the arguments pressed by these thinkers in "The Challenge of the Catechism" in *Church and Society* (New York: Fordham University Press, 2008), 157–74.

29 So Jean-Luc Marion writes, in a sentence that seems more Barthian than Catholic: "The Gxd who reveals himself has nothing in common [. . .] with the 'God' of the philosophers, of the learned and, eventually, of the poet." Legitimately, Marion wants to alert us to the irreducible heteronomy of God; but is a disjunction between faith and reason needed to protect God's otherness? See *God Without Being*, trans. Thomas Carlson (Chicago: University of Chicago Press, 1991), 52.

30 I discuss "foundationalism" in essay four of this volume, "Postmodernity and Five Fundamental Theological Issues."

Theology, then, can never be captive to any mode of reasoning, whatever its provenance, precisely because Christian thought has the obligation to purge every viewpoint of errors. Aquinas argues that theologians, in subjecting philosophy to the Christian faith, change water into wine. Similarly, Newman states that the Church is a vast treasure-house, cleansing erroneous ideas of their imperfections, then stamping them with the Master's image.[31] More recently, Balthasar, speaking of the theological use of Hegel, Schelling, and Fichte, insists that Christian thinkers must always adopt Mary's posture: *"deposuit potentes de sede."*[32]

This is the theoretical horizon within which one should understand Catholicism's frequent invocation of metaphysical themes. Metaphysics is helpful for defending the claims of the Catholic faith—especially the assertion that dogmatic statements are universally, definitively, and perpetually true. But it is always metaphysics adduced within the house of faith, as a way of explicating and supporting crucial doctrinal convictions. Catholic theologians would never say, then, as Barth does in his *Dogmatics*, that "The Lord who is visible in the *vestigia* [referring to the *vestigia Trinitatis* of the patristic era] we can only regard as a different Lord than the one so called in the Bible."[33] Even more pointedly, Barth says that the concept of God emerging from natural theology attempts "to unite Yahweh with Baal, the triune God of Holy Scripture with the concept of being of Aristotelian and Stoic philosophy."[34] In theological matters, philosophy is almost always regarded dyslogistically by Barth and his epigones. Philosophy (and metaphysics in particular) is a theoretical prison, neutering the Gospel of its salt, light and power—and demanding that the Christian faith establish its conceptual foundation in a general philosophy of being.[35]

In fact, the truly crucial issue for Catholic theology is this: How do the affirmations of the Christian faith find theoretical support in the philosophical order? This is assuredly not an attempt to justify divine revelation by

---

31 See John Henry Newman, *An Essay on the Development of Christian Doctrine* (London: Longmans, Green, and Co., 1894), 382.

32 Balthasar, *Love Alone Is Credible*, trans. A. Dru (New York: Herder and Herder, 1969), 34.

33 Barth, *Church Dogmatics* I/1, 399.

34 Barth, *Church Dogmatics* II/1, ed. G. W. Bromiley and T. F. Torrance (Edinburgh, T & T Clark, 1957) , 84.

35 Colin Gunton, for example, commenting on *Fides et ratio*, states that underlying the encyclical "is a conviction that the teaching of the Christian faith, dependent as it is on particularities, requires foundation in a general philosophy of being." See *Act and Being* (London: SCM, 2002), 5.

philosophy or to place theological claims in an alien Procrustean bed. It is, rather, to ensure that faith's claims are also able to satisfy the legitimate demands of human reason. Catholicism insists that its dogmatic teachings are perduringly and universally true. But can one philosophically defend the *very possibility* of the continuously and universally true, especially at a time when such ideas are under unrelenting attack from a variety of quarters? One argument consistently made in the following essays is that only philosophies with a metaphysical dimension are able to offer adequate support for the affirmations of Catholic doctrine.

Also important here is the traditional Catholic insistence that the natural order, including philosophy, has a "relative autonomy."[36] The natural order cannot be entirely subsumed into theology because meaning and truth have a visibility embedded within the *kosmos*, within the form of the world. Nonetheless, this autonomy is always relative in kind because all realities necessarily exist within the *unicus ordo supernaturalis*, the one and only order of grace. Vatican II captured this accent on the stability of the created order when it stated, "If by the autonomy of earthly affairs we mean that created things and societies themselves enjoy their own laws and values [. . .], then it is entirely right to demand that autonomy. [. . .] For by the very circumstance of their having been created, all things are endowed with their own stability, truth, goodness, proper laws and order."[37]

An example of philosophy's autonomy may be found in Aquinas's work, *"On the Unity of the Intellect against the Averroists."* St. Thomas states that he could overcome the errors of Radical Aristotelianism simply by citing the Church's faith. He insists, however, that he will argue from reason alone in order to prove that the soul is individuated in creatures.[38] The created order, Aquinas was convinced, could deliver much truth, even though its insights needed to be measured and completed by divine revelation.

John Paul II also defends the natural visibility of truth. For example, in his 1995 encyclical, *Evangelium vitae*, he argues that while the Gospel of

---

36 Of this relative autonomy, *Fides et ratio* states, "And just as in giving her assent to Gabriel's word, Mary lost nothing of her true humanity and freedom, so too when philosophy heeds the summons of the Gospel's truth its autonomy is in no way impaired." See John Paul II, *Fides et ratio*, no. 108. An extended discussion of the "relative autonomy" of the natural order may be found in essay seven of this volume, "Nature and Grace: Seeking the Delicate Balance."

37 Vatican Council II, *Gaudium et spes* (December 7, 1965), no. 36.

38 *On the Unity of the Intellect Against the Averroists*, trans. Beatrice H. Zedler (Milwaukee: Marquette University Press, 1968), 22.

Jesus Christ is intrinsically related to conclusions in the moral order, many of the same conclusions can be reached on the basis of arguments adduced by unaided reason. Therefore, he confidently affirms, "despite the negative consequences of sin [. . .] [the Gospel of Life] *can also be known in its essential traits by human reason*."[39] Benedict XVI, too, frequently averted to the "relative autonomy" of the natural order, even while insisting on the priority of revelation, faith, and grace. His speeches at Westminster Hall in London (2010) and at the Bundestag in Berlin (2011), for example, are minor masterpieces of philosophical reasoning in support of divine revelation.[40]

In all of this, the fundamental point is that the philosophical order has a rational validity—even apart from intrasystemic Christian belief—that allows it to support the affirmations required by divine revelation. It is never a matter of an either/or—either the Gospel or philosophy/metaphysics. Epistemic primacy is always accorded to divine revelation. At the same time, philosophies with a metaphysical dimension are essential for supporting Catholicism's (and much of Christianity's) claims that its dogmatic teachings are true universally and perpetually.

Of course, such claims are under relentless attack from postmodern thought—even the "moderate" postmodernity represented by Gadamer and Habermas. For these thinkers, metaphysics, whether of the classical type or the more recent transcendental variety, has been exposed as inappropriate and untenable. The newly-presenced horizons of socio-cultural embeddedness and contextualized rationality impose a conclusive argument against philosophies purveying universal and trans-cultural structures.

In the essays that follow it will be argued that Catholicism makes use of philosophical reasoning—particularly metaphysics—for several reasons: 1) metaphysics opens up the participationist structure of reality (the ascent to God by virtue of the intelligibility of the existing real); 2) it warrants the distinction between *esse* and essence, thereby allowing God to be

---

39 John Paul II, Encyclical Letter *Evangelium vitae* (March 25, 1995), no. 29. In *Acta apostolicae sedis* 87 (1995), 401–522, at 434.

40 For an analysis of these papal addresses, see Thomas G. Guarino, "Vattimo, Diversity and Catholicism," in *Justice Through Diversity?*, ed. Michael J. Sweeney, 533–50 (Lanham, MD: Rowman and Littlefield, 2016). See also the statement by the International Theological Commission of 2009, which appeals to the dialogue between Antigone and King Creon in Sophocles' famous work. Violating the command of the royal lawgiver, Antigone buries her dead brother. She justifies her action by appealing to a law that is "unwritten and immutable," not made by kings. See International Theological Commission, *In Search of a Universal Ethic: A New Look at the Natural Law* (2009).

understood as the intensive act of existing without potentiality (supporting the Church's understanding of God as the Unchanging One of Absolute Love); 3) it offers an anthropology that establishes an eidetically discernable nature or form (thereby explaining how meaning and truth are not swallowed up in the maw of socio-cultural contingency); and 4) it grounds the predication of names to God (by way of the *analogia entis*).

It is entirely understandable, therefore, that in the encyclical *Fides et ratio*, John Paul II states that philosophies which lack a metaphysical range "would be radically unsuited to the task of mediation in the understanding of Revelation."[41] Indeed, only with the help of metaphysics can the *intellectus fidei* give a "coherent account of the universal and transcendent power of revealed truth."[42] These are important magisterial statements since they indicate that only certain *kinds* of philosophies are able to support the universal doctrines proclaimed by the Catholic Church.

At the same time, it should be clearly stated that the term "metaphysics" is not intended to be restrictive. As *Fides et ratio* points out, it is a matter of cultivating philosophies with a "metaphysical range," namely philosophies able to fulfill the aforementioned "*officium congruum*." It is not a question, then, of a constricted understanding of the *philosophia perennis*. On the contrary, philosophy should be able to "propose anew the problem of being—and this in harmony with the demands and insights of the entire philosophical tradition, including philosophy of more recent times, without lapsing into sterile repetition of antiquated formulas."[43] In the last analysis, the "suitable office" which philosophy must fulfill is not limited to Thomism or Scholasticism but seeks instead a *legitimate plurality* of conceptual systems which are, nonetheless, supportive of, and commensurable with, the *depositum fidei*. A significant argument animating the essays that follow, then, is the essential role that metaphysics, broadly understood, plays in supporting the dogmatic tradition of the Catholic Church.[44]

---

41 John Paul II, *Fides et ratio*, no. 83.

42 *Fides et ratio*, no. 83.

43 *Fides et ratio*, no. 97.

44 Although it is not usually acknowledged, Vatican II was itself deeply shaped by Thomist ideas such as participation and analogy. That is why Yves Congar, one of the principal architects of the conciliar documents, could say, a mere two years after Vatican II ended: "It could be shown . . . that St. Thomas, the *Doctor communis,* furnished the writers of the dogmatic texts of Vatican II with the bases and structure [*les assises et la structure*] of their thought. We do not doubt that they themselves would make this confession." See *Situation et tâches présentes de la théologie*

CONCLUSION

In these essays, I seek to show which *philosophical forms are adequate to the content of salvation history as expressed in Christian doctrine*. Such supportive philosophies are essential so that the claims of Catholic doctrine are recognized as intellectually rigorous and not as fideistic, authoritarian assertions. Conversely, I show the weaknesses involved in attempting to elaborate theological positions without a strong metaphysical (and realist epistemological) horizon. Only determinate philosophies can be legitimately placed in service to the faith.

Many thinkers discussed in these essays, Gadamer and Habermas for example, believe they have advanced an "ontologically-appropriate" philosophy, that is to say, a philosophical form that is congruent with the sociohistorical-cultural-linguistic horizons that inexorably determine life and thought. They conclude that these horizons presage the demise of metaphysics and the universal realities associated with it. They end by agreeing with Nietzsche who famously declares that metaphysics is "the science that treats of the fundamental errors of mankind—but does so as though they were fundamental truths."[45] In fact, the hermeneutical philosophies that have been championed by these thinkers—while they have something to teach us about history and tradition—are ultimately fatal to Catholic theology and to the Catholic dogmatic tradition. It is precisely these foundational issues which these essays seek to explore and examine.

A NOTE

The essays in this volume appear in substantially the same form as when they were originally published. In some cases, a book or two has been added to the bibliography or a footnote has been updated. On a few occasions, a word or two has been changed for the sake of precision or a sentence slightly altered to make a point more clearly than in the original. The fresh introduction provided for each is intended to show how that particular study is relevant to the theme of the book as a whole.

(Paris: Cerf, 1967), 53. For an extended treatment of the role of analogy and participation at Vatican II, see Guarino, *Disputed Teachings of Vatican II*, 73–131.

45 Friedrich Nietzsche, *Human, All Too Human*, trans. R. J. Hollingdale (Cambridge: Cambridge University Press, 1986), no. 18.

Chapter One

Introduction to
Philosophia Obscurans? Six Theses
on the Proper Relationship between
Theology and Philosophy

as philosophy defaced and deformed solid Christian doctrine? Has Hellenism corrupted the clear message of the Bible? Has metaphysics obstructed and obscured the truth of divine revelation? At the root of each of these questions lies a fundamental issue: the proper relationship between theology and philosophy.

The correlation between the two ancient disciplines has been the subject of intense reflection through the ages and remains a living topic today. For example, Benedict XVI, in his memorable Regensburg Lecture of 2006, directly attacked the notorious claim of Adolf von Harnack, that Christianity had been corrupted by its encounter with Greek philosophy—that the simple message of Jesus Christ had been twisted into the metaphysical nightmare of the Trinity, involving eternal relations among divine persons. Against Harnack's onslaught, Benedict pronounced it deeply providential that St. Paul, finding the road to Asia blocked, journeyed north to Greece, thereby allowing the Church to utilize the riches of philosophical thought (citing Acts 16. 6–10). Ratzinger even speaks of "the intrinsic necessity of a rapprochement between Biblical faith and Greek inquiry."[1]

With these comments, Benedict aligns himself with a long Catholic tradition. In the third century, Origen argued that the Church, like the ancient Israelites, had been licensed to "despoil the Egyptians," using their philosophical "gold" for the glory of God. In the thirteenth century, St. Thomas, reflecting on Paul's claim that Christians are charged with "bringing into captivity every thought unto the obedience of Christ,"[2] insists those who

---

1 Benedict XVI, *Regensburg Lecture* (September 12, 2006). English translation: *Origins* 36 (September 28, 2006): 248–52.

2 2 Cor. 10:5.

use philosophy in service to the faith do not *mix* water with wine, but *change* water into wine.[3] In the nineteenth century, John Henry Newman, responding to the charge that Catholic doctrine had been corrupted by philosophy, teaches that the Church is heir to Our Lord's promise: Even if the disciples drank some deadly thing, it would not harm them.[4] In all these examples, the central claim is that the Church may use every form of thought for the elucidation of Christian doctrine, always recognizing, of course, that epistemic primacy belongs solely to the Gospel.

Another crucial issue addressed in this essay goes beyond the *use* of philosophy, to the *kind* of philosophy employed in theological reasoning. The Dogmatic Constitution on Divine Revelation, *Dei verbum*, states that what God has revealed will "abide perpetually in its full integrity and be handed on to all generations."[5] The International Theological Commission adds, "the truth of revelation [. . .] is universally valid and unchangeable in substance."[6] Given these statements, which merely summarize Catholic teaching, what is needed is a philosophy which *supports and confirms* the universal, trans-temporal, and trans-cultural claims of Catholic doctrine, that is, a philosophy which shows that the truth of divine revelation, as mediated by the Church, is both intelligible and defensible. Such a philosophy will defend the *very possibility* of universal truth and the *very possibility* of meaning-invariance over time. Absent such supportive philosophical warrants, doctrinal truth-claims easily degenerate into fideistic, authoritarian assertions.

This essay, then, argues that theology requires modes of reasoning that can protect and buttress, in the philosophical order, the Church's foundational doctrinal convictions. Metaphysical reasoning (commodiously understood) is essential for cogently defending the Church's faith.

---

3 St. Thomas Aquinas, *De Trinitate*, q. 2, a. 3, ad 5.

4 See John Henry Newman, *An Essay on the Development of Christian Doctrine* (London: Longmans, Green, and Co., 1894), 441. Page numbers refer to this volume.

5 Vatican Council II, *Dei verbum* (November 18, 1965), no. 7.

6 International Theological Commission, *On the Interpretation of Dogmas* (October 1989). An English translation may be found in *Origins* 20 (May 17, 1990): 9. Listed on the Vatican website as *The Interpretation of Dogma*.

Philosophia Obscurans? Six Theses on the Proper Relationship between Theology and Philosophy

I t has long been observed that 529 A.D. was a momentous date. In that year, the Emperor Justinian closed the Academy in Athens—thus symbolically bringing pagan antiquity to an end—while, according to tradition, St. Benedict established the abbey at Monte Cassino—indicating the flourishing of Christian life and practice. Along with Athens and Jerusalem in the early Church, and Paris and Assisi in the medieval Church, the Academy and Monte Cassino provide another trope for imaging the relationship between reason and faith.

For Catholic theology, this relationship remains of primatial importance, for understanding it properly means grasping how human beings may be intelligent and inquisitive thinkers, lifelong seekers after truth, as well as men and women of faith. Further, one cannot read any serious book of theology without coming up against the correlation between philosophy and Christian faith. Has some Church teaching been influenced by a particular philosophical position that is no longer acceptable? Has a distinct philosophical approach had a baleful influence on some later ecclesial formulation of the Gospel? Have theologians relied too strongly on certain thinkers, seduced by Siren songs of reason, when Ulysses-like, they should have strapped themselves to the mast so that they would not be captivated by alien forms of thought?

Of course, the criticism that mere human reasoning is tainting the Christian faith—that itching ears have traded the sound doctrine of the Gospel for the wisdom of the Greeks—has a long and distinguished pedigree. St. Paul straightforwardly told his readers that "God has made foolish the wisdom of the world" and again, "I will destroy the wisdom of the wise and the learning of the clever I will set aside. [. . .] For Jews look for signs

* This essay was originally published as "*Philosophia Obscurans?* Six Theses on the Proper Relationship between Theology and Philosophy," *Nova et Vetera* English edition 12, no. 2 (2014): 349–94. Republished with permission.

and Greeks for wisdom, but we preach Christ crucified."[7] Still again, "The wisdom of world is foolishness in the eyes of God."[8] St. Paul's concerns continue unabated through Tatian's attacks on philosophy in his "Address to the Greeks," through Tertullian's famous cleavage between Athens and Jerusalem, through Jacopone da Todi's mocking poems on the allurements of Parisian learning, through the stern *monitum* of Pope Gregory IX to the Parisian theology masters, through the condemnations issued by the bishop of Paris, Etienne Tempier, through the claims of Peter John Olivi that philosophical questions are "unworthy of the Christian's serious concern," through the harsh comments of Luther against Aristotle and Plato, through Pascal's famous dichotomizing of *le Dieu des philosophes et le Dieu d'Abraham, d'Isaac et de Jacob*, and through Karl Barth's philippics against theology's contemptuous toadying to foreign canons of rationality.[9] In all of these thinkers, one cannot fail to hear the comment by the long-forgotten Absalon of Saint-Victor (†1203) who insists, "*Non regnat spiritus Christi ubi dominatur spiritus Aristotelis,*" with Aristotle a proxy for any philosophy or philosopher who seeks to usurp the Gospel.[10]

In each of these cases, the wisdom taught by the prophets of Israel and by Jesus Christ needs no help from the Athenian Academy. Philosophy serves only to deface and deform the fiery message of the Gospel. If it is not baldly asserted that faith and reason are at antipodes, then at least it is claimed that theirs is an uneasy relationship, with philosophy and theology circling each other as wary and aggressive enemies, each girding itself for a likely strike.

While forceful reservations have been expressed about philosophy's influence over Christianity, the broader tradition has acknowledged a sal-

---

7 1 Cor. 1:19–23.

8 1 Cor. 3:19.

9 See Tatian, *Oratio ad Graecos*, ed. and trans. Molly Whittaker (Oxford: Clarendon, 1982). For Tertullian, *The Prescription against Heretics* in vol. 3 of *The Ante-Nicene Fathers*, ed. Alexander Roberts and James Donaldson (Grand Rapids: Eerdmans Publishing, 1957), 246, chap. 7. For Gregory IX's letter of 1228, see vol. 1 of *Chartularium Universitatis Parisiensis*, ed. H. Denifle, 114–16 (Paris, 1899). Also, *Enchiridion symbolorum*, 37th ed., ed. Heinrich Denzinger and Peter Hünermann (Freiburg im Breisgau: Herder, 1991), no. 824. For Olivi's attitude toward philosophy, see David Burr, "Petrus Ioannis Olivi and the Philosophers," *Franciscan Studies* 31 (1971), 41–71, at 46. For Tempier's comments at Paris in 1277, see David Piché with Claude LaFleur, *La condemnation parisienne de 1277* (Paris: Vrin, 1999), 74–75. For Jacopone's poems, see *Sons of Francis*, trans. Anne MacDonell (London: J.M. Dent and Co., 1902).

10 Absalon of Saint Victor, *PL* 211, 1855, col. 37 cited by Serge-Thomas Bonino, "*Qu'est-ce que l'antithomisme?*" *Revue Thomiste* 108 (2008): 9–38, at 15. For textual difficulties with Absalon's comment, see Bonino, 15n22.

utary confluence between faith and reason. One sees this position championed in those early Christian writers who spoke glowingly of the role of philosophy, such as Clement of Alexandria who insists that the Old Testament and Greek wisdom are twin rivers leading to Christ, Origen who boldly counsels Christians to take philosophical "spoils from Egypt," the Cappadocians who never finish with Hellenistic thought, Augustine's *De doctrina christiana* which reprises Origen's "spoils" trope for the West, and Boethius who, in a well-known discussion of the Trinity, counsels his interlocutor to "join faith to reason."[11]

Aquinas, of course, ardently defends the use of philosophy in theological reasoning, glossing St. Paul's biblical admonitions with the comment that the Apostle warns against trusting in one's personal erudition, not in human reasoning per se.[12] Aquinas's confidence in the conjunctive nature of faith and philosophy is also powerfully reflected in the *Summa contra Gentiles* I, 7. There, Thomas argues for the profound complementarity of faith and reason, principles restated by Vatican I, at a time when the Church sought a Christian via media between currents of rationalism and fideism dominating the eighteenth and nineteenth centuries. This medieval assurance in the congruency of faith and human wisdom was to be a guiding force in the founding of the great Western universities.

But the question remains: How does theology use philosophy so that the latter does not obscure or deform the Christian message? It is these two competing approaches, one arguing for evangelical purity and the other insisting on philosophical plenitude, which give rise to this essay. I will examine the proper relationship between philosophy and theology in six theses, arguing that: 1) the point continues to be made, at times zealously so, that philosophy obscures the Gospel message, offering only an alien narrative that deforms biblical teaching; 2) the broader tradition has insisted

---

11 Clement, *Stromateis*, 1, 29, in vol. 2 of *The Ante-Nicene Fathers* (Grand Rapids: Eerdmans Publishing, 1956), 341; Origen, "Letter to Gregory," in vol. 4 of *The Ante-Nicene Fathers* (Grand Rapids: Eerdmans Publishing, 1956), 393–94; Augustine, *De doctrina christiana*, II, 40. Boethius, "Letter to John the Deacon," in *The Theological Tractates*, The Loeb Classical Library, trans. H. F. Stewart and E. K. Rand (Cambridge, MA: Harvard University Press, 1962), 32–37, at 37. Boethius' comment, "insofar as you are able, join faith to reason" (*Fidem, si poterit, rationemque conjunge*) is found in his discussion of the principles of unity and diversity in the Trinity. Boethius argues that the terms "God," "truth," "omnipotence," and "immutability" can be formally predicated of the divine substance, but the terms "Father," "Son," and "Spirit" cannot be so attributed. Boethius asks his interlocutor to either confirm his investigations or, to proffer another opinion, one reconciling faith and reason.

12 Aquinas, *De Trinitate*, q. 2, a.3, ad 1.

that the Christian faith is always a "Jewgreek" enterprise, incorporating Hellenic and Hebraic traditions; 3) even while assimilating all forms of human wisdom, theology recognizes its need to performatively discipline every philosophical (and other) insight; 4) speculative philosophy has its own legitimate freedom and autonomy; 5) by its incorporative nature, Catholicism encourages authentic theological pluralism, and 6) some capacious metaphysical horizon is ultimately necessary to subserve properly theological reasoning.

THESIS ONE: PHILOSOPHY DEFORMS AND OBSCURES CHRISTIAN FAITH (THE HELLENIZATION THESIS)

While reservations about the role of philosophical thinking in theological reflection go back to St. Paul, it is Martin Luther who seized upon this critique in service to his mission of reforming the Church by purifying her of non-scriptural accretions. As Yves Congar has pointed out, the idea that all salvific truth was to be found in scripture had a long history before Luther, but Luther used the criterion of *sola scriptura* in a new way.[13] For the reformer's turn to scriptural exclusivity was accompanied by a deep suspicion of philosophy, particularly the Scholasticism that was seen as badly deforming the foursquare Gospel. Luther's attacks on philosophy resulted at times to formulations which, taken in isolation, seem jarringly irrational: "Whoever wishes to be a Christian must be intent on silencing the voice of reason [. . .] . To the judgment of reason they [the articles of faith] appear so far from the truth that it is impossible to believe them."[14] And again, "no one becomes a theologian, unless he becomes one without Aristotle."[15]

Luther's spirited critique of Pseudo-Dionysius serves as an example of his legitimate evangelical concerns. The primary salvo launched by the reformer against Dionysian thought is that it is philosophically rather than

---

13 Yves Congar, *Tradition and Traditions*, trans. Michael Naseby and Thomas Rainborough (New York: MacMillan, 1967), 107–18.

14 *Luther's Works* (hereafter *LW*) vol. 23, 99. For a discussion of Luther's mixed evaluation of philosophy, see Thomas G. Guarino, "Spoils from Egypt: Yesterday and Today," *Pro Ecclesia* 15 (2006): 403–17.

15 *LW* 31, 12. Denis R. Janz says that to call the reason the "Devil's whore" as Luther does (*LW* 40, 175 and *LW* 51, 374) "is to invite misunderstanding and caricature." But this phrase does not exhaust Luther's judgment on human reasoning. See "Whore or Handmaid?," in *The Devil's Whore: Reason and Philosophy in the Lutheran Tradition*, ed. Jennifer Hockenbery Dragseth, 47–52 (Minneapolis: Fortress, 2011).

biblically inspired, owing more to Plato than to the scriptures.[16] As Luther says in his commentary on Genesis, "Nowhere does he [Dionysius] have a single word about faith or any useful instruction from the Holy Scriptures."[17] Negative theology cannot be rooted in the Dionysian dialectic of affirmation and negation, in an ascent beyond being and non-being; it can only be rooted in the cross and the suffering of Christ crucified. Luther's clarion hermeneutical principle is *crux probat omnia*, the cross judges everything, or as he insists, "The Cross alone is our theology."[18] The reformer's searing critique of Dionysius's Platonism was essential because "neither darkness nor negative theology are ever linked to the cross of Christ in the Dionysian corpus."[19] Luther's assault on Dionysius is a good example of his desire to develop a theology rooted only in scripture and the central events of Christ's life. Only the Bible can teach us something about the true God. Dionysius, with his unending philosophical dialectic of negative and positive affirmations, "deserves to be ridiculed."[20]

Luther was followed in his attack on philosophy by the young Melanchthon who famously wrote, at the beginning of his *Loci Communes,* "how corrupt are all the theological hallucinations of those who have offered the subtleties of Aristotle instead of the teachings of Christ."[21] The young reformer argues that "From the philosophy of Plato was added the equally pernicious word 'reason.' For just as we in these latter times of the Church have embraced Aristotle instead of Christ, so immediately after the beginnings of the Church Christian doctrine was weakened by Platonic philos-

---

16 Partial confirmation of Luther's judgment comes from Alasdair MacIntyre who says, "Dionysius was as much of a Neoplatonist as it is possible to be while also being a Christian." See Alasdair MacIntyre, *God, Philosophy, Universities* (Lanham, MD: Sheed and Ward, 2009), 37.

17 *LW* 1, 235. Cited by Paul Rorem, "Martin Luther's Christocentric Critique of Pseudo-Dionysian Spirituality," *Lutheran Quarterly* 11, no. 3 (1997): 291–307, at 293.

18 *LW* 25, 287.

19 Rorem, "Martin Luther's Christocentric Critique," 300. At the same time, Rorem observes that Bonaventure is a precursor of Luther. While not hesitating to cite Dionysius's work, the Franciscan simultaneously accents the centrality of Christ crucified, thereby crossing from philosophical nescience to the depths of revelation. See Rorem, "Negative Theologies and the Cross," *Harvard Theological Review* 101 (2008): 451–64.

20 *LW,* 13, 111. Balthasar sympathetically evaluates Luther's critique of philosophy (and particularly of Dionysius) saying, "the showy splendor of such cosmic and mystical piety leads to a forgetting of Christ, and the world of beauty overshadows the mystery of the biblical glory and one must wait for Luther [. . .] to bring the sharpness of the crisis to consciousness." See *The Glory of the Lord,* vol. 4, trans. Brian McNeil, et al. (San Francisco: Ignatius, 1989), 320.

21 Philip Melanchthon, *Loci Communes Theologici (1521)* in *Melanchthon and Bucer,* ed. Wilhelm Pauck (Philadelphia: The Westminster Press, 1969), 19.

ophy."[22] Given this attack, it is unsurprising that both Luther and Melanchthon shied away from using analogical reasoning as a means of explaining the Trinity, and "even hinted that the [Trinitarian] doctrine may be contradictory to reason."[23]

In more recent times, it is Adolf von Harnack who is the well-known coryphaeus of the claim that philosophy increasingly deformed Christianity, leading to the *Abfall vom Evangelium* that defaced the primitive Church. Of long familiarity to theologians is Harnack's description of Christian teaching as "in its conception and development a work of the Greek spirit on the soil of the gospel."[24] His parallel assertion is that "the victory of the Nicene Creed was a victory of the priests over the faith of the Christian people."[25] According to Harnack, the philosophically educated clergy had forced an alien definition on the Gospel. Nicene faith itself is here called into question as a Hellenistic import that obscures and misshapes the simple Hebraic belief in the one God of Jesus of Nazareth. This Hebraic-Hellenistic disjunction has become an enduring trope, invoked over subsequent generations with varying levels of intensity. It is no surprise, then, that even at the remove of over a century, Benedict XVI at Regensburg felt compelled to attack Harnack's Hellenization thesis in direct terms.[26]

Despite his well-known differences with Harnack, Karl Barth echoes many of the same themes. For Barth, too, stands on restive guard for the purity of Scripture over and against the alleged philosophical accretions

---

22 Melanchthon, *Loci Communes*, 23. Several authors have noted that the later Melanchthon became somewhat more amenable to speculative theology. Oswald Bayer observes that at the height of Lutheran Pietism, Melanchthon was even accused of slipping Aristotle into the back door of theology. See Oswald Bayer, "Philipp Melanchthon," *Pro Ecclesia* 18, no. 2 (2009): 134–61, at 135. Also, E. P. Meijering, *Melanchthon and Patristic Thought* (Leiden: Brill, 1983).

23 Samuel M. Powell, *The Trinity in German Thought* (Cambridge: Cambridge University Press, 2001), 23. Powell notes that while Melanchthon was at first militantly opposed to any speculative explanation of the Trinity, he later adopted some use of the psychological analogy. This change leads Powell to conclude that "its bare presence in Melancthon's thought testifies to its enduring fascination, even among those most resolutely opposed to it." See Powell, *The Trinity in German Thought*, 28. On the other hand, a recent work about Luther states that "The difference between Luther and scholastic Trinitarian speculation is easily overemphasized." See Sammeli Juntunen, "Christ," in *Engaging Luther*, ed. Olli-Pekka Vainio, 60–61 (Eugene, OR: Wipf and Stock, 2010).

24 Adolf von Harnack, vol. 1 of *History of Dogma*, trans. Neil Buchanan (New York: Russell and Russell, 1958, orig. 1898), 20.

25 Harnack, *History of Dogma*, vol. 4, 106.

26 Benedict XVI, *Regensburg Lecture* (September 12, 2006). An English translation may be found in *Origins* 36 (September 28, 2006): 248–52.

that have mutilated Christian faith. One may simply point to the prole-gomena of Barth's *Church Dogmatics* where both the liberal Protestant axis of Schleiermacher-Hermann-Ritschl and the Catholic *analogia entis* are lumped together as pre-determining schemas inexorably distorting the Gospel through the imposition of foreign philosophical norms not drawn from the scriptures themselves. This is the basis of Barth's notorious asser-tion that the analogy of being is the invention of the anti-Christ precisely because it seeks to force the gospel of grace into a philosophical Procrus-tean bed.[27] Barth similarly argues that by considering first the divine nature, rather than the God revealed by Christ, the door was opened [in the Middle Ages] to the domination of theology by philosophy: "The fact that the life of God was identified with the notion of pure being, the fact that the idea of God was not determined by the doctrine of the Trinity, but that the latter was shaped by a general conception of God (that of ancient Stoicism and Neo-Platonism) was now avenged at the most sensitive spot." The philosophical idea of divine simplicity became an "all-controlling prin-ciple, the idol" which devoured everything concrete.[28] Even more devas-tatingly, Barth says that concept of God emerging from natural theology attempts "to unite Yahweh with Baal, the triune God of Holy Scripture with the concept of being of Aristotelian and Stoic philosophy."[29] And, he con-tinues, "The Lord who is visible in the *vestigia* [referring to the *vestigia Trinitatis* of the patristic era] we can only regard as a different Lord than the one so called in the Bible."[30]

While limiting ourselves to just a few thinkers, we can easily cite con-temporary theologians who have repeated this line of thought. Robert Jenson, for example, in his *Unbaptized God*, attacks Hellenism as a foreign metaphysics: "The great task of the theological and spiritual history that leads to the Christianity now divided is reinterpretation by the gospel of Hellenism's antecedent interpretation of God." He continues, "And the heart

---

27 Karl Barth, *Church Dogmatics* I/1, trans. G. T. Thomson (Edinburgh: T & T Clark, 1949), x. I have treated Barth's criticisms of analogy at length in *Foundations of Systematic Theology* (New York: T & T Clark, 2005), 224–30. Balthasar responded to Barth that the principles of causality and similarity (the ontological roots of analogical predication) exist only in the *unicus ordo supernaturalis* and so are never purely philosophical.

28 Barth, *Church Dogmatics* II/I, ed. G. W. Bromiley and T. F. Torrance (Edinburgh, T & T Clark, 1957), 329.

29 Barth, *Church Dogmatics* II/I, 84.

30 Barth, *Church Dogmatics* I/1, 399.

of what needed reinterpreting in antecedent Hellenic theology is its posit of eternity as timelessness, as *immunity* to time's opportunities and threats and so of being as *persistence*."[31] Jenson's stark claim that theology has conducted only an "incomplete exorcism" on "unbaptized Hellenism" finds echoes in other Protestant theologians who argue that philosophy has too often become a theoretical prison, neutering the Gospel of its salt, light, and power.[32] Philosophical reasoning is here regarded as a pernicious Trojan horse in the City of God, an alien conceptual foundation that befouls the salvific biblical economy.[33]

Although the Hellenization thesis has been principally associated with theologians in the Reformation tradition, the claim that philosophy has deformed revelation cannot be limited to Protestant thinkers. At times, Orthodox theologians adopt this line of thought as well (particularly when discussing Western theology). Sergius Bulgakov, for example, spends pages attacking the Catholic teaching on transubstantiation, observing that the doctrine is based on the Aristotelian distinction between *ousia (substantia)* and *sumbabekos (accidentia)*. Bulgakov concludes that in the Eucharistic doctrine, one notices "an inherent strangeness in such a degree of dependence of the core of this dogma on the purely philosophical doctrine of some philosopher, and especially a pagan one."[34] Of course, Bulgakov is fully alive to the early Church's use of philosophy and its adoption of terms such as *hypostasis* and *physis*; however, he insists that ancient Christianity employed these concepts in new ways. With the doctrine of transubstan-

---

31 Robert Jenson, *Unbaptized God* (Minneapolis: Fortress, 1992), 137–38.

32 So, for example, Colin Gunton, commenting on *Fides et ratio*, says that underlying the encyclical "is a conviction that the teaching of the Christian faith, dependent as it is on particularities, requires foundation in a general philosophy of being." See *Act and Being* (London: SCM, 2002), 5. Eberhard Jüngel argues that Luther's chief philosophical point is that metaphysics fails to understand Christ's cross, which necessarily negates the traditional divine attributes of immutability and impassibility. See *God as Mystery of the World*, trans. Darrell L. Guder (Grand Rapids: Eerdmans Publishing, 1983), 373. Pannenberg (gently) accuses Thomas of allowing philosophy to control his treatment of the Trinity in the *Summa Theologiae*. See Wolfhart Pannenberg, vol. 1 of *Systematic Theology*, trans. Geoffrey W. Bromiley (Grand Rapids: Eerdmans Publishing, 1988), 287–89.

33 On the other hand, Anna Williams insightfully remarks, "If Reformation theology was grounded on the sole foundation of scripture, and that of the schoolmen on a poisonous cocktail of tradition and human reason, it is hard to explain the marked similarities between the theology of the two periods." See A. N. Williams, *The Architecture of Theology* (Oxford: Oxford University Press, 2011), 97.

34 Sergius Bulgakov, *The Holy Grail and the Eucharist*, trans. Boris Jakim (Hudson, NY: Lindisfarne Books, 1997), 75.

tiation, on the contrary, "philosophy does not serve theology but theology is a slave to philosophy."[35]

A similar approach is taken by Christos Yannaras who nods in assent to Heidegger's claim that the Western theological tradition from Augustine to Aquinas has been typically philosophical: "God is the logically necessary first cause of all beings, and both the ontology and epistemology of the West were built on this logical necessity as a starting point."[36] Yannaras argues that the Western emphasis on a rational, conceptual theology—culminating in the proofs for God's existence found throughout the Western tradition— is rightly condemned by Heidegger as mere onto-theology, as the reduction of the transcendent God to a pedestrian *causa sui*. This has led, he concludes, to "a kind of 'spiritual schizophrenia' which basically characterizes the Western stance toward the world and history."[37]

Finally, Michael Azkoul has written that Augustine is the origin of "almost every religious opinion which separates Western Christendom from the Orthodox Church," including cataphatic theology, the filioque, and purgatory. Prompting all of these deviations is "Hellenism, the invisible hand behind Augustine's innovations."[38] Speaking of Augustine's theology, Azkoul says, "Hellenism [. . .] the elevation of 'faith' to rational knowledge—proved to be his undoing. He yielded to the same temptation [Platonism] by which Origen and other heretics were seduced."[39] Indeed, Augustine's "attraction to Platonism was very serious, perhaps fatal."[40]

---

35 Bulgakov, *The Holy Grail*, 76. Avery Dulles, on the other hand, pointedly argues that the change that occurs in the Eucharist "does not fit into the categories of Aristotle, who believed that every substantial change involved a change in the appearances" as well. Consequently, the Church uses the term transubstantiation "to designate a process that is unique and unparalleled." See Dulles, *Church and Society* (New York: Fordham University Press, 2008), 457.

36 Christos Yannaras, *On the Absence and Unknowability of God*, trans. Haralambos Ventis (London: T & T Clark, 2005; orig., 1967), 43.

37 Yannaras, "Orthodoxy and the West," *Eastern Churches Review* 111, no. 3 (1971): 286–300, at 288. In a later book with the same title, Yannaras argues that the Western reception of Aristotle is very different from that found in the Cappadocians or John Damascene. For the West fell into an epistemology which lionized autonomous reason apart from its social and experiential roots. See *Orthodoxy and the West*, trans. Peter Chamberas and Norman Russell (Brookline, MA: Holy Cross Orthodox Press, 2006), 52–54.

38 Michael Azkoul, *The Influence of Augustine of Hippo on the Orthodox Church* (Lewiston, ME: The Edwin Mellen Press, 1990), 265.

39 Azkoul, *The Influence of Augustine of Hippo*, 268.

40 Azkoul, *The Influence of Augustine of Hippo*, 129. But note the work of Reinhard Flogaus who argues that even Gregory Palamas was influenced by Augustine and such influence is not unimportant since for certain Eastern theologians, Augustine is "the chief villain, the heresiarch"

In the eyes of these Eastern Orthodox thinkers, the West is largely rationalist and conceptualist, profoundly under the sway of secular philosophy, and far removed from the mystical and apophatic East which glories in a theology accenting the transcendence and hiddenness of God. It is certainly true that the West and East *did* place the theological accent differently. James Gill, for example, relates that at the Council of Florence, the Greeks (even those well disposed toward Catholicism such as Bessarion) were suspicious of any Western argument which relied not only on biblical and patristic sources but also on syllogistic reasoning, giving rise to the Greek response that arguments are convincing only when citing "St. Peter, St. Paul, St. Basil, Gregory the Theologian; a fig for your Aristotle, Aristotle."[41] But cannot one admit, as did Vatican II, that Western and Eastern theologians have often developed different but complementary perspectives, without thereby entailing a division, or the claim that philosophy has disfigured Christian faith?[42]

Catholics themselves, while frequently the target of the Hellenization thesis, are not exempt from invoking it. While rarely issuing blanket condemnations of philosophy or Hellenism, Catholic thinkers nonetheless point to select theological teachings as having been obscured by philosophical intrusions. One well-known instance is the split between the dogmatic tracts *de Deo uno et de Deo trino*. This narrative stems from Theodore de Régnon, the French theologian who argued that Western theology begins with a divine unity that is rationally argued while Eastern thought originates from the triune relationality of God.[43] Fergus Kerr observes that in the Eng-

---

whose theological errors led the West to atheism and rationalism. See "Inspiration-Exploitation-Distortion: The Use of St. Augustine in the Hesychast Controversy," in *Orthodox Readings of Augustine*, ed. George E. Demacopoulos and Aristotle Papanikolaou (Crestwood, NY: St. Vladimir's Seminary Press, 2008) 63–80, at 68.

41 James Gill, *The Council of Florence* (Cambridge: Cambridge University Press, 1959), 227. This Florentine response seems somewhat naïve given the quantity of ancient philosophy which the Greek Fathers assimilated (and transformed).

42 Of course, not every Orthodox thinker adopts the Hellenization thesis vis-à-vis the West. But Paul Gavrilyuk observes that in the quest for a stronger contemporary identity, some Orthodox writers equate "Eastern Orthodox" with true and authentic, while "Western" becomes a marker for all that is distorted, misguided, or false. Gavrilyuk notes that "in [Vladimir] Lossky's scheme, the term 'Western' has a very strong connotation of 'doctrinally questionable.'" See Paul Gavrilyuk, "The Reception of Dionysius in Twentieth Century Eastern Orthodoxy," *Modern Theology* 24, no. 4 (2008): 707–23, at 709 and 715.

43 Régnon, *Etudes de théologie positive sur la Sainte Trinité* (Paris: Victor Retaux, 1892–1896). For an argument that de Régnon sought only to identify differing but complementary approaches in East and West, see Kristin Hennessy, "An Answer to de Régnon's Accusers: Why We Should Not Speak of 'His' Paradigm," *Harvard Theological Review* 100, no. 2 (2007): 179–97.

lish speaking world, the storyline usually goes as follows: Aquinas first considered the divine nature philosophically and only later discussed the three divine persons, thereby forgetting the specifically Christian God and, in the process, opening a path for Enlightenment deism and even atheism.[44] Karl Rahner is often invoked as one who decried the deleterious effects of this split between the one and the triune God.[45] Balthasar further accuses Aquinas of paying insufficient attention to the concrete events of salvation history; Barth, by contrast, is fully alive to theology as a *scientia de singularibus*.[46] In these instances, Aquinas's philosophical thought is seen as jeopardizing the specificity of revelation.

Also under discussion by Catholic theologians are the traditional divine attributes of immutability and impassibility. Are these reflective of biblical truth or are these attributes merely representative of the corrosive influence of Hellenism? The move toward advocating a passible Godhead had become so widespread in theology that by the 1980s, one author spoke of the "rise of a new orthodoxy."[47] As Paul Gavrilyuk has observed, "It has become almost commonplace in contemporary theological works to pass a negative judgment upon the patristic concept of divine impassibility."[48] Indeed, this traditional attribute has "often been caricatured as an alien Hellenistic concept."[49] Thomas Weinandy points out that even Catholic scholars with unimpeachably Thomist credentials, such as W. Norris Clarke, William J. Hill, and Jean Galot imply that Christian thought must, at the very least, plot some distinction between God's ontological immutability and actual relationality if a properly biblical understanding of the traditional attributes is to be preserved.[50] Immutability and impassibility continue to be dis-

44 Fergus Kerr, "Thomas Aquinas: Conflicting Interpretations in Recent Anglophone Literature," in *Aquinas as Authority*, ed. Paul van Geest, et al. (Leuven: Peeters, 2002), 168.

45 Kerr, "Thomas Aquinas," 168, citing Rahner's "Remarks on the Dogmatic Treatise '*De Trinitate*.'" Kerr notes that Balthasar (although less frequently adduced) also accuses Aquinas of a defective Trinitarian doctrine. See Kerr, "Thomas Aquinas," 169, citing Hans Urs von Balthasar, *The Theology of Karl Barth*, trans. Edward Oakes (San Francisco: Ignatius Press, 1992), 263–66.

46 Balthasar says that Scholasticism concentrates on natures and essences, which is the opposite of Barth's dictum, *esse sequitur operari*. See *The Theology of Karl Barth*, 191 and 266.

47 See Ronald Goetz, "The Suffering God: The Rise of a New Orthodoxy," *Christian Century* 103, no. 13 (1986): 385–89.

48 Paul L. Gavrilyuk, *The Suffering of the Impassible God* (Oxford: Oxford University Press, 2004), 2.

49 Gavrilyuk, *The Suffering of the Impossible God*, 5.

50 See Thomas Weinandy, *Does God Suffer?* (Notre Dame: University of Notre Dame Press, 2000), 136n69.

cussed, then, with theologians exploring the extent to which these predicates must be further disciplined with the Gospel if they are to bear fruit in Christian life.

Perhaps the highest profile Catholic case in recent decades to argue that theology has been defaced by philosophy is the signature work of Jean-Luc Marion, *God Without Being*. Sounding deeply Barthian in his condemnation of being-language, Marion argues that metaphysics is "idolic" rather than "iconic," screening and obscuring the donative phenomenon of revelation. For Marion, the philosophical notion of being, long a pillar of Catholic theology, is an affront to a proper understanding of the Godhead because it establishes a constricting horizon within which the gratuitously given phenomenon of revelation must appear. Following Heidegger, Marion insists that this approach is nothing less than onto-theology, the inappropriate wedding of theology and metaphysics.[51] Marion has bluntly stated that "conceptual idolatry" has a site (metaphysics), a function (theology in ontotheology), and a definition (*causa sui*).[52] He does not hesitate to add, echoing Pascal, that, "The Gxd who reveals himself has nothing in common [. . .] with the 'God' of the philosophers, of the learned and, eventually, of the poet."[53] This Heidegger-like polemic against metaphysics has been softened by Marion in his later works (after some pointed criticism), but the theme has not disappeared from his thinking.[54]

Despite the various criticisms that have been lodged, it remains correct to say that the broad Catholic tradition ardently defends the thesis that theology legitimately assimilates philosophical thought, even if it needs to discipline it and to mold it in the image of the Gospel. And this gives rise to the second thesis.

51 See Marion, *God Without Being*, trans. Thomas Carlson (Chicago: University of Chicago Press, 1991). Also, Marion, "Metaphysics and Phenomenology: A Summary for Theologians," in *The Postmodern God*, ed. Graham Ward, 279–96 (Oxford: Blackwell, 1997).

52 Marion, *God Without Being*, 36.

53 Marion, *God Without Being*, 52.

54 Marion, "Saint Thomas et l'onto-théologie," *Revue Thomiste* 95, no. 1 (1995): 31–66. But Marion can still say, "In order to approach the question of charity, it is above all important not to suffer the influence of what metaphysics has thought about love." See Marion, *Prolegomena to Charity*, trans. Stephen E. Lewis (New York: Fordham University Press, 2002), 168.

THESIS TWO: THEOLOGY ASSIMILATES PHILOSOPHY (AND ALL WISDOM)

Of course, the claim that philosophy has deformed theology presupposes the prior theological assimilation of philosophical wisdom. Of this assimilation the Catholic tradition offers overwhelming evidence so we will pass over this thesis quickly.[55]

As everyone knows, a vital synthesis occurred between Christianity and Greco-Roman thought in the early years of the Church. In the third century, Origen used the term "spoils from Egypt" to describe, in biblical terms, the Christian use of ideas emanating, not only from Plato and Aristotle, but even from opponents of Christianity like Celsus.[56] Christians should act as did the Israelites at the time of the Exodus: "With the spoils taken from the Egyptians [. . .] were made the movable Holy of Holies, the arc with its cover [. . .] and the vessel of gold to hold the manna, the food of angels. These objects were truly made from the most beautiful gold of Egypt." Under Origen's influence, "spoils from Egypt" gradually became the major image sanctioning the use of Greek reasoning in Christian thought.[57]

Augustine borrows Origen's trope and popularizes it in the West: "If those who are called philosophers, and especially the Platonists, have said anything that is true and in harmony with our faith, we are not only not to shrink from it, but to claim it for our own use from those who have unlawful possession of it."[58] And in book five of his *De Trinitate* Augustine strives mightily to defend the eternal relations among the divine persons by utilizing (and transforming) Aristotelian categories. This appropriation of philosophy is possible because for Augustine, as MacIntyre observes, "philosophical enquiry, even unaided by faith, is a work of natural reason and nature is never wholly corrupted." The African's final verdict on the philosophers of Greece and Rome, "was that, although they had made various mistakes, 'nature itself has not permitted them to wander too far from the path of truth' in their judgments about the supreme good."[59]

---

55 For examples, see Guarino, *Foundations of Systematic Theology*, 269–310. Also, Z. P. Thundy, "Sources of *Spoliatio Aegyptiorum*," *Annuale mediaevale* 21 (1981): 77–90.

56 Origen, "Letter to Gregory," 393–94.

57 Gregory of Nyssa adduced Moses as the paradigmatic example of "taking spoils" for, as Acts 7:22 testifies, Moses "received a *paideia* in all the *sophia* of the Egyptians." See Jaroslav Pelikan, *Christianity and Classical Culture* (New Haven: Yale University Press, 1993), 10.

58 Augustine, *De doctrina christiana*, II, 40.

59 See Augustine, *De Civitate Dei*, 19. 1. Cited by MacIntyre, *God, Philosophy, Universities*, 31–32.

Aquinas, of course, was one of the most accomplished theologians at assimilating the philosophical wisdom of the ancients, freely pursuing "spoils" from the classical world. To those lodging objections against borrowing from pagan thinkers, St. Thomas counters that the Bible itself sanctions the use of ancient authors with St. Paul citing Epimenides and Menander (in Titus 1:12 and 1 Cor. 15:33). Given these Scriptural warrants, Aquinas asserts, "It is therefore licit for other doctors of divine Scripture also to make use of the arguments of the philosophers."[60] Sounding much like Origen, Thomas affirms, "Whatever its source, truth is of the Holy Spirit."[61]

Six centuries later, John Henry Newman argues persuasively that assimilating new perspectives is an essential part of Christian life and an inexorable dimension of the Church's proper development. The Christian "idea" must inevitably meet and absorb other points of view. This is the case because "whatever has life is characterized by growth" and any idea grows "by taking into its own substance external materials; and this absorption and assimilation is complete when the materials appropriated come to belong to it or enter into its unity."[62] He continues that "the idea never was that throve and lasted, yet [. . .] incorporated nothing from external sources."[63] Assimilation is not without dangers, to be sure, but it must be undertaken: "Whatever be the risk of corruption from intercourse with the world around, such a risk must be encountered if a great idea is duly to be understood, and much more if it is to be fully exhibited."[64]

In his response to those claiming that Christianity is a twisted amalgam of faith and philosophy, Newman memorably asserts: "They [his opponents] cast off all that they find in Pharisee or heathen; we conceive that the Church, like Aaron's rod, devours the serpents of the magicians. They are ever hunting for a fabulous primitive simplicity; we repose in Catholic fullness [. . .]. They are driven to maintain, on their part, that the Church's doctrine was never pure; we say that it can never be corrupt."[65] Newman concludes that no matter the falsehood attached to a particular system of thought, the Church can always extract good from evil because she is heir

60 Aquinas, *De Trinitate*, q. 2, a. 3, *sc.*

61 Aquinas, *Summa Theologiae*, I–II, q.109, a. 1, ad 1. Cited by John Paul II, Encyclical Letter *Fides et ratio* (September 14, 1998), no. 44.

62 See Newman, *Christian Doctrine*, 185.

63 Newman, *Christian Doctrine*, 186.

64 Newman, *Christian Doctrine*, 39–40.

65 Newman, *Christian Doctrine*, 382.

to the Lord's promise: "If they [his disciples] drank any deadly thing, it should not hurt them."[66]

A century after Newman, Henri de Lubac reprises Terence by insisting that "nothing authentically human, whatever its origin, can be alien to her [the Church]."[67] Cyril of Alexandria rightly made use of Plato, as did Ambrose of Seneca, Aquinas of Aristotle, and Matteo Ricci of Confucius. Such was the audacity of early Christians that they even incorporated the pagan image of the *"Magna mater"* (applied to the Church) into Catholic theology. This was "a typical example of the boldness of Christian thought which was strong enough to seize, without contamination, everything which could serve to express it [the faith]."[68] This daring, de Lubac insists, must be duplicated in our own day, with ideas harboring even Marxist and Nietzschean elements finding a place in some new theological synthesis, for "in the Church, the work of assimilation never ceases, and it is never too soon to undertake it!"[69] If the salt of Christianity is to maintain its tang, there must be an unending appropriation of human wisdom. The Church cannot simply revive the Middle Ages or even primitive Christianity; there must be a continual assimilation of new ideas.

Hans Urs von Balthasar similarly insisted that Catholic theology must open itself to every field of thought: "Why did Aquinas devote himself to Arabic and Aristotelian philosophy? Why did Möhler avail himself of Hegel, Newman, of Locke and Hume? In all cases they did so as to transpose natural philosophy to the supernatural order."[70] Balthasar pleads for the renewal of the assimilative imagination in Catholic theology, noting that Aquinas made full use of Plato, Aristotle, and the Stoics. Surely, "if he had known Buddha and Lao-Tse, there is no doubt that he would have drawn them too into the *summa* of what can be thought and would have given them the place appropriate to them."[71] Theology must absorb all that is living, whether one finds this is in Kant or Hegel, in Scheler or Heidegger.

---

66 Newman, *Christian Doctrine*, 441.

67 Henri de Lubac, *Catholicism*, trans. L. Sheppard (New York: Longmans, Green, and Co., 1950), 149–53.

68 See *The Motherhood of the Church*, trans. Sr. Sergia Englund (San Francisco: Ignatius Press, 1982), 54.

69 De Lubac, *The Drama of Atheist Humanism*, trans. E. Riley (London: Sheed and Ward, 1949), vi.

70 Balthasar, "On the Tasks of Catholic Philosophy in Our Time," translated by Brian McNeil, *Communio: International Catholic Review* 20, no. 1 (1993; orig., 1946): 155.

71 Balthasar, "Catholic Philosophy in Our Time," 158–59.

The plea of the *noveaux théologiens* for a renaissance of the absorptive imagination was, undoubtedly, a criticism of neo-scholasticism's attempt to foreshorten the process of assimilation by limiting itself to Aquinas's Aristotelianism, as if any further theological advance would require nothing more than extended glosses on Thomas's achievements. In this sense, the *nouvelle théologie* sought to move in two directions: to recover early Christian thought and to engage in an enriching dialogue with contemporary philosophical movements such as existentialism, personalism, and phenomenology.

In his controversial Regensburg Lecture, Benedict XVI dealt head-on with the issue of assimilation, directly attacking Harnack's Hellenization thesis and pronouncing it providential that St. Paul journeyed north to Greece (with its philosophical riches) while his path to Asia was blocked (citing Acts 16:6–10). Benedict has also praised the Church's gradual incorporation of Enlightenment themes, noting that, while one must exclude philosophies that eliminate God, one should nonetheless, "welcome the true conquests of the Enlightenment, human rights, and especially the freedom of faith and its practice, and recognize these also as being essential elements for the authenticity of religion."[72] Even though the Enlightenment, in its most radical form, was developed *against* Christianity, it, too, has borne good fruit that the Church must admire, pursue, and use. Perhaps one may see just here a reprise of Ovid's insight, *Fas est et ab hoste doceri*, "It is right to learn, even from an enemy,"[73] a position which has characterized the Church at least since Origen's careful weighing of Celsus's pointed criticisms of Christianity.

There is no need to multiply examples since the thesis that the Church has assimilated philosophical reasoning, for weal or for woe, is uncontested. But the truly crucial theological question remains. How are Athens and Jerusalem properly related? Is theology more Greek than Jew, or more *pistis* than *logos*? And precisely which kind of correlation exists between these terms?

THESIS THREE: THEOLOGY MUST PERFORMATIVELY DISCIPLINE PHILOSOPHY (AND ALL WISDOM)

The critical task in the theological absorption of philosophy (and other disciplines) involves the incorporation of new insights and perspectives without the concomitant loss of substantial identity. How is Christianity a

---

72 Benedict XVI, *Christmas Address to the Roman Curia* (December 22, 2006).

73 Ovid, *Metamorphoses*, IV, 428.

broadly capacious idea which takes every thought captive to Christ, as St. Paul counseled?[74] This is a particularly important point in the post-Enlightenment epoch when certain philosophers (the early Jürgen Habermas, for example) endorse precisely the opposite view: Every thought needs to be taken captive to the Enlightenment, since all religious claims need to be "publicly redeemed" if they are to have any role in societal discourse.[75]

The early Christian writers continuously insist on the theological disciplining of secular reasoning. Origen, as we have seen, boldly encourages taking "spoils from Egypt," yet argues that this project must be undertaken with caution: "Rare are those who have taken from Egypt only the useful, and go away and use it for the service of God. There are those who have profited from their Greek studies, in order to produce heretical notions and set them up, like the golden calf, in Bethel."[76] St. Augustine likewise cautioned that while the Egyptians undoubtedly yielded valuable spoils, they also possessed "idols and heavy burdens which the people of Israel hated and fled."[77] As John Rist has noted, Augustine's deep attraction to the Latin text of Isaiah 7:9, *Nisi credideritis, non intellegetis*, implies that the solutions offered by the philosophers are incomplete because lacking the guidance of Scripture and the Church.[78] St. Basil argues that while Christians are permitted to entertain the accounts of some classical poets, others should cause them to stop their ears, like Odysseus before the Sirens. All Christians, Basil counsels, should learn from the bees, who extract only honey from the flower. Like them, we should cull the best from pagan writers, while passing over the rest.[79] For all these thinkers, of course, the salient point is that philosophical wisdom may be used, but always subject to the Gospel. As St. Gregory Nazienzen stated, the Fathers theologized, "'in the manner of the Apostles, not in that of Aristotle,' *alieutikos, ouk aristotelikos.*"[80]

---

74 2 Cor. 10:5.

75 In recent years, however, Habermas has taken a much more benign view of religious belief. For a good overview of his developing attitude towards religious discourse, see Maureen Junker-Kenny, *Habermas and Theology* (New York: T & T Clark, 2011).

76 Origen, "Letter to Gregory," 393–94.

77 Augustine, *De doctrina christiana*, II, 40.

78 John Rist, *Augustine: Ancient Thought Baptized* (Cambridge: Cambridge University Press, 1994), 13.

79 Basil, "Address to Young People on Reading Greek Literature," in vol. 4 of *The Letters*, trans. R. Deferrari and M. McGuire (Cambridge, MA: Harvard University Press, 1934), 391–93.

80 Gregory Nazianzen, *Hom.* 23. 12. Cited by Georges Florovsky, vol. 1 of *The Collected Works of Georges Florovsky* (Belmont, MA: Nordland, 1972), 108.

As earlier noted, there is no greater example of this process of assimilation and transformation than that offered by Aquinas himself. But St. Thomas nonetheless insists that one is in error employing critical reason if one is "willing to believe nothing except what could be established by philosophical reasoning; when, on the contrary, *philosophy should be subject to the measure of faith* as the Apostle says 'Bring into captivity every thought to the obedience of Christ.'"[81] Aquinas then offers his own image, intended to complement the traditional "spoils" trope: those who use philosophical doctrines in service to the Christian faith do not *mix* water with wine, but *change* water into wine.[82] For Aquinas, all human learning can be of service to the faith, but it must be adduced wisely and judiciously, avoiding the dangers of philosophical imperialism.[83] Unsurprisingly, then, St. Thomas sounds the traditional caution: "In divine matters, natural reason is greatly deficient."[84] And he insists that no discipline can be a competitor to theology's claims, for these derive their authority and certitude not from fallible human reason, but from divine revelation.[85]

We have already seen that in the nineteenth century, Newman firmly endorsed the theological incorporation of all human wisdom. Only by casting a wide net could the idea of Christianity properly flourish, ripen, and develop. Yet Newman was also insistent on the performative disciplining of reason by faith. An idea surely grows by the absorption of external materials, but these very materials are "subjected to a new sovereign."[86] And while the Church is a vast treasure house of wisdom, she is always "casting the gold of fresh tributaries into her refiner's fire or stamping upon her own, as time required it, a deeper impress of her Master's image."[87] The Church, then, is always ingesting new ideas and perspectives—and, indeed, needs such nov-

---

81 Aquinas, *De Trinitate*, q. 2, a. 3, c, emphasis added.

82 Aquinas, *De Trinitate,* q. 2, a. 3, ad 5. Armand Maurer notes that Bonaventure quickly challenged this image, warning that, in any such mixture, the pure wine of Scripture is in danger of being reduced to philosophical water—the worst of miracles! See Aquinas, *Faith, Reason and Theology: Questions I–IV of the* De Trinitate *of Boethius,* trans. Armand Maurer (Toronto: Pontifical Institute of Medieval Studies, 1987), xv, no. 24.

83 For Aquinas's warnings against philosophical colonization, see John Wippel, *Mediaeval Reactions to the Encounter between Faith and Reason*, The Aquinas Lecture (Milwaukee: Marquette University Press, 1995), 14–28.

84 Aquinas, *Summa theologiae*, II-II, q. 2, a.4.

85 Aquinas, *Summa theologiae*, I, q. 1, a. 5, ad 2.

86 Newman, *Christian Doctrine*, 186.

87 Newman, *Christian Doctrine*, 382.

elty to thrive and properly develop. At the same time, the Church molds and measures human wisdom by the Word of God. Such theological measuring is essential, otherwise the Church's faith would be "depraved by the intrusion of foreign principles." For Newman, the "original type" of Christianity must always be preserved, even while the Church gains vital nourishment from every form of thought.[88]

Henri de Lubac, as earlier noted, boldly called for the assimilation of new philosophies, insisting that even ideas with a Marxist or Nietzschean stamp would find a place in some new theological synthesis. But to mark the proper relationship between faith and reason, De Lubac liked to cite Augustine's recollection of the divine voice in the *Confessions*, "*Non tu me in te mutabis, sicut cibum carnis tuae, sed tu mutaberis in me.*" (You will not transform me into you [the Lord says], as with your fleshly food; rather, you will be transformed into me.)[89] Balthasar, too, although an early champion of assimilative theology, insisted that every concrete philosophy must be measured by its relationship to the one God in Jesus Christ.[90] The sovereign and free Lord of the Bible cannot be encompassed by any system, whether it is Hegel's *Geist*, Schopenhauer's *Wille*, or Schelling's *intellektuelle Anschauung*. In opposition to philosophical notions seeking to control divine revelation, Balthasar invokes Mary's Magnificat: *deposuit potentes de sede.*[91]

Joseph Ratzinger similarly argues that the Church's absorption of philosophy always involves a transformation. In his well-known book on eschatology, for example, Ratzinger attacks the oft-repeated claim that the concept of an "immortal soul" is simply an alien import from Platonic philosophy.[92] In fact, Ratzinger avers, the Church's teaching on immortality was determined by Christology. It was Christian belief that made assertive claims upon philosoph-

---

88 Of course, the crucial theological issue lies in determining how this "original type" is preserved, even while allowing for the growth and development that necessarily occurs over time. As Newman realized, this process involves a variety of *loci theologici*, including the work of theologians, the *sensus fidelium*, and the magisterium.

89 De Lubac, *A Brief Catechesis on Nature and Grace*, trans. R. Arnandez (San Francisco: Ignatius Press, 1984), 69. For Augustine, see *Confessions*, VII, 10.

90 Balthasar, *The Theology of Karl Barth*, 257.

91 Balthasar, *Love Alone Is Credible*, trans. A. Dru (New York: Herder and Herder, 1969), 34.

92 The Lutheran-Catholic dialogue in the United States quotes a contemporary Protestant theologian who says that "the battle against the concept of immortality [. . .] has dominated German Protestant theology for the last half-century." See Gerhard Sauter, *What Dare We Hope? Reconsidering Eschatology* (Harrisburg: Trinity Press, 1999), 188. Cited by the US Lutheran-Roman Catholic Dialogue, *The Hope of Eternal Life* (Minneapolis: Lutheran University Press, 2011), 11n42.

ical anthropology, not the other way around.[93] While Aquinas undoubtedly uses Aristotelian *language*—speaking of the soul as *"forma corporis"*—this takes on an entirely different *meaning* than it had in Aristotle's philosophy. For the Stagirite, the soul is entirely bonded to matter, while St. Thomas protects the biblical affirmation that union with Christ overcomes death. In Aquinas, then, philosophical concepts are marshaled in order to champion what amounts to an impossibility in Aristotle's own thought. As Ratzinger would later say in the Regensburg Address, the Greek heritage forms an integral part of the Christian faith, but it does so only as "critically purified."[94]

What is at stake in all of these examples is the epistemic primacy of theology, a discipline which nonetheless relies on and uses philosophy, and, indeed, all of the sciences. It is just this primacy (and precisely how it is understood) that gives rise to pressing contemporary questions: How does Catholic theology properly assimilate evolutionary biology, quantum mechanics, liberation theology, feminist thought, bioethical advances, Nietzschean postmodernity, Whiteheadian process philosophy, Heideggerian hermeneutics, and so on? How does it refine and utilize every idea while stamping it, as Newman counseled, "with a deeper impress of [the] Master's image"? The best theologians are well aware that assimilative efforts must be continually underway, for theology, if it is to flourish, must be in profound dialogue with all of the academic disciplines. Without such a dialogue, Newman recognized, the Christian "idea" could not thrive and develop, could not become a powerful stream with a broad and capacious riverbed. The theological enterprise, then, must engage the entire treasury of human wisdom, not only because of Catholicism's decided commitment to the conjunction of faith and reason, but also to ensure the continuing intelligibility of Christianity itself.

But it is one thing to insist on the incorporative nature of theology, and on the ultimate primacy of the Gospel. There is little argument on these points, even from those stressing theology's mutually correlational dimensions. It is another matter entirely to determine if *some particular and concrete use* of philosophy or other discipline is fully congruent with the Christian faith, that is, if it leads to some complementary development which is architectonically and harmoniously related to the earlier doctrinal

---

93 Joseph Ratzinger, *Eschatology*, trans. Michael Waldstein (Washington, DC: The Catholic University of America Press, 1988), 143–47.

94 Benedict XVI, *Regensburg Lecture*.

tradition. This latter determination is usually not immediately visible and requires an extended process of discernment; it is the work of time, thought, and the Holy Spirit. *Gaudium et spes* affirms that "the recent studies and findings of science, history and philosophy raise new questions which affect life and which demand new theological investigations."[95] More recently, John Paul II, in his *Letter on Galileo*, chided theologians to keep up with developments in science and, if necessary, to make adjustments to their teaching. Rahner observed that the assimilative process (which at times requires the elimination of long-held conceptual models) is so sensitive that some friction inevitably accompanies this arduous but essential procedure.[96] The continuing theological task is to balance absorption and purification, learning from every quarter of human knowledge, even while maintaining "identity of type" over time.

THESIS FOUR: THE *RELATIVE* AUTONOMY OF THE PHILOSOPHICAL ORDER

Whereas theology assimilates and disciplines philosophy (and all human wisdom), it must be equally affirmed that other fields have their own legitimate autonomy; they cannot simply be subsumed under, or made lackeys of, theological reasoning. Indeed, there exists a long Catholic tradition acknowledging the comparative independence of the natural, created estate. One reason for such recognition was the indefeasible evidence that a host of ancient philosophers, without the palpable benefit of Judeo-Christian revelation, had penetrated deeply into the *logos*-structure of the universe, and into the existing moral order. Vatican II affirmed this tradition when stating, "For by the very circumstance of their having been created, all things are endowed with their own stability, truth, goodness, proper laws and order."[97] And again, "If by the autonomy of earthly affairs we mean that created things and societies themselves enjoy their own laws and values which must be gradually deciphered, put to use, and regulated by men, then it is entirely right to demand that autonomy."[98] These statements display the

---

95 Vatican Council II, *Gaudium et spes* (December 7, 1965), no. 62.

96 See Rahner, "Yesterday's History of Dogma and Theology for Tomorrow," in vol. 18 of *Theological Investigations*, trans. Edward Quinn (Chestnut Ridge, NY: The Crossroad Publishing Company, 1983), 13.

97 *Gaudium et spes*, no. 36.

98 *Gaudium et spes*, no. 36.

classical Catholic theme that the natural sphere possesses an integral excellence and intrinsic stability.

More recently, the relative independence of the natural order was ardently defended by John Paul II in his 1998 encyclical *Fides et ratio*. In this letter, the pope insists that philosophy and reason have a legitimate autonomy that cannot be suppressed (*comprimere*), even by the content of revelation.[99] And he reminds readers that the ancient discipline is "rightly jealous" of its independence. The pope's intention here is transparent: the philosophical order—and the created estate generally—possess an authentic autonomy and freedom even "apart" from revelation. So earnestly does the pope defend this position that he eschews, at least theoretically, the venerable term for philosophy as *ancilla theologiae*, lest the impression be given that philosophical reasoning does not have a legitimate sovereignty within its own estate.[100] Reason, though embedded in the *unicus ordo supernaturalis*, has an actual, if not total, independence.

This insistence on the autonomy of the philosophical order has been taken up by Benedict XVI in several venues.[101] For example, in his (abortive) 2008 discourse to the faculty and students of the University of Rome, the pope speaks of the "autonomy which [. . .] has always been part of the nature of universities, which must be tied exclusively to the authority of truth." And he eulogistically invokes Aquinas who "highlighted the autonomy of philosophy, and with it, the laws and responsibility proper to reason." The pope even invokes the council of Chalcedon, observing that "philosophy and theology must be interrelated 'without confusion and without separation.'"[102]

A careful reading of both John Paul II and Benedict XVI reveals that while they endorse the independence of the natural order, they acknowledge this as a *relative*, not absolute autonomy. As *Fides et ratio* states, in the light of divine revelation philosophy itself must undergo "profound transformations." And the encyclical makes a clear distinction between the valid

---

99 John Paul II, Encyclical Letter *Fides et ratio* (September 14, 1998) , no. 79. In *Acta apostolicae sedis* 91 (1999), 5–88. An English translation may be found in *Origins* 28 (October 22, 1998): 317–47. See also the supporting comments found at nos. 48 and 67. Of course, John Paul II also makes clear that philosophy has no *ultimate* "self-sufficiency." Therefore, one fittingly refers to philosophy's *real but relative* autonomy.

100 John Paul II, *Fides et ratio*, no. 77.

101 I have adduced several "Benedictine" examples defending the relative autonomy of the natural sphere in essay seven of this volume, "Nature and Grace: Seeking the Delicate Balance."

102 See *Lecture of Benedict XVI at the University of Rome 'La Sapienza'* (January 17, 2008). In *Acta apostolicae sedis* 100 (2008), 107–14.

autonomy of philosophy and its *illegitimate* self-sufficiency.[103] This is to say that while the philosophical sphere has an authentic liberty, it must ultimately be enlightened by the Gospel. One may conclude, then, that *Fides et ratio* is endorsing the fuller maxim concerning philosophy's traditional role: *ancilla theologiae sed non ancilla nisi libera*. Philosophy can properly serve theology only if she is free and independent, always exploring new realms of thought, entirely without constraint. Of course, what is said here of philosophy applies equally to the sciences and to other disciplines.

It is precisely because of philosophy's authentic autonomy that reason and faith can enrich each other, as *Fides et ratio* states, with a mutually "purifying critique."[104] Joseph Ratzinger expanded on this point in his 2004 dialogue with Jürgen Habermas: "I would speak of a necessary relatedness between reason and faith and between reason and religion, which are called to purify and help one another. They need each other, and they must acknowledge this mutual need."[105]

This marked accent on the autonomy of the philosophical order makes me hesitant about unreservedly endorsing the claim of the well-known Thomist, Victor Preller, who states, "Aquinas is always writing as *catholicae doctor veritatis* [. . .]. And in his interpretation of Aristotle [. . .] he tells us what Aristotle would say *after* his errors were corrected in the light of the *truth* of the Catholic faith."[106] Preller's formulation properly notes the priority of revelation in Aquinas's thought. But one wonders if his comment entirely protects the autonomy of the philosophical order as Aquinas understood it. Was St. Thomas always writing (explicitly) as a Catholic theologian? Or did he recognize that a significant amount of truth was delivered by philosophical reasoning alone? At times Aquinas appears to defend positions on purely philosophical grounds, positions he was convinced that philosophers had safeguarded without the light of revelation.[107]

In just this regard, one turns to Aquinas's campaign against radical Aristotelianism, particularly its position on the nature of the intellect. Against

103 John Paul II, *Fides et ratio*, nos. 75, 77.

104 *Fides et ratio*, no. 100.

105 Joseph Ratzinger and Jürgen Habermas, *The Dialectics of Secularization*, trans. Brian McNeil (San Francisco: Ignatius Press, 2006), 78.

106 Victor Preller, "Water into Wine," in *Grammar and Grace*, ed. Jeffrey Stout and Robert Mac-Swain, 253–69 (London: SCM Press, 2004), 262.

107 On Aquinas as a philosopher, see John F. Wippel, *Metaphysical Themes in Thomas Aquinas II* (Washington, DC, The Catholic University of America Press, 2007), 240–71.

the monopsychism of his fellow Parisian master, Siger of Brabant, St. Thomas argues that there exists a diversity of intellects in diverse beings. He states that he could easily prove his case by relying on the truth of the Christian faith. But he will display the error by arguing on philosophical grounds alone.[108] Does Aquinas argue this way only because he saw the truth of this matter on the basis of faith? Or did proper philosophical reasoning also deliver to him this correction of radical Aristotelianism? After all, Aquinas did not hesitate to affirm philosophy's powers, even while acknowledging that they fall short of the contents of faith.[109] Indeed, at the very outset of his magnum opus, St. Thomas insists that philosophy's unfettered autonomy is called into question for one reason only: "Eye has not seen, O God, what you have prepared for those who wait for you."[110] While philosophy cannot be the last word about the world and humanity, the relative autonomy of the philosophical order is never evacuated.

Preller's comment may well reflect the tendency of certain thinkers to worry about the relative autonomy of the philosophical estate, thinking that to insist even on limited independence is to open the door to what an earlier generation called "separated philosophy."[111] There is also the further fear that this accent on philosophical liberty—even in a mitigated sense—leads to the kind of rationalism associated with the radical Enlightenment. For if philosophy, science, and the created estate generally enjoy a substantial independence, cannot one fairly conclude that revelation and faith are superfluous accoutrements, prostheses for which contemporary men and women have no need? Why not live *etsi Deus non daretur*?

Precisely this fear of an imperious cultural rationalism—with secular Archimedean principles seeking either to supervise or to ignore the world of faith—appears to animate statements found in certain theologians. George Lindbeck, for example, concludes his influential *The Nature of Doctrine* by stating that the world must be absorbed into the biblical narrative.[112] In one sense

---

108 See *On the Unity of the Intellect Against the Averroists*, trans. Beatrice H. Zedler (Milwaukee: Marquette University Press, 1968), 22. It is true that in this instance Thomas modifies Aristotle in light of the Christian faith (and on its face this is supportive of Preller's thesis), but Aquinas is convinced that he is arguing on grounds that are entirely accessible philosophically, not only theologically.

109 Aquinas, *De Trinitate*, q. 2, a. 3, c.

110 Aquinas, *Summa theologiae* I, q. 1, a. 1.

111 See, for example, Jacques Maritain, *An Essay on Christian Philosophy*, trans. Edward H. Flannery (New York: Philosophical Library, 1955).

112 George Lindbeck, *The Nature of Doctrine* (Philadelphia: Westminster Press, 1984), 135.

this is true since heteronomous and alien standards of thought cannot ultimately judge revelation. However, neither can philosophy lose its proper autonomy by being simply absorbed into theology. For instance, D. Stephen Long, in a generally excellent work, exhibits some of these same concerns. He worries about a Catholic thought that divides philosophy, particularly metaphysics, "too thoroughly" from theology.[113] While Long is right that philosophy must ultimately be theologically disciplined, his work, at times, appears to suffer from the fear of even the *relative* autonomy of the philosophical estate.

Instructive about this entire issue of the comparative independence of the natural order is the thinking of Leo Strauss, who insists on philosophy's *complete* autonomy, with no contribution whatsoever from revelation. For Strauss, Christianity has only hampered thinking by continually assimilating philosophy into decidedly theological narratives.[114] Because of the theological colonization of philosophy, Strauss continues, thinking today is much more difficult than it was at the time of Plato. Plato held that humanity must emerge from a natural cave, but Strauss argues that there are now *two* caves obscuring philosophy's ascent to truth: the cave of natural ignorance, and the cave of a tradition based on revelation. This second cave cannot be attributed to Judaism or Islam because in these religions there is a decided difference between human wisdom and the eternal dictates of Divine Law. For Strauss, "it is clear that Christianity alone has 'stepped into the world of philosophy.'"[115] It has subjected philosophy to theological control, thereby deforming the classical tradition and creating unnatural conditions for thought.

Ironically, Strauss's work purveys the Hellenization thesis in reverse. It is not Greek thought that has obscured Christianity. Rather, Christian revelation, with its incorporation of philosophy into a master theological narrative, has damaged the ancient discipline. It is no surprise, therefore, that "Strauss never ceases to highlight what he takes to be the fundamental opposition between Athens and Jerusalem."[116] Strauss argues that philosophical reasoning needs absolute and unfettered autonomy if it is to reach

---

113 See D. Stephen Long, *Speaking of God: Theology, Language, and Truth* (Grand Rapids: Eerdmans Publishing, 2009), 65, 258.

114 For an excellent analysis of Strauss's understanding of the relationship between philosophy and religious thought, see John Ranieri, *Disturbing Revelation: Leo Strauss, Eric Voegelin, and the Bible* (Columbia: University of Missouri Press, 2009), 23. Also illuminative is Clark A. Merrill, "Leo Strauss's Indictment of Christian Philosophy," *The Review of Politics* 62, no. 1 (2000): 77–105.

115 Ranieri, 23.

116 Ranieri, 17.

truth. His position, then, throws into high relief the fundamental claim of Catholic thought: while accenting the freedom and liberty of the philosophical and scientific order, theology nonetheless insists that the light of revelation must clarify and illuminate philosophical discussion.

In summary, Catholic theology holds for the *real but relative* autonomy of the created estate. Nature has only a relative autonomy because it is always embedded in the one and only sphere of grace. In the middle of the notorious nature/grace controversy of the 1940s, Balthasar gave a subtle response to both neo-scholasticism and Karl Barth on just this point, insisting that, because all of creation is embedded in the supernatural sphere, the deeply Aristotelian term "nature" could be invoked only analogically. At the same time, Balthasar held that there is a certain stability and integrity in the natural, philosophical estate itself, even if it is always transformed and irradiated by divine revelation.[117]

In certain segments of contemporary theology, there is a strong accent on the recovery of biblical and patristic sources, on the entire project of *ressourcement.*

This recovery, which legitimately accents the graced world of revelation and faith, should not be placed at antipodes with the autonomy belonging to philosophy and science. Nor should this renascence be naively opposed to modernity and the Enlightenment, as if these later movements contained nothing but errors and blind alleys. The Enlightenment's mistake was not its affirmation of an independent and free reason. Such autonomy is essential and the great medieval theologians affirmed it. Its error was that, by its positivism and radical empiricism, the existing real was entirely severed from the *fons et origo* of being itself.[118] This is what de Lubac meant when he remarked towards the end of his life that modernity will always *know* more, it will always *explain* more, but it will never *understand* more, because it has refused mystery.[119] But it would be an unfortunate mistake to allow

---

117 For a discussion of Balthasar on this point, see Guarino, *Foundations of Systematic Theology,* 224–31.

118 Or, as Alvin Plantinga argued, the Enlightenment's error was its insistence that revelation justify itself before the bar of reason. But one cannot give a non-circular rational argument establishing that reason itself is reliable. Why, then, must the sources of religious belief justify themselves before the bar of rational intuition? See Plantinga, *Where the Conflict Really Lies* (Oxford: Oxford University Press, 2011), 48–49.

119 Henri de Lubac, *A Theologian Speaks* (Los Angeles: Twin Circle, 1985), 25. This publication is an English translation of an interview of de Lubac by Angelo Scola which first appeared in the Italian journal *30 Giorni* (July 1985).

the Christian reaction to modernity's errors to evacuate philosophy of its proper autonomy and the *natural* visibility of truth that belongs to the created estate.

THESIS FIVE: THE ASSIMILATION OF "SPOILS" FROM EVERY SOURCE INDICATES THE NECESSITY OF THEOLOGICAL PLURALISM

The capacious absorption of "spoils" means, as we have seen, that the Church assimilates all human wisdom to her evangelical perspective. Precisely because the Church casts a wide net, this incorporative action inexorably leads to theological pluralism. Already in the 1930s and 1940s, the *nouvelle théologie* sought to overcome a conceptually univocal neo-scholasticism that had been hegemonic since *Aeterni Patris* (1879) in order to restore a broader assimilative imagination to theological reasoning. M.-D. Chenu and Henri Bouillard argued at length for the pluralism characteristic of the earlier theological tradition, while Yves Congar pointed to the unique witness of Eastern Christianity as displaying authentic plurality at the very heart of the ancient Church. Diversity and unity could not be placed at antipodes.[120]

Bouillard was attacked (and ultimately disciplined after *Humani generis* was published in 1950) for writing in 1944 that a simple study of history shows that, over the course of time, the Church borrows various philosophical concepts in order to express her faith. For example, when speaking about grace and justification, the concepts used by the evangelists, by Augustine, by Aquinas, and by post-Tridentine theologians, differ significantly. But, Bouillard adds, these varying formulations are not incongruously diverse; they are united by a fundamental affirmation: We are justified by God's grace in Jesus Christ, who empowers us to live holy lives. Bouillard argues, in other words, that the Church maintains doctrinal unity in and through a variety of philosophical forms and semantic lexica. The same is true of the term

---

120 For Chenu, see *Le Saulchoir: Une école de théologie* (Kain-Lez-Tournai: Le Saulchoir, 1937). A 1985 reprint was issued by Les editions du Cerf, Paris. For Bouillard, *Conversion et Grâce chez S. Thomas d'Aquin: Étude Historique* (Paris: Aubier, 1944). For Congar, *After Nine Hundred Years* (Westport, CT: Greenwood Press, 1978). Also, *Diversity and Communion*, trans. John Bowden (Mystic, CT: Twenty-Third Publications, 1985). Of the many recent books on the *nouvelle théologie*, I have found helpful Hans Boersma, *Nouvelle Théologie and Sacramental Ontology: A Return to Mystery* (Oxford: Oxford University Press, 2009). Also, Boersma, "Nature and the Supernatural in *la nouvelle théologie*: The Recovery of a Sacramental Mindset," *New Blackfriars* 93, no. 1043 (2012): 34–46.

"transubstantiation." Catholicism did not always use the Aristotelian language of substance and accident to explain the Real Presence of Christ in the Eucharist (and Eastern Christianity did not use these concepts at all). Nor does Catholicism require the language of hylomorphic theory (as used at the fourteenth century council of Vienne) to elucidate the unity of the human person embedded in Christian anthropology. Newer philosophical forms could and should be sought to mediate Christian teaching precisely because the Church of every epoch must express its faith in formulations that are intelligible to the men and women of their time. There exists, then, a continuing process of reconceptualization which allows for authentic diversity even while protecting the substantial identity of doctrine.[121]

Bouillard, with the *nouvelle théologie* generally, was urging theology to widen its philosophical compass beyond the conceptual and lexical monism of neo-scholasticism in order to engage in a more robust dialogue with the existentialism, personalism, and phenomenology that were sweeping European thought in the forties. The markedly neo-Augustinian philosophy of Maurice Blondel was important to the *nouveaux théologiens* as was the invigorating dialogue with modern thought conducted by Joseph Maréchal. And there were pressing pastoral concerns as well. When de Lubac published *Catholicism* in 1938 he was clearly uneasy that France was becoming increasingly Marxist and anti-religious. One reason for this was that the Church's scholastic-tinged formulations failed to resonate with men and women of the day, while various political movements had appropriated the traditional Christian concepts of brotherhood and the unity of humanity. So, when the series *Sources chrétiennes* was founded in 1943 to propagate the thought of early Christian writers, and when Daniélou argued that neo-scholasticism was largely outdated, this was not a full-scale attack on Thomism, but reflected a marked desire to repristinate the faith, restoring its evangelical vigor by widening the store of "spoils" beyond Thomas's Aristotelianism.[122] This is why de Lubac spoke of the need for contemporary styles in theology

121 I discuss Bouillard's position at length, as well as the entire debate over the context/content approach to pluralism, including the philosophical warrants necessary to sustain it, and the objections lodged against it, in *Foundations of Systematic Theology*, 141–67.

122 See Jean Daniélou, "Les orientations preésentes de la pensée religieuse," *Études* 79 (1946): 5–21. The first English translation of this article of which I am aware is "The Present Orientations of Religious Thought," *Josephinum Journal of Theology* 18, no. 1 (2011): 51–62. For a compact treatment of the issues surrounding the *nouvelle théologie*, see Brian Daley, "The *Nouvelle Théologie* and the Patristic Revival: Sources, Symbols, and the Science of Theology," *International Journal of Systematic Theology* 7, no. 4 (2005): 362–82.

and why he championed the ancient axiom *"Diversi sed non adversi,"* a maxim indicating that there can be diverse approaches to theological issues without thereby sanctioning adversarial and incommensurable paths.[123]

Of course, the importance of authentic pluralism had been defended on several fronts. Gilson had shown, in his careful studies of Aquinas, Bonaventure, and Scotus, that significant dimensions of plurality had already existed in medieval philosophy, with very different theoretical visions underlying a common faith. And Congar had vigorously argued in 1937, in his groundbreaking *Chrétiens désunis,* that Christians often affirmed the same mystery from different perspectives.[124] Well before the *nouvelle théologie,* one could find this same theme in the writings of Johann Evangelist Kuhn of Tübingen, who insisted that the Church's faith could never be a "a monotone spiritless repetition of the same concepts and expressions." Kuhn argues, rather, that the Church's preaching and theology must be *geistlich* and *zeitgemäß,* speaking the ancient Christian faith in the language of the times and making full use of the surrounding culture.[125] As is well-known, the authentic theological plurality championed by Kuhn and the *nouvelle théologie* was explicitly confirmed at Vatican II.[126] In my judgment, the *nouvelle théologie* and Vatican II (as well as Kuhn earlier), sanctioned what may be called "commensurable pluralism" meaning by this term that there exists a fundamental unity of Christian doctrine (taking account of all the necessary qualifications, e.g., the hierarchy of truths and theological notes), but that doctrine is now expressed in wide variety of concepts, forms, and lexica. History itself had witnessed to the fact that diversity and communion are co-existing realities. The council intended to recover the traditional theological absorption of new philosophies, cultures, and languages, all in service to authentic plurality.

---

123 See de Lubac, "A propos de la formule: *Diversi, sed non adversi," Recherches de science religieuse* 40 (1952): 27–40, and Hubert Silvestre, *"Diversi sed non adversi," Recherches de théologie ancienne et médiévale* 31 (1964): 124–32.

124 See Yves Congar, *Divided Christendom* (London: Centenary, 1939).

125 J. E. Kuhn, *Einleitung in die katholische Dogmatik,* 2 vols. (Tubingen, 1846–1847).

126 The most obvious official support for this position is found in the opening speech of John XXIII (repeated in *Gaudium et spes,* no. 62), with its distinction between the *depositum fidei* and the *modus quo veritates enuntiantur* leading Yves Congar to remark that these few words summarize the meaning of the entire council. See Congar, *A History of Theology,* trans. Hunter Guthrie (Garden City, NY: Doubleday, 1968), 18–19. Giuseppe Alberigo has called this distinction one of the decisive motifs of the council. See Alberigo, "Facteurs de 'Laïcité' au Concile Vatican II," *Revue des sciences religieuses* 74, no. 2 (2000): 211–25.

This conciliar distinction between the meaning of a Christian doctrine and the formulation or concept through which it is expressed is entirely traditional. Already in the early fifth century, Vincent of Lérins was fully alive to this distinction, exhorting Christians, *dicas nove non dicas nova*.[127] John Damascene endorsed this position in the eighth century, as did Aquinas five centuries later.[128] Such authentic pluralism, of course, is never simply iterative repetition. A new concept or *Denkstil* necessarily throws into relief unseen aspects of a doctrine's truth, bringing forth perspectives and insights which may have been languishing in obscurity (or adding a welcome and complementary supplement). By admitting that the traditional affirmations of doctrine could be expressed in new philosophical and cultural forms, the council sought to make the faith more intelligible to the times, to expose previously hidden dimensions of the mystery of faith, to allow for legitimate doctrinal development, and, crucially, to acknowledge that the formulations of Orthodox and Protestant Christians might differently, but complementarily, mediate the truth of Christian doctrine.

Of course, precisely *how* the identical meaning is preserved over time and in new formulations requires nuance and sophistication. Rahner clearly recognized the difficulties attending this process, warning that "context" and "content" are not easily discernable and separable.[129] At the same time, Rahner insisted that, even within the process of reconceptualization, one "must of course make simultaneously clear that the sameness of dogma in the old sense is assured and the effort to do this must not be regarded in principle as dubious, as a feeble and cowardly compromise [. . .]."[130] The

127 *Commonitorium*, no. 22. Vincent argues that while the words *homoousios* and *Theotokos* are not found in the earliest tradition, they perfectly express biblical faith. Vincent sanctioned not only re-expression; he was an early and vigorous champion of doctrinal development, *eodem sensu eademque sententia*.

128 See John of Damascus, *On the Divine Images*, trans. David Anderson (Crestwood, NY: St. Vladimir's Seminary Press, 1980), 71. Gregory Nazianzen expresses the same thought in the fourth century when he says that there exists "a great deal of diversity inherent in names" for it is a matter of "meanings rather than words." See *Oration* 31.24. For Aquinas, see *Summa Theologiae*, I, 29, 3, ad 1, where he argues that new words are necessary to express the ancient faith.

129 I outline Rahner's cautious thought on the form-content distinction in *Revelation and Truth* (Scranton: University of Scranton Press, 1993), 49–55 and, more briefly in *Foundations of Systematic Theology*, 192–93. Rahner chided the CDF's 1973 declaration, *Mysterium Ecclesiae*, for making things easy for itself with the form/content distinction. Although Rahner himself used this approach, he was well-aware of the difficulties attending the facile invocation of it. See Rahner, "*Mysterium Ecclesiae*," in vol. 17 of *Theological Investigations*, trans. Margaret Kohl (Chestnut Ridge, NY: The Crossroad Publishing Company, 1981), 151.

130 See Rahner, "Yesterday's History of Dogma and Theology for Tomorrow," 13.

underlying issue here is always the same: How can there be a series of new philosophical forms and concepts which allows the Christian faith to speak robustly and vigorously in every age—the new wine of the Gospel always in fresh skins?

More recently, *Fides et ratio* endorses philosophical pluralism at great length, a pluralism that ineluctably leads to theological diversity. The encyclical insists that the Church has no philosophy of her own, relativizes St. Thomas (even if he remains a unique master), and calls for a new philosophy which takes account of the entire prior tradition. This emphasis on authentic pluralism was further strengthened in 2001 when the Congregation for the Doctrine of the Faith rehabilitated the thought of Antonio Rosmini, acknowledging that his desire to surpass neo-scholastic language and concepts led to the illegitimate condemnation of theses drawn from his works.[131]

One significant fruit of theological reflection from *Aeterni Patris* in 1879, through the *fin de siècle* Modernist crisis, through the *nouvelle théologie*, and down to Vatican II and afterwards, has been to show that one need not be a neo-Thomist or neo-scholastic to protect, explore, or fruitfully develop the mysteries of faith. The truth of revelation is dependent on neither conceptual nor cultural univocity. Each epoch "performs" the truth of revelation in its own day, even while in doctrinal continuity with the Church of earlier centuries. Theology, then, fruitfully explores and assimilates philosophy, and every academic field of inquiry, since penetrating reason can always further illuminate (and creatively develop) the mysteries of faith.

THESIS SIX: THE UNIQUE ROLE OF METAPHYSICS (COMMODIOUSLY UNDERSTOOD) IN CATHOLIC THEOLOGY

Surely it smacks of a performative contradiction to insist that theology must be vigorously pluralistic, and then to contend for the essential role of metaphysics—capaciously understood—in theological thinking. Yet that is the argument offered here. For while theology must constantly incorporate fresh ideas, foster authentic diversity, and remain in lively dialogue with an extensive variety of perspectives, metaphysics, broadly speaking, provides the essential theoretical spine, buttressing (in the philosophical sphere) theology's universal and trans-cultural claims.

---

131 I have treated of the intricacies of the CDF's statements on this case in "Rosmini, Ratzinger, and Kuhn: Observations on a Note by the Doctrinal Congregation," *Theological Studies* 64, no. 1 (2003): 43–68.

Metaphysics under Assault

Although the Hellenization thesis extends to several forms of philosophy, it is metaphysics, in particular, that has been regarded as the primary enemy of biblical teaching and so, of revelation itself. As we have seen, the principal *theological* charge is that metaphysics is an alien ideology, a pre-existing Procrustean bed which seeks to shape and mold the Christian faith according to its own foreign and intrusive norms. But metaphysics, of course, has been attacked on philosophical grounds as well.

Louis Dupré has provided a useful typology for the assault. He notes that the ancients were constructivists only to the extent that a pre-existing nature or essence could be further refined and cultivated. With Descartes and Kant, however, there develops a gradual loss of the intelligibility mediated by the form-giving principles of *kosmos* and *physis*, of the truth mediated by nature. The accent is placed, rather, on the subject's own intense, form-shaping role. Humanity itself, not a pre-existing cosmic structure, is the measure of all things. For post-Kantian voluntarism (including, one might add, postmodernity), nature—and, indeed, any insistence on a discernable *logos*-structure of the world—gradually becomes the enemy of emancipatory freedom since it tries to shape the subject according to pre-existing norms. But only the autonomous person in his or her sovereign liberty is the proper locus of meaning and truth.[132]

By the time one reaches Nietzsche, meaning is entirely and without remainder bestowed by human subjectivity. In his parable, "How the World Became a Fable," Nietzsche says that the "true world" was first available to the wise man, the follower of Plato. Later, the truth was promised to the Christian, the one who was committed to a virtuous life. In Kantian philosophy, the true world became unknowable, with reality itself (the noumenon) escaping humanity's cognitive grasp. Today, Nietzsche adds, even positing an "objective world" no longer makes sense; it is entirely superfluous. In other words, the "world" does not possess a pre-existing *ratio,* nor do human beings have a given nature or essence; intelligibility is *created* by every person who has the fortitude to establish his or her own self-propelled meaning (the very definition of the *Übermensch*).[133]

---

132 Louis Dupré, *Passage to Modernity* (New Haven: Yale University Press, 1993).

133 Friedrich Nietzsche, *Twilight of the Idols*, trans. R. J. Hollingdale (London: Penguin, 1990), 50–51.

This attack on the metaphysical structure of reality is also exemplified by Wilhelm Dilthey, an early champion of the antipodean Hellenic-Hebraic typology. In his *Introduction to the Human Sciences* of 1833, Dilthey argues that St. Augustine was an early opponent of the truth mediated by *physis* and *kosmos*, recognizing that the interior life of the spirit is the measure of all things. Crucial here is Augustine's famous cry, "I wish to know God and the soul." When Reason asks, "nothing more?" Augustine responds, "nothing at all."[134] Dilthey takes this dramatic plea of the Augustinian soul as the evaporation of cosmology, the dissolution of metaphysical objectivity. The great theologian presciently recognized that the interior dynamics of the spirit, not a pre-existing "nature," is the primary purveyor of meaning.[135]

Dilthey concedes that Augustine's work remains scarred by classical thought. Because the Church was the only remaining power after the fall of the Western Empire, the responsibility for maintaining civilization fell to Christianity, and this entailed the adoption of Greek philosophy. To some extent, then, Augustine's thought remains bound by the fetters of (neo-Platonic) antiquity. But the essential turn has already been made. There is a palpable move away from Hellenic objectivity (the cosmic-metaphysical path) toward an accent on subjectivity and interiority. Augustine's interest in the soul's relationship to God gradually dissolves and corrodes the "metaphysical" dimension of Greek thought.

One may see the influence of Dilthey on the young Heidegger who, in his early works adopts this oppositional Hebraic-Hellenic narrative.[136] For example, in *The Phenomenology of Religious Life* (lectures delivered from 1918–1921), Heidegger argues that St. Paul's original apocalyptic attitude is gradually buried under the weight of Hellenic thinking. In several New Testament passages, such as Paul's second letter to the Thessalonians, there exists a tangible sense of uncertainty and judgment, of instability and eschatological expectation. But this biblical attitude is gradually crushed by the fixed thought of metaphysics; a hardened philosophical *ousia* slowly betrays the primordial experience of the early Church. Indeed, the original

---

134 Augustine, *Soliloquies*, Book, I, 7.

135 Wilhelm Dilthey, *Introduction to the Human Sciences*, trans. Ramon J. Betanzos (Detroit: Wayne State University, 1988), 231–39. Dilthey insists that Augustine's profound concern for self-consciousness "swallows up all interest in studying the cosmos." See Dilthey, *Human Sciences*, 234.

136 The early Heidegger's religious writing is discussed at length by Gianni Vattimo in *After Christianity*, trans. Luca D'Isanto (New York: Columbia University Press, 2002), 123–37.

Pauline sense of foreboding is no longer grasped in late antiquity and the Middle Ages following the penetration of Greek thought into Christian faith. And so, Heidegger concludes, "already at the end of the first century, the eschatological was covered up in Christianity. In later times one misjudged all original Christian concepts. In today's philosophy, too, the Christian concept-formations are hidden behind a Greek view."[137] Theology has turned away from the genuinely biblical attitude toward the fixed, the objective, the always-already at hand (*Vorhandenheit*) and, thus, toward the "onto-theological."

When Heidegger publishes *Being and Time* a few years later, the explicitly biblical language disappears although the fundamental themes remain the same. The entire post-Socratic tradition has been a "forgetting of Being." The philosophical tradition has been perniciously saturated with *ousia, energeia, actualitas, essentia*. But these philosophies of substance have led only to the objectification and reification of Being, confusing one episodic "appearance" of being in history (Hellenic thought) with Being itself. Being is now conceived of as that which is substantial and ready-to-hand, rather than as irruptive, epiphanic, and evanescent.[138]

So, Heidegger famously argues, to speak of God in terms of causality, or as *Ipsum Esse Subsistens*, is to name a god before whom one cannot dance and sing, a god of the philosophers, but not God himself. This is why theology can never be a founding and primordial discipline—*for it does not and cannot think Being*. It thinks within particular, epochal, ontic, and regionalized forms of being.[139] Philosophy alone is the true *ontological* discipline, thinking the very fountainhead of Being, the very source of the Being/beings distinction. Heidegger's conclusion is that theology is not truly thought; it is inattentive to the primordial nature of Being, to its transitory and evanescent disclosures in time. In his conclusions about theology, then, Heidegger comes close to the position espoused by Leo Strauss: theology is another "cave" from which true thinking must emerge.

Heideggerian anti-metaphysical thought lives on in contemporary postmodern thinkers such as Gianni Vattimo and John Caputo. Vattimo, for

---

137 Martin Heidegger, *The Phenomenology of Religious Life*, trans. Matthias Fritsch and Jennifer Anna Gosetti-Ferencei (Bloomington: Indiana University Press, 2004), 67–82, at 73.

138 Heidegger, *Being and Time*, trans. John Macquarrie and Edward Robinson (New York: Harper and Row, 1962).

139 For Heidegger's remarks on theology as a regional discipline, see *The Piety of Thinking*, trans. J. Hart and J. Maraldo (Bloomington: Indiana University Press, 1976), 6.

example, has long argued that philosophical interest in being, in the *ontos on,* has waned over time. Indeed, Vattimo's "weak thought" (his signature idea) holds that strong claims concerning the "*logos*-structure" of reality, or the "universal natural law," are no longer tenable. In fact, the history of Western philosophy (which comes to fruition in Nietzsche and Heidegger) may be read precisely as the progressive dissolution of objectivity and metaphysical assertion. Virtually every educated person now concedes that there exists no sure grasp of "truth" that is not already deeply encased within historically bound predispositions. It is precisely this lesson that accounts for the contemporary ascendency of hermeneutical thought which adopts as its slogan, "it's interpretation all the way down." By deconstructing the alleged "structure" of the world, by exposing the historicity and socio-cultural horizons attending all thought, hermeneutics has been unveiled as a truly *emancipatory* philosophy, one that does not force us to conform to a preexisting "nature" or cosmic *ratio.*[140]

What survives in the educated Christian West, then, is not *veritas,* with its aggressively metaphysical implications, but *caritas* (read as tolerance of all non-violent viewpoints). It is precisely "tolerance" which describes how the Christian tradition has been "received" by the great majority of Western Europeans and significant numbers of North Americans. This is why Vattimo can say, much like Dilthey, "Christianity is a stimulus, a message that sets in motion a tradition of thought that will eventually realize its freedom from metaphysics."[141] Properly understood (as *caritas*), Christianity encourages us to understand humanity as an *historical project* with the ability and freedom to create its own norms. With the demise of metaphysics, we have learned that so-called "objective and universal structures" are mere artifice; rather, "postmodern nihilism constitutes the actual truth of Christianity."[142]

One sees in Vattimo's work (and Caputo's) an adoption of the traditional Hellenization thesis, with metaphysics, in particular, detrimentally infecting

---

140 I have examined Vattimo's thought at length in *Vattimo and Theology* (London: T & T Clark, 2009). On the demise of metaphysics, see also the suggestive study of Santiago Zabala, *The Remains of Being* (New York: Columbia University Press, 2009). For Vattimo's extended comments on metaphysical dissolution, see Vattimo, *A Farewell to Truth,* trans. William McCuaig (New York: Columbia University Press, 2011).

141 Vattimo, "Toward a Nonreligious Christianity," in John Caputo and Gianni Vattimo, *After the Death of God,* ed. Jeffrey W. Robbins (New York: Columbia University Press, 2007), 35.

142 Richard Rorty and Gianni Vattimo, *The Future of Religion,* ed. Santiago Zabala (New York: Columbia University Press, 2005), 47.

enlightened Christianity.[143] The danger lurking in these thinkers is that one kind of philosophy (the Heideggerian-Derridean approach), accenting the provisional event of Being, the *Ereignis*, the Impossible, is simply exchanged for another. Since metaphysics must be eschewed as ontologically inappropriate, faith's creedal claims should now be understood as epiphanic and transitory rather than as definitive and lasting. In making this move, however, doctrinal teachings are stripped of their cognitive yield, making them fallibilistic at best and nihilistic at worst. Does such an exchange truly "free" theology from philosophy? Or is theology now simply enslaved by new masters?

As Caputo says, theology is a "Jewgreek" enterprise—and so it has always been.[144] But is not the Vattimo-Caputo proposal merely an exchange of metaphysical for non-metaphysical "Greeks"? And are the non-metaphysical Greeks truly more congruent with biblical claims? Further, does not this postmodern dissolution of historical Christianity into *caritas* simply duplicate the quintessential move of modernity, defanging religion by dissolving its "hard" cognitive claims, thereby allowing religion to play a public, societal role only when it is jejune and toothless? The truly crucial question is this: which Greeks—that is to say, which philosophical form—best serves the revelatory demands of the God of Israel who has come near to us in Jesus of Nazareth?

Metaphysics (Commodiously Understood) Is Necessary for Theology

It is my contention that some capacious metaphysical approach is essential to Catholic theology for the following reasons: (1) Metaphysics points to the participationist structure of reality whereby the mind ascends, by way of the theatre of the world and the intelligibility of the existing real, to the

---

143 Without minimizing differences between them, I regard Caputo's thought as similar to Vattimo's insofar as both thinkers urge theology to abandon its metaphysical captivity. Caputo counsels theology to temper its Hellenistic traditions by fostering Israel's prophetic spirit. See Caputo, "Philosophy and Prophetic Postmodernism: Toward a Catholic Postmodernity," *American Catholic Philosophical Quarterly* 74, no. 4 (2000): 549–67.

144 Caputo borrows the expression "Jewgreek" from Jacques Derrida who in turn borrowed it from James Joyce. The term accents the fact that the Christian tradition is "miscegenated," always a combination of biblical (Hebraic) and philosophical (Hellenic) thinking. See Caputo, *Demythologizing Heidegger* (Bloomington: Indiana University Press, 1993), 6–8. Derrida explains the term in his essay "Violence and Metaphysics," in *Writing and Difference*, trans. Alan Bass (Chicago: University of Chicago Press, 1978) , 79–153, at 153 and at 320n92.

fons et origo of being and truth; (2) metaphysics, in the form of the *analogia entis*, philosophically grounds the predication of names to God. Without the structure of analogy, all divine attribution is either reduced to pure metaphor or simply asserted as true absent the further dimension of intelligibility (precisely *how* may human concepts denominate the Infinite) that analogical language (and its ontological underpinning, the analogy of being) provides; and (3) metaphysics allows for an anthropology that establishes an eidetically discerned human nature or form which helps to explain why stable textual meanings (such as those found in the Nicene Creed) may be reliably transmitted over millennia, and are not swallowed up in socio-cultural-linguistic contingency.[145]

Catholicism has traditionally taught, and *Dei verbum* reaffirms, that in its essential dimensions revelation is universally, perpetually, and normatively true. As Vatican II says, "God has seen to it that what he has revealed will abide *perpetually* in its full *integrity* and be handed on to all generations.[146] The substance of this conciliar citation could be easily duplicated, but the point is transparent: The Church's foundational teachings are trustworthy and authoritative across generations and cultures. As the International Theological Commission has stated in one of its most insightful documents, "the truth of revelation . . . is universally valid and unchangeable in substance."[147] The point of these statements is that if revelation is truly God's *self*-manifestation, then it entails an irreducibly cognitive dimension that is perpetual and irreversible.

It is no surprise, then, that in *Fides et ratio*, John Paul II states that a "theology which shuns a metaphysical approach is unsuited for mediating divine revelation."[148] Why is this the case? Because theology requires modes of reasoning that can protect and substantiate, in the philosophical order, the Church's fundamental doctrinal convictions. Christian truth claims, as found for example in the Nicene-Constantinopolitan creed, are intended

---

145 I can only mention these points briefly here. I have defended them at length in *Foundations of Systematic Theology.*

146 *Dei verbum*, no. 7, emphasis added.

147 ITC, *On the Interpretations of Dogmas*, 9. Catholicism, of course, is not alone in this belief. Orthodoxy holds the same for the creeds and councils of the early Church and, as Geoffrey Wainwright has said, "For classical Protestants, at least, the Apostles' Creed and the conciliar Creed of Nicaea, Constantinople and Chalcedon [. . .] have always been taken as the irreversible deliverances and continuing guides of the Tradition." See Wainwright, *Is the Reformation Over?* (Milwaukee: Marquette University Press, 2000), 39.

148 John Paul II, *Fides et ratio*, no. 83.

to be transcultural and enduring. While reappropriated and recon-
ceptualized in every generation, the Church's teachings perdure from epoch
to epoch in their fundamental meaning. But such a belief would make no
sense whatsoever if one could not speak intelligibly about the very *possibility*
of substantially enduring meanings over time. This is why *Fides et ratio*
states that "philosophy should confirm the intelligibility and universal truth
of its [theology's] claims."[149] Absent such a "confirming" philosophy (that
is to say, absent the ability to defend philosophically the very *possibility* of
the universally true, and the very *possibility* of meaning invariance over
time), Christian doctrine would rightly be perceived as nothing more than
authoritarian, or even irrational, assertion. But philosophies with a metaphysical range consistently protect the universality of truth and the stable
identity of meaning in and through vast socio-cultural-linguistic diversity.

One must immediately add that this defense of the metaphysical
dimension of thought is *not* intended to tie theology to the thirteenth
century or to some constricted understanding of the *philosophia perennis*.
Doing so would be to ignore the insights of Vatican II about authentic
plurality. This is why one more cogently speaks of philosophies with
metaphysical horizons rather than simply metaphysics *sensu stricto*. Several
philosophies are protective of such dimensions without being neo-scholastic
in kind, as the case of Rosmini (noted above) clearly indicates.

Further, one traditional and obvious defect of metaphysics was that it
failed to take adequate account of the irrepressible horizons of historicity
and subjectivity.[150] It was just this failure that led Karl Rahner and Bernard
Lonergan to enter into an animated philosophical dialogue with modernity.
It is why Rahner concluded, "I also believe that one can say that neo-scholastic theology and philosophy, for all their accomplishments, are quite
passé today."[151] But recognizing the defects of neo-scholasticism led neither
Rahner nor Lonergan to an abandonment of metaphysics, but to its rediscovery in a transcendental (and to some extent hermeneutical) key. Reveal-

---

149 *Fides et ratio*, no. 77.

150 I have criticized *Fides et ratio* because, while calling for capacious philosophical options, it
largely ignores approaches which, although broadly committed to metaphysical thought,
seriously engage historicity and human subjectivity. Guarino, *"Fides et Ratio*: Theology and Contemporary Pluralism," *Theological Studies* 62, no. 4 (2001): 675–700. This essay may be found
in chapter two of this volume.

151 Rahner, *I Remember*, trans. Harvey D. Egan (Chestnut Ridge, NY: The Crossroad Publishing
Company, 1985), 88.

ingly, Rahner found Heidegger's thought deficient and continued to defend metaphysical themes, including the universal anthropology found in his earlier philosophical works.[152] Both Rahner and Lonergan insisted that historicity and metaphysics need not be enemies.

For all theologians, the fundamental issue is this: Which philosophies can sustain faith's claims? If Catholicism insists (as it surely does, with all the necessary qualifications) that certain of its teachings are universally true, substantially identical over generations and cultures, then which philosophies can support this bold assertion? It is just here that narratives with metaphysical dimensions seem particularly congruent with the Catholic faith.

Of course, the objections to metaphysics must be taken seriously. Above all, there exists the concern that metaphysically inspired philosophies will "freeze the flux," marginalizing the profound effects of historicity and cultural specificity, thereby dismissing as extraneous and accidental the political and social interests integral to thought. Is it not possible that metaphysics, which claims to express the foundational principles of reality, will end by defending time-bound structures reflective not of truth but of shopworn ideology? Given this possibility, prominent Catholic thinkers have warned about the dangers of metaphysical approaches. One need only witness Jean-Luc Marion's Heideggerian concern that a metaphysics of presence too easily treats God as a reified object, thereby missing the gratuitous phenomenon of revelation itself. David Tracy, for his part, has developed the notion of "fragment" as a theological form resistant to rationalist totality and enclosure, seeking in apocalyptic and eschatological models elements assuring that a steely metaphysics will not simply bury the "Other" under a reductive system.[153]

It is important, then, not only to reiterate the necessity of authentic pluralism, but to insist that theological reflection must incorporate all that has been learned from phenomenology, from analytical and evolutionary thought, and from various modes of liberative and emancipatory reasoning. If theology must *ultimately* eschew philosophies such as Heidegger's, it must nonetheless admit that hermeneutics in general has forced the discipline to think, and profoundly so, about human embeddedness in history, culture,

---

152 Rahner states, "Heidegger himself was, of course, convinced that after the pre-Socratics [. . .] a philosophy was being carried out that was based on an ultimate misunderstanding of being. I cannot share this opinion. I consider it false." See Harvey Egan, ed. and trans., *Karl Rahner in Dialogue* (Chestnut Ridge, NY: The Crossroad Publishing Company, 1986), 311.

153 See Tracy, "Fragments," in *God, the Gift and Postmodernism*, ed. John Caputo and Michael Scanlon, 170–84 (Bloomington: Indiana University Press, 1999).

language, and tradition. Together with postmodernism, hermeneutical philosophy has rightly challenged the ahistorical and wooden conceptualism that was often a hallmark of metaphysics.

However, if theology were to bypass metaphysical thinking entirely, it would have only two options: to assert Church teaching fideistically, without finding theoretical support in the natural, philosophical order, for the universality and perpetuity of doctrinal claims or, conversely, to concede that Church teachings are, indeed, circumscribed in scope by the deeply incommensurable layers of socio-cultural-linguistic diversity. In this latter option, theology would need to jettison its defense of the universality, material identity, and relative meaning-invariance of Christian doctrine over time. Catholicism has rightly avoided this path since embracing it would entail an abandonment of doctrine's universal and perpetual truth claims (and, necessarily, would lead to a complete reinterpretation of the very notion of revelation as *locutio Dei*). One may conclude, then, that nonmetaphysical approaches, while ultimately unacceptable, make their own contributions, challenging theology to examine its philosophical convictions so that the decided effects of historicity and contingency are neither ignored nor diminished.[154]

CONCLUSION

The Catholic theological tradition places a strong accent on the assimilation of every mode of thought, even those which are seemingly opposed to the Christian faith. This approach is essential because there can exist no fundamental opposition between Athens and Jerusalem, between *logos* and *pistis*. But the process of thoughtful assimilation is neither quick nor easy. The theological incorporation of classical antiquity was a journey of some twelve centuries, from the time of the earliest Fathers right up until Aquinas. With Vatican II, the Church began the official sifting and absorption of the fruits of the Enlightenment, a reception that will likely continue for decades and perhaps centuries.

This process of assimilation (and purification) must be bold and undaunting. Echoing de Lubac's plea to use the thought even of Marx and Nietzsche, *Fides et ratio* encourages theology to enter into "demanding crit-

---

154 This means that theology must take account not only of Heidegger's primordial notion of historicity, but also of Wittgenstein's cultural-linguistic web of experience, of Gadamer's *phronesis*-based rationality, and of Habermas's neo-pragmatic communicative theory, all of which provide salutary cautions to metaphysical thinking.

ical dialogue with both contemporary philosophical thought and with the philosophical tradition in all its aspects, whether consonant with the word of God or not."[155] This openness to every idea, no matter its provenance, is also enunciated in John Paul II's statement on the Galileo case: "It is a duty for theologians to keep themselves regularly informed of scientific advances in order to examine, if such be necessary, whether or not there are reasons for taking them into account in their reflection or for introducing changes in their teaching."[156] Many of these same themes are also found in John Paul's 1988 letter to George V. Coyne, SJ. While lauding those theologians who utilized "spoils" from Aristotle, the pope says,

> Contemporary developments in science challenge theology far more deeply than did the introduction of Aristotle into Western Europe in the thirteenth century. Yet these developments also offer to theology a potentially important resource. [. . .] Can we not hope that the sciences of today, along with all forms of human knowing, may invigorate and inform those parts of the theological enterprise that bear on the relation of nature, humanity, and God?[157]

The vital and vigorous appropriation of new ideas, then, is a living one in Catholic theology, encouraged by the popes themselves. As earlier noted, however, such absorption rarely occurs without a certain amount of tension and friction. One need only recall the thirteenth-century University of Paris to see this process, with all its attendant difficulties, at work. More recently, Karl Rahner has observed that "friction and struggle" is an integral part of the process when deciding if some aspect of Christian teaching is essential, or is simply part of an historically conditioned model (using the example of original sin and monogenism). In service to continuing assimilation, theologians have offered speculative works in liberation theology, feminist hermeneutics, evolutionary biology, postmodernity—and so the list continues.

The Catholic Church must encourage this exercise of critical reasoning, recognizing the essential role of the *schola theologorum* in understanding

---

155 *Fides et ratio*, no. 105.

156 John Paul II, *Address to the Participants in the Plenary Session of the Pontifical Academy of Sciences* (October 31, 1992), no. 8. This English translation can be found at "Lessons of the Galileo Case," *Origins* 22 (November 12, 1992): 371–73, at 372. Needless to add, what the pope says about the physical sciences is true, *mutatis mutandis*, for the human sciences as well.

157 John Paul II, "Letter to George V. Coyne, S.J.," Director of the Vatican Observatory," *AAS* 81 (1989): 274–83, at 282.

and architectonically developing the Christian faith. One profitably turns here to John Henry Newman who acknowledged at great length the important role of theological speculation.[158] Newman was well aware that a too-quick resolution of knotty issues illegitimately foreshortens the essential process of theological debate. Judging whether or not some position is harmoniously congruent with the Gospel often takes decades of thought, debate, and reflection. The authority of the Roman see is properly invoked, Newman believed, at the end of a protracted process, after an idea had been debated by a wide variety of theological courts.[159] For this very reason he insists that the theologian needs liberty; otherwise, "he would be fighting, as the Persian soldiers, under the lash, and the freedom of his intellect might truly be said to be beaten out of him. But this has not been so. [. . .] Zosimus treated Pelagius and Coelestius with extreme forbearance; St. Gregory VII was equally indulgent with Berengarius; by reason of the very power of the popes they have commonly been slow and moderate in their use of it.[160] Extended theological reflection is essential precisely because authentic development requires "the slow, painful, anxious taking up of new truths into an existing body of belief."[161]

The contemporary physicist, Peter E. Hodgson, echoed just this point when discussing the difficulties that Galileo faced:

> The consultors were theologians trained in the theology of Aquinas that was thoroughly integrated with Aristotelian cosmology. The synthesis of Aristotle had stood for two millennia [. . .] and was congruent with Catholic beliefs. [. . .] To them [theologians] it was simply inconceivable that Galileo, simply by looking through a little tube with lenses at either end, could overthrow this majestic synthesis. [. . .] It did not take them long to decide that Galileo's views were absurd and indeed heretical.[162]

---

158 In his important preface of 1877, Newman famously says, "Theology is the fundamental and regulating principle of the whole Church system." See Preface, vol. 1 of *The Via Media of the Anglican Church*, 3rd ed. (London: Longmans, Green, and Co., 1901), xlvii.

159 Newman, *Apologia Pro Vita Sua* (London: Longmans, Green, and Co., 1895), 267. Originally published in 1864, a new edition appeared the following year. See also, Newman, *Via Media*, xlvii.

160 Newman, *Apologia*, 267–68.

161 Newman, *Christian Doctrine*, 366.

162 Peter E. Hodgson, "Galileo the Theologian," *Logos: A Journal of Catholic Thought and Culture* 8, no. 1 (2005): 28–51, at 42–43. For a careful examination of the Galileo case, subverting several popular narratives, see Jerome Langford, *Galileo, Science and the Church*, 3rd ed. (Ann Arbor: University of Michigan Press, 1992).

Hodgson's point, like Newman's and Rahner's before him, is that the assimilation of new ideas is never easy, particularly when a specific paradigm or model has been in long use in the Church. While the magisterium has been entrusted with making the ultimate decision about the successful absorption of philosophy and the disciplines, it must extend due freedom to theologians as well. And, of course, the magisterium speaks with varying levels of authority so the judgments rendered, while authentic, are often contingent and provisional rather than final and determinative.

Deep within the heart of Catholicism is the recognition that faith and reason, theology and the disciplines, *pistis* and *logos*, are one reality, reflective of the supernatural order instituted by the Creator. It is precisely through the incorporation (and purification) of new insights in philosophy, the sciences, and other fields that the *mysterium fidei* is more fully penetrated and that architectonic doctrinal development properly occurs. It is in theology's unending assimilation and transformation of human wisdom, with every thought taken captive to Jesus Christ, that "the Church, through the unrolling centuries, continuously tends toward the fullness of divine truth until the words of God come to fulfillment in her."[163]

---

163 *Dei verbum*, no. 8.

Chapter Two

Introduction: *Fides et ratio*: Philosophy, Theology, and Contemporary Pluralism

In 1998, Pope John Paul II issued the most significant magisterial statement on the relationship between faith and reason since Vatican I's dogmatic constitution, *Dei Filius*, of 1870. This rich and wide-ranging encyclical, *Fides et ratio*, is crucially important for understanding the constitutive hallmarks of any theology capable of mediating the Catholic faith.

Of profound significance for this papal letter is the symbiotic relationship between the two ancient disciplines, philosophy and theology. While philosophy needs theology to illumine its path of inquiry, theology needs philosophy in order "to confirm the intelligibility and universal truth of its claims." In other words, Catholic theology cannot simply *assert* its normative truth-claims—claims that are based, of course, on divine revelation—as universally and perpetually true. Absent continuing and sustained reflection, that would be fideism in its baldest form. Theology must also provide warrants showing that its claims to universal and perpetual truth can also be philosophically supported. If doctrinal assertions are as true in twenty-first century Nairobi and New York as they were in fourth-century Nicaea—a bedrock claim of Catholic theology—then, the very *possibility* of transcultural truth and universal validity, as well as fundamental meaning-invariance over time, must be philosophically defended.

In order to provide theoretical support for these kinds of assertions, John Paul argues that theology needs philosophies that have a "metaphysical range," that is to say, philosophies *capable of reinforcing the claims to perpetuity, universality, and meaning-invariance affirmed by the Catholic faith.* The pope's firm insistence on metaphysics is noteworthy precisely because metaphysics has been under attack from many quarters: postmodernism; hermeneutical thought; neo-pragmatism; and, from a theological perspective, Barthianism. But absent metaphysics, Catholic theology would be left with only two alternatives: on the one hand, a fideistic assertion of the universal and perpetual truth of the Christian faith, but without philosophical warrants supportive of these bold claims; or, on the other, an abdication of theology's insistence that it represents universal truth since theology, too, would now purvey only fragmentary, culture-bound, and contextualized "truths." This is why John Paul II, in a forceful statement, asserts that any philosophy "which shuns metaphysics would be radically unsuited to the task of mediation in the understanding of Revelation."[1]

At the same time, the encyclical does not assert that the only path to Christian philosophy must go through St. Thomas. While acknowledging Aquinas's unique role in integrating faith and reason, John Paul II also endorses philosophical pluralism, insisting that he is not speaking of metaphysics "in the sense of a specific school."[2] Thomism, while an elevated model for theological thinking, is not alone in fulfilling the demands of what may be called a revelationally-appropriate philosophy. The encyclical's advocacy of pluralism affords a wide berth to philosophical speculation, always circumscribed, of course, by the Church's faith.

Fides et ratio, with its strong endorsement of metaphysics and realism, has extraordinary strengths. Are there any weaknesses in the document? I think there are. The encyclical gives the impression that the only two philosophical alternatives today are either metaphysics or nihilism. But this misses the attempts by contemporary philosophers—hermeneutical and neo-pragmatist thinkers particularly—to avoid both alternatives, seeking a middle path which defends rationality, but with reason now encircled by and embedded deeply within, history, culture, and language. This attempted via media, I argue, is unsuitable for Catholic theology; nonetheless, its insights and concerns must be directly addressed.

Despite this weakness, *Fides et ratio* will long stand as a lasting monument to Catholicism's confidence both in the claims of divine revelation, and in reason's ability to adduce the warrants needed to support them.

---

1 John Paul II, Encyclical Letter *Fides et ratio* (September 14, 1998), no. 83.

2 *Fides et ratio*, no. 83.

Fides et ratio:
Philosophy, Theology, and Contemporary Pluralism

The publication of the encyclical *Fides et ratio* (*FR*) has met with general but by no means uncritical theological approval.[3] Several questions have been raised about the document: Is it an unabashed defense of an out-dated philosophy of being? Does its emphasis on certitude invoke the ghost of Descartes? Is it foundationalist in nature? Are its assertions sufficiently apophatic? Are its intentions premodern? Is it naïve about contemporary thought? Does it sufficiently recognize the debilitating effect of the Fall on human reason? The task of this article is to examine the principal theses of *Fides et ratio*, to answer some of the questions raised about it, to raise several of my own, and, in so doing, to discuss the wider implications of *FR* for fundamental theology and theological thought at large. In particular, I evaluate the letter in light of its own repeated exhortations for theology to be fully engaged with contemporary philosophical currents and cultural ideas.

Precedents for an encyclical of this type are well-known. Envisioning the proper relationship between faith and reason runs the gamut from Ter-

---

* This essay was originally published as *"Fides et Ratio*: Theology and Contemporary Pluralism,"* Theological Studies* 62, no. 4 (2001): 675–700. Republished under terms of SAGE author re-use policy.

3 The encyclical is dated September 14, 1998. The official Latin text may be found in *Acta apostolicae sedis* 91 (1999), 5–88. An English translation may be found in *Origins* 28 (October 22, 1998): 317–47. A partial list of articles on the encyclical includes: the entire issue of *Communio: International Review* 26 (Fall 1999); John Galvin, "Fides et Ratio," *The Downside Review* 118, no. 410 (2000): 1–16; Peter Phan, *"Fides et Ratio* and Asian Philosophies," *Science et esprit* 51, no. 3 (1999): 333–49; André Dartigues, "À propos de la vérité philosophique. En echo à encyclique *Fides et Ratio,"* Bulletin de littérature ecclésiastique* 101, no. 1 (2000): 15–36. John Webster attacks the encyclical from a Reformed, Barthian position, claiming that the document does not take full account of human sinfulness, in *"Fides et Ratio*: Articles 64–79," *New Blackfriars* 81, no. 948 (2000): 68–76. Thomas Weinandy defends the encyclical in *"Fides et Ratio*: A Response to John Webster," *New Blackfriars* 81, no. 951 (2000): 225–35. Alvin Plantinga also claims that the encyclical does not seriously wrestle with the Fall's effects in "Faith and Reason," *Books and Culture* 5 (July/August 1999): 32–35. A well-wrought reading of *Fides et ratio* from a Jewish perspective is offered by Leon Klenicki, "Se il rabbino commenta l'enciclica," *Studi Cattolici* 44 (October 2000): 660–72.

tullian's Athens vs. Jerusalem dichotomy to Aquinas's unbreakable cementing of the two in the *Summa contra gentiles*. Certainly, Vatican I's *Dei Filius*, despite its well-known shortcomings, was an important document both for combating rationalism and for offering a potent apophaticism even today not fully exploited by theology. The encyclical *Pascendi dominici gregis* (1907), despite its poor reputation, was an important decree given its determined attempt to diagnose and expose the epistemological roots of Modernism. *Humani generis* (1950) contains significant philosophical sections including a strong *monitum* about pluralism and its dangers. *Mysterium ecclesiae* (1973), issued by the Congregation for the Doctrine of the Faith, offers several important statements germane to theological epistemology, especially with regard to the role of historicity in dogmatic formulations. Finally, the statement of the quasi-magisterial International Theological Commission (ITC), *On the Interpretation of Dogmas* (1989), includes a nuanced treatment of history and the hermeneutics of dogmatic statements.

If the *Sitz im Leben* of *Dei Filius* was the struggle with rationalism and fideism, if *Pascendi* was inspired by an alleged Modernism, if *Humani generis* was fearful that Aquinas would be marginalized, and if *Mysterium ecclesiae* and the ITC statement were inspired by the increasing recognition of history's inexorable twinning with truth, then what is the motive for *Fides et ratio*? Surely the ascendancy of postmodernism and allied tendencies in contemporary thought is one reason. Another is the fear of the deleterious effects of fashioning a theology apart from a consciously held philosophy. Still another reason is the continuing decline of metaphysics, a central theme of the encyclical, as a legitimate philosophical/theological option. As John Paul II notes, there exists a "deep-seated distrust of reason which has surfaced" to the point that there is talk of the "end of metaphysics."[4]

According to *Fides et ratio*, this "distrust of reason" has forced philosophy to circumscribe its ambitions: " [. . .] little by little [reason] has lost the capacity to lift its gaze to the heights, not daring to rise to the truth of being."[5] For contemporary thought has concentrated less on the human capacity to know the truth; instead accenting ways in which reason is "limited and conditioned."[6] One might add that present-day thought has not just understood reason as conditioned and limited but also as embedded,

4 *Fides et ratio*, no. 55.
5 *Fides et ratio*, no. 5.
6 *Fides et ratio*, no. 5.

contextualized, situated, and paradigm based along with a host of other descriptions indicating the historical, cultural, and social circumscription of human rationality. For a significant part of contemporary thought, human subjects and human rationality are deeply, if not entirely, shaped by the cultural and linguistic circumstances in which they are embedded.

The legacy of circumscribed reason extends ultimately back to Kant and finds defenders today not only among postmodernists, but also among neo-pragmatists and hermeneutical thinkers of various stripes. Constructivist elements in both the humanities and the philosophy of science have served to intensify the Promethean claim that humanity is primarily the shaper rather than the receiver of meaning.[7] But while Kant kept the transcendental subject as the basis for meaning and truth, the analyses of Heidegger and Wittgenstein have unmasked that subject as itself rooted in a tangled web of historical and linguistic existence. And Heidegger and Wittgenstein have in turn given rise to significant postmetaphysical, post-transcendental, postmodern diagnoses such as the decentering, "erasive" thought of Derrida, the *phronesis*-based rationality of Gadamer and the neo-pragmatic communicative discourse structures of Habermas. For all of these thinkers, the ability of reason to universalize on the basis of a common human nature or unshakeable first principles, the hallmarks of metaphysics, has been severely questioned. Jean Bethke Elshtain has summed up recent currents of thought by asking if the notion of humanity as *imago Dei* has been "consigned to the conceptual scrap heap as so much debris labeled 'Western metaphysic,' 'Western logocentrism,' 'patriarchal hegemony' or a combination of all these?"[8]

Fides et ratio intends to challenge several of these newer philosophical directions as inappropriate to the Catholic understanding of revelation.

THE *OFFICIUM CONGRUUM* OF PHILOSOPHY

Fides et ratio is, in effect, a long treatise on the congruency and symbiotic relationship between philosophy and theology. Theology needs philosophy as a partner in dialogue in order to "confirm the intelligibility and universal

---

7 For a masterful exposition of the history of constructivism from its beginnings in medieval nominalism to its intensification in Descartes and Kant, see Louis Dupré, *Passage to Modernity: An Essay in the Hermeneutics of Nature and Culture* (New Haven: Yale University Press, 1993).

8 Elshtain, "Augustine and Diversity," in *A Catholic Modernity? Charles Taylor's Marianist Award Lecture and Four Responses*, ed. James Heft (Oxford: Oxford University Press, 1999) , 95–104, at 96.

truth of its claims."[9] Without philosophy, theology is deprived of rational warrants and ultimately regresses to an unwitting fideism,[10] for as Augustine aptly notes, "If faith does not think, it is nothing."[11] The document, then, has little use for the claim that theology is a discourse answerable only to rules that it defines. Of course, theology's epistemic primacy remains undisputed; however, the discipline's autonomy does not free it from responding to, at least to a certain extent, the legitimate criteria imposed by philosophical thinking. Indeed, as the encyclical boldly notes, in a statement with profound implications, "The content of Revelation can never debase [*comprimere*] the discoveries and legitimate autonomy of reason."[12]

Just as theology without philosophy is shallow and ineffective, philosophy without the *lumen revelationis* is incomplete and partial, for "revealed truth offers the fullness of light and will therefore illumine the path of philosophical inquiry."[13] Further, Christian revelation is the "absolute truth," the "true lodestar of men and women."[14] Because of revelation's primacy, any particular philosophy must ultimately be congruent with theological teaching. What is needed, the encyclical insists, is a philosophy "*cum Dei verbo congruens*"[15] or "*verbo Dei conveniat.*"[16] Only a philosophy that is suitable and commensurate with the word of God can properly mediate the truth that revelation offers. Only such a philosophy is appropriate for fulfilling the *officium congruum.*[17]

What kind of philosophy can satisfy this "office" or "function"? What kind of philosophy, according to *Fides et ratio*, is "revelationally-appropriate"? The encyclical outlines three essential elements: In the first place, any such philosophy must have a *sapiential* dimension, that is, it must be a search for the ultimate and overarching meaning of life. Such a philosophy cannot rest easy with fragmentation nor can it limit itself to the intensive development of discrete and local areas of thought. It must, instead, have

9 *Fides et ratio*, no. 77.

10 *Fides et ratio*, nos. 55, 77.

11 *Fides et ratio*, nos. 79, 95.

12 *Fides et ratio*, no. 79.

13 *Fides et ratio*, no. 79.

14 *Fides et ratio*, no. 15.

15 *Fides et ratio*, no. 79.

16 *Fides et ratio*, no. 81.

17 *Fides et ratio*, no. 83.

the courage to provide an ultimate and unitive framework. Only an over-arching philosophy can resist functional or utilitarian goals and begin to converge on true wisdom. Secondly, a suitable philosophy is one that verifies the "human capacity *to know the truth*, to come to a knowledge which can reach objective truth by means of the *adaequatio rei et intellectus* to which the Scholastic Doctors referred."[18] To what extent this rather specific statement commits philosophy to Thomism or allows for the philosophical pluralism trumpeted by the document will be further discussed. What seems certain, however, is that this second criterion demands that any adequate epistemology must be ultimately wedded to some sort of realism. Finally, a philosophy consonant with the word of God will have a "*genuinely metaphysical* range, capable [. . .] of transcending empirical data in order to attain something absolute, ultimate, and foundational in its search for truth."[19] Thought can never stop at experience alone; its movement must be from "phenomenon to foundation." The pope quickly notes, however, that he is not speaking of metaphysics "in the sense of a specific school or particular historical current of thought." On the contrary, his intention is to affirm the human capacity to know the "transcendent and metaphysical dimension in a way that is true and certain, albeit imperfect and analogical."[20]

According to the encyclical, these three dimensions are essential if a particular philosophy is to be deemed revelationally appropriate, if it is to be judged capable of performing the *officium congruum* or "stewardship" of adequately mediating the truth of revelation. Unsurprisingly, the type of philosophy here envisioned is one that protects and undergirds the fundamental characteristics of doctrinal teachings. The three essential elements adduced by the document are intended to support doctrine's universality, continuity, objectivity, and perduring identity over the course of time. Such

---

18 *Fides et ratio*, no. 82. Vatican II is here adduced as endorsing realism: "Intelligence [. . .] can with genuine certitude attain to reality itself as knowable, though in consequence of sin that certitude is partially obscured and weakened." Vatican Council II, *Gaudium et spes* (December 7, 1965), no. 15.

19 *Fides et ratio*, no. 83.

20 *Fides et ratio*, no. 83. The analogical dimension of theological language, while never fully developed, is a theme noted throughout *Fides et ratio*. For example, the encyclical, citing the famous passage from Lateran IV, claims that human language is capable of expressing divine reality in a universal way, "analogically it is true, but no less meaningfully for that" (no. 84). It goes on to add, "our vision of the face of God is always fragmentary and impaired by the limits of our understanding" (no. 13). A fine statement of the analogical nature of language and the limits of theological understanding may be found in Karl Rahner, "Experiences of a Catholic Theologian," *Theological Studies* 61, no. 1 (2000): 3–15.

is how the encyclical views the traditional hallmarks of Catholic teaching.[21]
A philosophy fulfilling its appropriate office, then, must be able to sustain,
for example, the continuity and objectivity of dogmatic claims such as the
mystery of the Trinity and the humanity/divinity of Christ.

Given the type of philosophy that *Fides et ratio* regards as properly supportive of revealed truth, it is not surprising that metaphysics plays a major
role. For metaphysics buttresses both the overarching framework and the
realistic epistemology identified by the encyclical as fundamental linchpins.
It also grounds those unique characteristics that the encyclical identifies,
sometimes explicitly, sometimes implicitly, as authentic hallmarks of Catholic doctrine. It comes as no surprise, then, when *Fides et ratio* notes that an
"intimate relationship" exists between faith and metaphysical reasoning.[22]
Even more forcefully, the document asserts that any philosophy which shuns
a metaphysical dimension "would be radically unsuited to the task of mediation in the understanding of Revelation."[23] Only with the help of metaphysics can the *intellectus fidei* give a "coherent [*congruenter*] account of the
universal and transcendent power of revealed truth."[24] In fact, the encyclical
holds that dogmatic theology is only able to perform its task appropriately
when it is able to rely on the contributions of a philosophy of being.[25]

It is clearly the case that this very strong emphasis on the enduring significance of philosophies with a universal and metaphysical dimension is
the precise opposite of much contemporary thought that seeks to underscore the local and heteromorphous character of truth. The encyclical, on

---

21 It is for this reason that the encyclical repeatedly invokes certain words and themes. Of universality, *Fides et ratio* notes the importance of arguing according to "rigorous rational criteria
to guarantee [. . .] that the results attained are universally valid" (no. 75). The document also
speaks of the necessity of neither obscuring nor denying the "universal validity" of the contents
of faith (no. 84), and of the "universal and transcendent value of revealed truth" (no. 83). Of continuity and perpetuity, the encyclical says, "To every culture Christians bring the unchanging
truth of God [*immutabilem Dei veritatem*]" (no. 71) and notes that "certain and unchangeable
doctrine" must be more profoundly understood. Equally important in this regard is the letter's
criticism of historicism whereby "the enduring validity of truth is denied. What was true in one
period [. . .] may not be true in another" (no. 87). Of objectivity, the encyclical inveighs against
the nihilistic "denial of all foundations and the negation of all objective truth" (no. 90). In the
same section, the document notes that, philosophically speaking, "the neglect of being inevitably leads to losing touch with objective truth and therefore with the very ground of human
dignity."

22 *Fides et ratio*, no. 97.

23 *Fides et ratio*, no. 83.

24 *Fides et ratio*, no. 83.

25 *Fides et ratio*, no. 97.

the contrary, asserts that a philosophy that is truly revelationally appropriate must be able to reason from the empirical to the universal; it must, in fact, be able to "transcend the boundaries of space and time."[26] This qualification is essential "lest the prime task of demonstrating the universality of faith's content be abandoned."[27] It is understandable, then, that Pentecost is adduced as the model for discerning the universal in the particular. The "unchanging truth of God" is brought to men and women of every culture without harming their local identity, without stripping particular cultures of their native riches, or imposing alien forms upon them.[28]

Given the encyclical's emphasis on metaphysics, and its attendant concepts of universality and objectivity, one may ask if *Fides et ratio* is simply a restatement of Thomism, an updated endorsement of *Aeterni Patris*? It is true that, throughout the document, Aquinas is lauded for his ability to integrate faith and reason, to harmonize nature and grace; nonetheless, Thomas is always contextualized as one possible, although certainly elevated, model for theology.[29] He is extolled for his signal dialogue with Arab and Jewish thinkers and noted for defending "the radical newness introduced by Revelation without ever demeaning the venture proper to reason."[30] Does Aquinas' thought provide a conceptual framework that can perennially articulate the truths of the Catholic faith? The encyclical responds that Thomism remains one system adequately mediating Christian truth; Thomism, however, does not exhaustively fulfill the demands of a revelationally appropriate philosophy.[31]

In fact, *Fides et ratio* suggests that while central elements of Aquinas' *corpus* remain essential, a new conceptual framework is needed which

---

26 *Fides et ratio*, no. 85.

27 *Fides et ratio*, no. 69.

28 *Fides et ratio*, no. 71.

29 *Fides et ratio*, no. 43.

30 *Fides et ratio*, no. 78.

31 Of course, the adequacy, but not exhaustiveness, of Thomism was already argued by the *nouvelle théologie* against those holding that Thomism was, in fact, the consummate mediation of the faith. Henri Bouillard, in particular, was at pains to defend the possibility of conceptual pluralism even while defending Thomistic adequacy. Aidan Nichols correctly concludes that the neo-scholastics of the forties were " [. . .] wrong in allowing so little *droit de cité* to the *nouvelle théologie*. It is not the case that, grudgingly, the other theologies [or philosophies] are permitted to exist until Thomism has absorbed their better insights (whereupon, like the Marxist State, they can wither away)." See "Thomism and the *Nouvelle Théologie*," *The Thomist* 64, no. 1 (2000): 1–19, at 19.

acknowledges and incorporates advances in thought since the Middle Ages.

The encyclical calls for a contemporary synthesis that, while taking account of early Christian thinkers, the Scholastics, and modern thought as well, is able to fashion a new relationship between faith and reason.[32] In a similar vein, the document claims that philosophy should be able to "propose anew the problem of being—and this in harmony with the demands and insights of the entire philosophical tradition, including philosophy of more recent times, without lapsing into sterile repetition of antiquated formulas."[33] One hardly sees in statements of this sort a return to neo-scholasticism or to a narrow understanding of the *philosophia perennis*. On the contrary, remarks such as these, while clearly staying within a metaphysical horizon, nonetheless open out onto the wider conceptual pluralism important to theological development. The "suitable office" which philosophy must fulfill, then, is hardly limited to Thomism or to Scholasticism but seeks instead a multiplicity of conceptual systems which are, nonetheless, commensurable with the deposit of faith.[34]

Considering the strong endorsement that *Fides et ratio* gives to philosophies having a "metaphysical range," it seems that the Heideggerian call for the "end of metaphysics" and the demise of ontotheology would be seen by the encyclical as inappropriate and untenable.[35] After all, as Merold Westphal noted, ontotheology is the position that there is a highest being who is key

---

32 *Fides et ratio*, no. 85.

33 *Fides et ratio*, no. 97.

34 One recent endorsement of metaphysics as essential for theological reasoning comes from the Anglican theologian, John Milbank, and the movement known as "radical orthodoxy." Seeking to create a post-liberal, post-secular theology, Milbank traces the roots of secularism to Duns Scotus, claiming that Scotus's univocal notion of being created the conditions for an ontology prior to and unconstrained by theology itself. Being was now an abstraction drawn from the twin notions of created and creating being. Once philosophy had arrogated to itself this knowledge of being, theology was reduced to a "regional, ontic, positive science" leading, necessarily, to a reason/revelation dichotomy. See John Milbank, "The Theological Critique of Philosophy in Hamann and Jacobi," in *Radical Orthodoxy*, ed. John Milbank, Catherine Pickstock, and Graham Ward (London: Routledge, 1999), 24. For Milbank, anti-metaphysical theologies, such as Barth's, foster a reduction in breadth of the discipline's scope. "Therefore, while the Barthian claim is that post-Kantian philosophy liberates theology to be theological, the inner truth of his theology is that by allowing legitimacy to a methodologically atheist philosophy, he finishes by construing God on the model, ironically, of man without God" (22).

35 For Heidegger's thought on "overcoming metaphysics," see "The End of Philosophy and the Task of Thinking," in *Basic Writings*, ed. David Farrell Krell, 427–49 (San Francisco: HarperCollins, 1993). Also, "Overcoming Metaphysics," in *The Heidegger Controversy: A Critical Reader*, ed. Richard Wolin, 67–90 (Cambridge, MA: The MIT Press, 1993).

to the meaning of the whole of being, a point central to every Christian the-ology.[36] At the same time, Westphal and others agree that Heidegger's con-demnations of "ontotheology" are often concerned with not reducing the God of mystery to a mere *causa sui*, with not remanding God to the level of predicamental and categorical beings.[37] Insofar as this is the proper concern of Heidegger, then the encyclical may be said to be in agreement with him.[38]

One might also legitimately wonder about the relation of *Fides et ratio* to Jean-Luc Marion's severe critique of idolic ontotheology in *God Without Being*. Marion argues that the notion of being purveyed by the Scholastic tradition exchanges the iconic representation of God, eminently displayed by the Pseudo-Dionysian trajectory of love and unknowing, for the more objectified, calculative, and idolic trajectory of *Ipsum Esse Subsistens*. As has been pointed out by several commentators, however, Marion makes a cat-egory mistake regarding Aquinas's notion of being, as Barth himself did in his anti-analogy philippics, seeing being as a category encircling both God and creatures and, therefore, as representative of the "idolic imagination."[39]

---

36 Merold Westphal, "Overcoming Onto-theology," in *God, the Gift, and Postmodernism*, ed. John Caputo and Michael Scanlon, 146–69 (Bloomington: Indiana University Press, 1999). See also his "Postmodernism and the Gospel: Onto-theology, Metanarratives, and Perspectivism," *Perspectives: A Journal of Reformed Thought* 15, no. 4 (2000): 6–10.

37 As Gadamer says of Heidegger: "Not a Christian theologian, he did not feel qualified to speak of God. It was clear to Heidegger that it would be intolerable to speak of God like science speaks about its objects; but what that might mean, to speak of God—this was the question that moti-vated him and pointed out his way of thinking." See *Heidegger's Ways*, trans. John Stanley (Albany: State University of New York Press, 1994), 170. Cited by John Arthos, "Gadamer at the Cumaean Gates," *American Catholic Philosophical Quarterly* 74, no. 2 (2000): 247.

38 Of course, there are certainly elements in *Fides et ratio* with which Heidegger would take serious issue, primarily the encyclical's failure to wrestle with the inescapability of historicity. Early on, Heidegger, in a well-known letter, recognized the conflict between his own notion of metaphysics and that utilized by Catholic thought: "Epistemological insights, extending as far as the theory of historical knowledge, have made the *system* of Catholicism problematic and unacceptable to me—but not Christianity and metaphysics [the latter, to be sure, in a new sense]." Cited by John Caputo, "Heidegger and Theology," in *The Cambridge Companion to Hei-degger*, ed. Charles Guignon (Cambridge: Cambridge University Press, 1993), 272. Caputo adds that Aquinas's "metaphysics of *actualitas* is basically at odds with the meditative savoring of the original sense of Being as presencing." See *Heidegger and Aquinas: An Essay on Overcoming Metaphysics* (New York: Fordham University Press, 1982), 201. Whether *actualitas* and disclosure need to be at antipodes is a debatable point, but certainly Aquinas's understanding not only of history, but also of nature and creation, clearly separates him from Heidegger.

39 David Burrell has noted some of Marion's shortcomings in "Reflections on 'Negative Theology' in the Light of a Recent Venture to Speak of '*God Without Being*,'" in *Postmodernism and Chris-tian Philosophy*, ed. Roman T. Ciapalo, 58–67 (Mishawaka, IN: American Maritain Association, 1997). In particular, Burrell notes that Marion reduces Aquinas's understanding of being to Scotus's univocity. At the same time, it should be noted that Marion is properly concerned that

Marion has subsequently acknowledged that, indeed, Aquinas escapes the charge of ontotheology, carefully distinguishing the manner in which *esse* subsists on the predicamental and transcendental levels.[40] Insofar as the encyclical follows Aquinas on this point, one must acquit the document of the charge of reificatory, ontotheological thought.

Not only does *Fides et ratio* defend philosophies with a metaphysical horizon, it also worries about the nihilism resulting from the "denial of all foundations" evident in some contemporary thought.[41] Given that concerns about foundationalism abound in contemporary philosophical and theological reflection, it is legitimate to ask if the encyclical holds that some kind of foundationalist philosophy is alone revelationally appropriate. Only a brief *tour d'horizon* of the foundationalist debate can be offered, but one that will, perhaps, shed light on the document's concerns.[42]

There are two broadly identifiable uses of the term "foundationalism." On the one hand, philosophers and theologians rooted in the empirical-analytical tradition of philosophy tend to equate foundationalism with the Cartesian view of adherence to a rigorous epistemic standard. So, for example, one author notes: "By foundationalism, I mean here the philosophical view that a belief is justified only if it is itself certain, or is derivable from premises that are certain."[43] Along the same lines, Bruce Marshall describes foundationalism as demanding that "justified beliefs (including Christian ones) must either be tied [. . .] to self-evident or incorrigible data, or logically grounded in beliefs which are."[44] When criticized theologically, this type of foundationalism is normally scored for giving the impression that some standard *external to theology* is now proposed as the final criterion

---

sterile formulas can result in an idolic reification, reducing God to the lifeless *causa sui* of an inappropriate ontotheology.

40 See Marion, "Saint Thomas d'Aquin et l'onto-théo-logie," *Revue thomiste* 95, no. 1 (1995): 31–66.

41 *Fides et ratio*, no. 90.

42 For more on foundationalism, consult Timm Triplett, "Recent Work on Foundationalism," *American Philosophical Quarterly* 27, no. 2 (1990): 93–116, wherein he identifies over fifteen kinds of foundationalist thought.

43 Sally Haslanger, "Feminism in Metaphysics: Negotiating the Natural," in *The Cambridge Companion to Feminism in Philosophy*, ed. Miranda Fricker and Jennifer Hornsby (Cambridge: Cambridge University Press, 2000) , 107–26, at 112.

44 Bruce D. Marshall, *Trinity and Truth* (Cambridge: Cambridge University Press, 2000), 50. For a similar definition, see Amos Yong, "What Evangelicals Can Learn from C. S. Peirce," *Christian Scholar's Review* 29, no. 3 (2000): 563–88.

for truth and certainty. Theology is now called upon to justify itself before the bar of secular foundations (often some form of empiricism or logically derivable proposition) in order to attain validity. Normative epistemic primacy is now accorded to nontheological criteria.[45]

Alvin Plantinga decries precisely this kind of thinking, "classical foundationalism" he terms it, which holds that "at least in principle, any properly functioning human beings who think together about a disputed question with care and good will, can be expected to come to agreement."[46]

For this type of thinker, some propositions are properly basic and clearly accepted by all, while other propositions are not. Those propositions that are not basic must be traceable back, on the basis of evidence, to properly basic statements. As a Christian philosopher, Plantinga is concerned because "the existence of God [. . .] is not among the propositions that are properly basic; hence a person is rational in accepting theistic belief [according to classical foundationalism] only if he has evidence for it."[47] Plantinga, for a variety of reasons, thinks that classical foundationalism is rooted in an unacceptable evidentialism seeking to marginalize theism as a warranted basic belief. But this kind of foundationalism, which allows philosophy to erect nontheological criteria that theology itself must answer to, or which forces theology into an evidentialist Procrustean bed, is hardly the kind of foundationalist thinking defended by the encyclical.[48]

---

45 This was also the concern of Ronald Thiemann in *Revelation and Theology* (Notre Dame: University of Notre Dame Press, 1985) and George Lindbeck in *The Nature of Doctrine* (Philadelphia: The Westminster Press, 1984). Both authors wish to demonstrate, correctly, that the Word of God need not ultimately justify itself before other epistemic criteria. Their books may sound excessively Barthian to Catholic ears, however, in that they seem to rely on divine agency alone, rather than on the search for proper philosophical warrants as well, in order to undergird logically the truth of Christian doctrine. See also chapter 4 of this book.

46 Plantinga, *The Analytic Theist: An Alvin Plantinga Reader,* ed. James F. Sennett (Grand Rapids: Eerdmans Publishing, 1998), 333.

47 Plantinga, *The Analytic Theist,* 129.

48 Plantinga does think that Aquinas is a classical foundationalist because his natural theology relies on the evidence of the senses as a condition for proper basicality. Consequently, Plantinga avers, Aquinas shares with nontheists like Flew and Russell the position that belief in God is only basic when sufficiently justified and warranted. Joseph Greco argues against Plantinga that Aquinas was not a classical foundationalist in "Foundationalism and the Philosophy of Religion," in *Philosophy of Religion,* ed. Brian Davies, 34–41 (Washington, DC: Georgetown University Press, 1998). For the argument that Aquinas was not a foundationalist of any kind, see Eleonore Stump, "Aquinas on the Foundations of Knowledge," *Canadian Journal of Philosophy,* 17, Supplement (1992): 125–58. *Fides et ratio,* following Vatican I, affirms the natural knowability of God (nos. 8, 53). Whether this is necessarily reducible to the type of evidentialist foundationalism

On the other hand, the term "foundationalism" is also used in a wider, more general, and less restrictive sense. In this usage, any type of *prima philosophia*, whether of the ontological, transcendental, or empirical variety, is regarded as foundationalist in kind. Here, the entire axis of Western thought, whether Aristotelian, Thomistic, Kantian, or Husserlian, is understood as trying to establish some kind of "foundation" for philosophy, not specifically epistemological or Cartesian, to be sure, but nonetheless given to isolating a first principle, a metaphysical or transcendental foundation for thought and reality. Nonfoundationalist critics claim that this type of thinking both calcifies reality and, more seriously, betrays ignorance of the wider cultural and historical horizons displayed by Heidegger and Wittgenstein. Heidegger's primordial notion of historicity, Wittgenstein's cultural-linguistic web of experience, Derrida's destabilization of textual meaning, Gadamer's *phronēsis*-based rationality and Habermas's explicitly postmetaphysical, neo-pragmatic communicative theory all serve to deconstruct foundationalist metaphysics and transcendental gnoseologies as legitimate philosophical options. Among contemporary philosophers, Rorty, Bernstein, Vattimo, and Caputo may be adduced as thinkers opposing attempts at universalizing metaphysical and epistemological systems which only serve to "freeze the flux" of historical thought.[49]

While *Fides et ratio* hardly defends foundationalism in the (basic) evidentialist sense, or in the sense that epistemic primacy is accorded to some criterion other than revelation itself, it does defend, precisely within the parameters of revelation, the importance of philosophical warrants for the truth of the Christian faith. As such, the encyclical holds that the Catholic view of revelation requires a certain metaphysical structure or range to support logically doctrinal teaching, as well as the traditional hallmarks

---

that Plantinga decries is another question, especially given the various interpretations of both Aquinas's arguments and the statements of Vatican I itself.

49 Richard Rorty has defended this position in many works since the publication of his *Philosophy and the Mirror of Nature* (Princeton: Princeton University Press, 1979); Richard Bernstein has similarly done so, characterizing the tradition as saturated with "ontological anxiety" in his *Beyond Objectivism and Relativism* (Philadelphia: University of Pennsylvania Press, 1983); John Caputo has condemned Western philosophy's search for fundamental *principia* and *archai* in several publications including *Radical Hermeneutics* (Bloomington: Indiana University Press, 1987) and Gianni Vattimo, a well-known Italian exponent of *pensiero debole* (as opposed to the *pensiero forte* of metaphysics), seeks to move beyond the "violence" of traditional metaphysical thought in his *Belief*, trans. Luca D'Isanto and David Webb (Stanford: Stanford University Press, 1999).

associated with this teaching such as its universality and material identity over time. Only a philosophy with some kind of metaphysical horizon is able to fulfill the *officium congruum*, to be revelationally appropriate, to provide suitably logical warrants for the *depositum fidei*. Failing to seek such warrants will lead in the direction of either a deconstructive historicism or an assertive fideism both rejected by the encyclical. One may say, then, that the kind of "foundationalism" defended by *Fides et ratio* is quite specific and always elaborated within the household of faith. Attempts to establish a *prima philosophia* are demanded by revelation, never done apart from it, and are ultimately subject to theological criteria. The type of foundationalism sanctioned by the document, then, should always be understood as the "second moment" within the *auditus fidei, intellectus fidei* synthesis.

Even if the encyclical endorses some kind of metaphysics and some kind of foundationalism, it is equally clear that it emphasizes the importance of contemporary philosophy, rejects univocal answers, and seeks new and creative syntheses to express the truth of the Christian faith. How wide is this pluralistic endorsement?

PHILOSOPHICAL PLURALISM

The pluralism endorsed by *Fides et ratio* is inextricably intertwined with the encyclical's continual assertion that philosophy is an autonomous discipline,[50] one with its own methods of which it is "rightly jealous."[51] And, as noted earlier, the encyclical boldly asserts that "the content of revelation can never debase the discoveries and legitimate autonomy of reason."[52] Theology, then, can never simply dictate to philosophy without regard for the authentic demands and claims of reason itself.[53] At the same time, the encyclical makes a distinction between the "valid autonomy" of philosophy and its "self-sufficiency." While the former remains true, the latter is invalid

---

50 *Fides et ratio*, no. 77.

51 *Fides et ratio*, no. 13.

52 *Fides et ratio*, no. 79.

53 John Paul II made this point in his statement on the Galileo case: "It is a duty for theologians to keep themselves regularly informed of scientific advances in order to examine, if such be necessary, whether or not there are reasons for taking them into account in their reflection or for introducing changes in their teaching." See his *Address to the Participants in the Plenary Session of the Pontifical Academy of Sciences* (October 31, 1992), no. 8. This English translation may be found at "Lessons of the Galileo Case," *Origins* 22 (November 12, 1992): 372. What is indicated for the physical sciences is surely the case, by extension, for the human sciences as well.

because it refuses the "truth offered by divine Revelation."[54] Truth is one and undivided; consequently, philosophy can never be "separated" or "absolutely independent of the contents of faith."[55] Indeed, "when philosophy heeds the summons of the Gospel's truth, its autonomy is in no way impaired."[56] Of course, distinguishing the legitimate autonomy of philosophy from a misguided self-sufficiency is no easy task. As such, it calls forth the question: what kind of pluralism respects philosophical autonomy while remaining revelationally appropriate?

Clear indications of the scope and kind of pluralism envisioned are available in a catena of citations from *Fides et ratio.* The encyclical says, for example, that Christianity first encountered Greek philosophy "but this does not mean at all that other approaches are precluded."[57] Even more strongly the document asserts that "the Church has no philosophy of her own nor does she canonize any one particular philosophy in preference to others."[58] The encyclical also claims that "no historical form of philosophy can legitimately claim to embrace the totality of truth."[59] Still again, "I have no wish to direct theologians to particular methods, since that is not the competence of the Magisterium."[60] Finally, "there are many paths which lead to truth [. . .] [and] any one of these paths may be taken, as long as it leads [. . .] to the Revelation of Jesus Christ."[61] In fact, the pope notes that the magisterium's interventions in philosophical questions "are intended, above all, to prompt, promote and encourage philosophical enquiry."[62] The document also

---

54 *Fides et ratio,* no. 75.

55 *Fides et ratio,* no. 45.

56 *Fides et ratio,* no. 108. On earlier debates over the autonomy of philosophy vis-à-vis theology, see John Wippel, "Thomas Aquinas and the Problem of Christian Philosophy" in *Metaphysical Themes in Thomas Aquinas,* 1–33 (Washington, DC: The Catholic University of America Press, 1984). On this question with specific reference to *Fides et ratio,* see Avery Dulles, "Can Philosophy Be Christian?" *First Things* 102 (April 2000): 24–29.

57 *Fides et ratio,* no. 72.

58 *Fides et ratio,* no. 49. Here, the encyclical, in note 54, cites *"Humani generis," AAS,* 42 (1950): 566 as a supporting document. But one is hard pressed to read anything quite like the sentence indicated here. The theme of that passage is that although the terminology used in the Schools is capable of further perfection and refinement, it is clearly the case that such philosophy provides a sturdy foundation for church teaching.

59 *Fides et ratio,* no. 51.

60 *Fides et ratio,* no. 64.

61 *Fides et ratio,* no. 38.

62 *Fides et ratio,* no. 51.

proffers a variety of possible models, indicating by example the plurality of philosophical approaches sanctioned by the Church. At different times, one finds cited favorably the expected classical thinkers such as Augustine, Pseudo-Dionysius, the Cappadocians, Anselm and Aquinas, as well as modern theologians and philosophers such as Newman, Rosmini, Soloviev, Florensky, Lossky, and Stein. Even Pascal and Kierkegaard receive favorable mention for their epistemological humility in the face of rationalism. Of course, the thinkers adduced here are representative rather than exhaustive examples of those whose philosophy and theology is in "organic continuity with the great tradition" while developing "an original, new and constructive mode of thinking."[63]

What is clear is that the great Catholic philosophical tradition of the past, as well as the one envisaged for the future by *Fides et ratio*, is hardly identical with Thomism or Scholasticism.[64] At the same time, the encyclical leaves no doubt that the pluralism envisioned is one which, like Thomism, is revelationally appropriate and capable of fulfilling the *officium congruum*. This kind of pluralism may be termed "commensurable pluralism."

Commensurable pluralism allows for a diversity of philosophical systems, frameworks, and perspectives, all of which, however, must be fundamentally commensurable with the *depositum fidei*. Just as Augustine, the Cappadocians, Aquinas, and Bonaventure used varying philosophical approaches while protecting the unity of faith, so this type of unity in multiplicity, similarity in diversity, sameness in otherness, must be present in conceptually fitting contemporary thought as well. Different conceptual systems will be perennially adequate as possible mediations and expressions of the Christian faith. They will not be, however, given various limiting factors such as human historicity and finitude, exhaustive of either philosophical or theological truth.

Of course, the *nouvelle théologie* had already called into question the conceptual univocity of Scholasticism sanctioned by *Aeterni Patris* and

---

63 *Fides et ratio*, no. 85. John Galvin, in the article cited earlier (no. 1), has identified many others who, as John Paul II has elsewhere noted, have enriched the church with their thought. See Galvin, "*Fides et Ratio*," 16n18. The variety of names invoked by the pope indicates the wide berth afforded to theological and philosophical pluralism.

64 As Peter Henrici has written, "The two explicit references to Anselm of Canterbury (nos. 14, 42) and the allusions to the many Church Fathers who engaged in philosophy, as well as a series of more recent, and not altogether thomistic, Christian philosophers, can already generally be read as a certain relativising of the monopoly position of Thomism and Scholasticism." Henrici, "The One Who Went Unnamed: Maurice Blondel in the Encyclical *Fides et Ratio*," *Communio: International Catholic Review* 26, no. 3 (1999): 610.

reinforced by the Modernist controversy. Vatican II followed this lead by holding, in several well-known passages, for the possibility of legitimate theological pluralism, a trajectory followed in the postconciliar period as well.[65] Most recently, the 1995 statement of the Pontifical Council for Promoting Christian Unity regarding differing Eastern and Western formulations of the eternal procession of the Holy Spirit and, more dramatically, the Lutheran-Roman Catholic Joint Declaration on the Doctrine of Justification, testify to the actuality of varying conceptual systems that are themselves, nonetheless, commensurable with the *depositum fidei*.[66]

Among those reasons allowing for commensurable conceptual pluralism is the superrintelligibility of being itself. The mystery and ineffability of being necessarily supersedes its various conceptualizations; one conceptual system, one perspective on reality, can hardly exhaust its intelligibility. This is especially the case insofar as concepts themselves represent abstractions, at a certain remove from the intelligibility offered by the existing real. This is hardly to aver that the concept is devoid of cognitive value. It is to say that the intelligibility offered by the concept is ultimately limited in light of the fuller actualization provided by the dynamic reality of the *actus essendi*.[67]

If the abstracted concept is never a moment of pure presence, without an admixture of absence, if it affords a real but limited dimension of intel-

---

65 At Vatican II, one finds this embrace of theological pluralism in *Gaudet mater ecclesia*, the opening speech of John XXIII. For an exhaustive analysis, see Giuseppe Alberigo, "Formazione, contenuto e fortuna dell'allocuzione *Gaudet Mater Ecclesia*," in *Fede tradizione profezia*, ed. G. Alberigo, et al., 187–222 (Brescia: Paideia, 1984). One finds it clearly as well in *Unitatis redintegratio*, nos. 4, 6, and 17; and in *Gaudium et spes*, no. 62. During the postconciliar period, one may cite as supportive of pluralism, by way of a partial list, critical passages of the 1973 declaration, *Mysterium ecclesiae* and the encyclical of 1995, *Ut unum sint*, no. 57.

66 "The Greek and Latin Traditions regarding the Procession of the Holy Spirit," *Information Service* 89 (1995/II-III): 88–92; for an English translation of the Joint Declaration, see *Origins* 28, no. 8 (July 16, 1998): 120–27. Along the same lines, the agreements made by Paul VI and John Paul II with the ancient non-Chalcedonian churches provide additional examples. In both cases, the content of Chalcedon was affirmed within different formulations and conceptual frameworks. See Walter Kasper, *Theology and Church*, trans. Margaret Kohl (Chestnut Ridge, NY: The Crossroad Publishing Company, 1989), 144–45. See also his, "Unité ecclesiale et communion ecclésiale dans une perspective catholique," *Revue des sciences religieuses* 75, no. 1 (2001): 6–22.

67 One sees this argument made consistently by William Hill, *Knowing the Unknown God* (New York: Philosophical Library, 1971), chapters three and four. For the historical background to the discussion, see Gerald McCool, *Catholic Theology in the Nineteenth Century* (New York: Seabury Press, 1977) and *From Unity to Pluralism: The Internal Evolution of Thomism* (New York: Fordham University Press, 1989). This issue is also treated in Thomas G. Guarino, *Revelation and Truth* (Scranton: University of Scranton Press, 1993), chapter four.

ligibility, then the Church can never be wedded to one conceptual system as if one alone truly mediates the Christian faith. Varying conceptual systems may be incommensurable among themselves, Augustine's and Aquinas's for example, but equally commensurable with the fundamentals of Christian belief. Each conceptual system is adequate; neither is exhaustive. As the encyclical notes, "Revelation remains charged with mystery."[68] Even more strongly Vatican I stated, the "divine mysteries [. . .] so excel the created intellect that, even when they have been communicated by revelation and received by faith, they remain covered by the veil of faith itself and shrouded as it were in darkness."[69]

One intention of the encyclical, then, is to indicate that various conceptual frameworks may be used to mediate the truth of Christianity. *Fides et ratio* makes this clear when it notes that the term "Christian philosophy" "in no way intends to suggest that there is an official philosophy of the Church, since faith as such is not philosophy."[70] This, taken together with the earlier claim that the Church does not "canonize any one particular philosophy in preference to others,"[71] indicates that the magisterium sanctions no specific conceptual system, and that several may indeed be *congruens verbo Dei*, commensurable with the deposit of faith.

When the encyclical notes that the "Church cannot abandon what she has gained from her inculturation in the world of Greco-Latin thought,"[72] or that "certain basic concepts retain their universal epistemological value and thus retain the truth of the propositions in which they are expressed,"[73] this should be understood as meaning that the thought forms drawn from the ancient philosophical world, especially those used in dogmatic definitions, are perennially adequate, even if not exhaustively so, for mediating the faith. It also means that certain elements from Greek philosophy, such as its emphasis on the universality of truth and its fundamental realism, are, in fact, uniquely accordant with Christian belief.

But if it's true that the Church has had centuries to judge what is worthy in ancient thought, it is no less true that the task of judging whether con-

---

68 *Fides et ratio*, no. 13.

69 Denzinger-Hünermann, *Enchiridion symbolorum*, 3016.

70 *Fides et ratio*, no. 76.

71 *Fides et ratio*, no. 49.

72 *Fides et ratio*, no. 72.

73 *Fides et ratio*, no. 96.

temporary methodologies are commensurable with the *depositum fidei* also takes time. This should alert both theologians and the magisterium to what Thomas Kuhn referred to as the phenomenon of "masking."[74] The adequacy or inadequacy of new conceptual systems is not always readily apparent. New systems of thought, using unfamiliar concepts or paradigms, take time to develop consistency and to account for all of the data. This should be borne in mind when judging whether a new theology or philosophy is, in fact, commensurable with Catholicism.[75]

EVALUATION

While one can agree with the desire of *Fides et ratio* to encourage revelationally appropriate philosophies, certain blind spots in the encyclical lessen the chances for conceptual pluralism, for the adequate but not exhaustive systems that the document itself encourages. Some of these weaknesses will now be treated, even while recalling the encyclical's pertinent claim that it has not offered a complete picture of contemporary philosophy.[76]

In the first place, as previously noted, the encyclical identifies the ability to "know the truth," to "reach objective truth,"[77] as essential for any revelationally appropriate thought. It adds that this should be done by means of the "*adaequatio rei et intellectus* to which the Scholastic Doctors referred."[78] Indeed, a defense of some kind of realism seems philosophically and theologically essential to revelation, for realism alone allows the Church to defend Christian doctrine as not only symbolic and disclosive but also as ontologically true. Inasmuch as Christianity is concerned with mediating states of affairs, human and divine, some form of philosophical realism, profoundly stamped by the subjective and constructive dimensions intrinsic

---

74 Thomas Kuhn, *The Structure of Scientific Revolutions*, 2nd ed. (Chicago: University of Chicago Press, 1970). Also relevant is an earlier paper by Kuhn that, bearing witness to the function of masking in science, is applicable to theology as well. See "The Function of Dogma in Scientific Research," in *Scientific Change*, ed. A. C. Crombie, 347–69 (New York: Basic Books, 1963).

75 Both Kuhn's comments on "masking" as well as the pope's statement on Galileo should be appropriately recalled during the process of implementing *Ex Corde Ecclesiae*. Both authors warn of the danger of precipitously determining the boundaries of truth in the face of new evidence or of new conceptual systems. At the same time, this does not call into question the magisterium's *ultimate* authority to determine whether new theological systems are, in fact, congruent with the Christian faith.

76 *Fides et ratio*, no. 91.

77 *Fides et ratio*, no. 82.

78 *Fides et ratio*, no. 82.

to knowing and productive of it, and equally stamped by the apophatic nature of theological language, must be adduced. Just as theological language has analogical, apophatic, and doxological dimensions, it has ostensive and "representational" ones as well.[79] The breakdown of realism leads, seemingly, to unfettered constructivism, to conceptual pragmatism, or to a narrative unsure of its precise ontological status. This is why the encyclical insists that theological language and interpretation cannot simply "defer" in the Derridean sense but must ultimately offer us "a statement which is simply true; otherwise there would be no Revelation of God, but only the expression of human notions about God [. . .]."[80]

However, should realism be as tightly bound to the *adaequatio* as *Fides et ratio* seemingly requires? This appears both to limit the very pluralism the encyclical supports and to contradict the varying thinkers espoused by it. Was Newman representative of a bare *adaequatio*? Was Lossky, who is mentioned favorably by the encyclical, and who had such deep reservations about Aristotelianism and Western theological "rationalism"? Is it not precisely the Aristotelico-Thomistic notion of the *adaequatio* itself that, at least in certain aspects, needs rethinking? Most importantly, in defending realism, should the Christian theologian and philosopher be bound to thirteenth-century conceptual apparatus? This is hardly in the spirit of developing philosophies that proceed through the Fathers and Scholastics and also take account of modern and contemporary thought.[81] Robert Sokolowski, for example, clearly defends a realistic epistemology without resorting to the conceptual categories of another age.[82]

---

79 Needless to add, the representationalism proper to knowledge of created realities is essentially different from that proper to theology. The entire understanding of the analogical nature of theological language is built upon this premise.

80 *Fides et ratio*, no. 84. At the same time, Aquinas's important statement should be invoked: We cannot grasp what God is, but only what he is not and how other things are related to him (*Summa contra gentiles*, I, chap. 30). Even if this classic text, omitted from the encyclical, refers to our inability to know God quidditatively, it reminds us of Thomas's own profound apophaticism and the danger of naïve representationalism.

81 *Fides et ratio*, no. 85.

82 In this defense, Sokolowski employs not the *adaequatio*, but Husserlian themes such as the intentionality of consciousness, registration, the display of affairs in disclosure, and the correlation between things and the dative to whom they are manifested. By so doing he takes the anti-Cartesian dimension of phenomenology in a realistic direction. See Sokolowski, *Introduction to Phenomenology* (Cambridge: Cambridge University Press, 2000). It may also be asked whether the encyclical would not have been further strengthened had it noted, as Dupré does, that while correspondence should not be rejected, speaking about truth as "disclosure" serves to protect the truly religious nature of truth while standing at some distance from the

Related to the issue of realism and objectivity is the matter of human subjectivity in knowing truth. The encyclical ignores, for the most part, important dimensions of the noetic act which, of themselves, do not necessarily frustrate the realism or objectivity *Fides et ratio* wishes to defend. One sees very little, for example, about the turn to the subject, horizon analysis, theory-laden interpretation, the constructive dimension of knowledge, or the tacit and intuitive elements of epistemology. This failure to acknowledge the subjective element in knowing counts as a significant omission in a document discussing human rationality and its relationship to faith. Perhaps the encyclical should be credited for bypassing some of the blind alleys found in the epistemology of modernity. One wonders, however, if by ignoring the anthropological dimensions of knowing prominent in modern thought, the encyclical does not ignore modernity itself, thereby militating against its own goal of establishing a new synthesis which takes account of the entire philosophical tradition.[83]

It is legitimate to read Vatican II as the gradual and requisitely cautious incorporation of certain positive elements of modernity into Catholicism. This is true with regard to the conciliar concern for freedom of conscience

---

subjectivism of modernity. Louis Dupré, *Religious Mystery and Rational Reflection* (Grand Rapids: Eerdmans Publishing, 1998), 19–40. Noteworthy in this context is Lonergan's classic essay on the dehellenization of dogma, which is hardly a naïve restatement of the *adaequatio*, but remains, in fact, a sophisticated defense of realism. See "The Dehellenization of Dogma," in *A Second Collection*, ed. William Ryan and Bernard Tyrrell, 11–32 (Philadelphia: The Westminster Press, 1974), especially 14–17. The encyclical does, at one point, try to place the truth-question in a wider context (nos. 28–34). Its observations, however, remain at the level of adumbration.

83 It has been noted that Blondel and Maréchal, two thinkers who knew the tradition well and yet sought to incorporate the "fundamental achievements of modern and contemporary thought" (no. 85) are not mentioned in the encyclical. One reason for this may well be the document's relative disinterest in the subjective dimensions of knowing. *Fides et ratio* speaks pejoratively of an "immanentist habit of mind" (no, 15) but the immanentism (no. 91) and phenomenalism characteristic of Kant can hardly be predicated of either Blondel or Maréchal. Henrici's claim that the encyclical did not wish to bind thinkers strictly to Blondel (or to anyone else) as *Aeterni Patris* had bound them to Aquinas appears to be too benign an interpretation. See Henrici, "Maurice Blondel," 620–21. While Blondel is implicitly endorsed when the document applauds those who produced philosophies "starting with an analysis of immanence [. . .] " (no. 59), one nonetheless wonders if Garrigou-Lagrange's charge that Blondel understood truth as nothing more than an *adaequatio vitae et mentis* rather than a true correspondence finds a certain resonance in the encyclical. As for Maréchal, one may well take note of von Balthasar's claim in 1946: "The methodology carried out by Joseph Maréchal can be adduced as the most perfect example of such a clarifying transposition [spoils from Egypt] in the present age. [. . .] Kant has never been understood more deeply and thoroughly by a Catholic philosopher—understood and at the same time applied and overcome." See Balthasar, "On the Tasks of Catholic Philosophy in Our Time," trans. Brian McNeil, *Communio: International Catholic Review* 20, no. 1 (1993): 161.

as well as for the moderate egalitarianism (rooted in baptism, undoubtedly, but also influenced by modernity) found in the documents. This same modest incorporation may also be found in the conciliar emphasis on theological pluralism. But if Vatican II began the long journey of the Church's careful evaluation of modernity, then this process will be necessarily protracted—as demanded both by the "spoils from Egypt" tradition and by the fact that virtually all thinkers now recognize that modernity itself is a mixed blessing. Perhaps Origen and the Cappadocians can serve here as helpful paradigms. They began the theological assimilation of the intellectual heritage of antiquity, a journey completed only with Aquinas. The Church's long period of relative peace, shattered first by the Reformation and then by modernity itself, must now be restructured by gradually absorbing the fruits of these movements into the life of faith. If the magisterium's first response was mere rejection, this is perhaps understandable inasmuch as the Enlightenment was often a reaction against Christianity in a way that was not true for the ancient world. But the process of incorporation has definitively begun and will inevitably continue. The inability of the encyclical to come to grips with serious philosophical issues raised by modernity, such as the role of subjectivity and historicity in knowing, represents an unnecessary hesitation in the Church's attempt to enrich her intellectual and spiritual heritage with all that is true and human.

A second weakness of *Fides et ratio*, in my judgment, is that it tends to ascribe the contemporary distrust of reason to "nihilism" and to a diminished belief in the "human capacity to know the truth."[84] To this distrust it consistently opposes as an antidote a renewed metaphysics. Here a major problem of the encyclical surfaces. For *Fides et ratio* fails to address the fact that many contemporary thinkers are searching for a third option, beyond nihilism and metaphysics, an option which indeed calls attention to reason's limitations, but without a concomitant rejection of reason's capacities or a turn toward epistemological or metaphysical despair. What is sought is a properly contextualized reason or what may be called an ontologically appropriate understanding of rationality.

With the encyclical, many contemporary philosophers and theologians are seeking to overcome both relativism and anarchic irrationalism. But they wish to do so without metaphysics, without even a renewed metaphysics, which they deem philosophically untenable. These thinkers seek

84 *Fides et ratio*, no. 5.

to develop an understanding of human rationality adjusted to the newly-presenced horizons of historicity and linguisticality. Recognition of both the proper limits and the proper capabilities of human reason avoids, in their judgment, a flaccid relativism, a cynical nihilism and an unwarranted foundationalism. When the pope asserts, then, that the human sciences should not "marginalize philosophy"[85] or when he rejects all forms of relativism,[86] it is in fact the case that many philosophers and theologians agree with him, without necessarily turning to metaphysics as the only alternative.

These thinkers argue that Heidegger and Wittgenstein have conjointly shown that traditional metaphysical discourse is inappropriate because it rests on a fallacy concerning both the radical nature of historicity as well as the logic and language of culturally constituted communities. Philosophers and theologians, then, must search out new understandings of truth and rationality similar to Gadamer's *phronesis* and Habermas's "rocking hull" of communicative discourse. It may legitimately be argued that *Fides et ratio*, Gadamer, and Habermas all reject aspects of modernity and aspects of postmodernity. But while the encyclical turns to a renewed metaphysics as the remedy for philosophy's defects, Gadamer, Habermas, and others turn towards a postmetaphysical, posttranscendental, post-Enlightenment philosophy that fully recognizes human immersion in the socially constructed web of history and culture. This kind of practical reasoning is suspicious of universal metaphysical claims, but it is not distrustful of reason itself. With *Fides et ratio*, this type of reasoning seeks to overcome a strong and militant postmodernism, but, in a departure from the encyclical, wishes to add that reason itself is limited by and embedded in language and history and should, therefore, abandon its former, ontologically inappropriate, pretensions.

Of course, the encyclical does note that revelation is "immersed in time and history,"[87] but one wonders if the document appropriates this idea other than by way of *obiter dicta*. This is certainly not to say that *Fides et ratio* must concur with those distrustful of metaphysical claims. To do so leads to a very different understanding of revelation than has traditionally been the case. It is to say, however, that it is not nihilism, irrationalism, or the postmodern "destructive critique of every certitude"[88] that is, at bottom,

85 *Fides et ratio*, no. 61.
86 *Fides et ratio*, no. 80.
87 *Fides et ratio*, no. 11.
88 *Fides et ratio*, no. 91.

the major challenge to metaphysics as the chief philosophical linchpin of Christian dogmatic truth traditionally conceived. The major challenge, rather, is the attempted via media between metaphysics and postmodernity, the attempt to limit rationality to practical reason that issues forth in a hermeneutical approach seeking to understand doctrine in a more protean and fluid sense than the tradition heretofore.

The encyclical, then, despite its length and profundity on many issues, misses the sustained reflections on history and culture, as well as the differing notions of truth and rationality, that are presently flourishing and that, in fact, constitute the chief remonstrance to the renewed metaphysics that *Fides et ratio* itself champions. Insofar as the encyclical seeks to engage contemporary currents of thought, it here misses a significant opportunity.

A third weakness of the encyclical may be found in its understanding of the contemporary hermeneutical task. Since Vatican II, the primary way in which Catholicism has officially thought about theological pluralism is through the form/content or context/content distinction. The intention of this distinction is to allow a fundamental content, the *depositum fidei*, to be expressed through a variety of perspectives and terminologies. This is the distinction invoked by John XXIII in his opening address, *Gaudet mater ecclesia*, and, in different places and in varying ways, by the conciliar documents themselves.[89] After the council, the Congregation for the Doctrine of the Faith issued the declaration *Mysterium ecclesiae* further reinforcing the form/content hermeneutical approach.[90] Soon after Vatican II ended, Congar hailed the distinction between the deposit of faith and the way in which it is expressed, noting that the entire council echoed these few words.[91] More recently, Giuseppe Alberigo has asserted that the context/content distinction is one of the decisive motifs of the council.[92] Of course, one of the reasons theologians have welcomed this approach is because it allows for a variety of conceptual systems and frameworks, thereby encour-

---

89 *Gaudium et spes*, no. 62; *Unitatis redintegratio* (November 21, 1964), nos. 6, 17.

90 *AAS* 65 (1973): 403. "The truths which the Church intends to teach through her dogmatic formulas are distinct from the changeable conceptions of a given age and can be expressed without them." Other comments about dogmatic formulas, found in section five of thse declaration, are equally pointed.

91 Yves Congar, *A History of Theology*, trans. Hunter Guthrie (Garden City, NY: Doubleday, 1968), 18–19.

92 Giuseppe Alberigo, "Facteurs de 'Laïcité' au Concile Vatican II," *Revue des sciences religieuses*, 74, no. 2 (2000): 211–25. See also his "Fedeltà e creatività nella ricezione del concilio Vaticano II. Criteri ermeneutici," *Cristianesimo nella storia* 21 (2000), 383–402, at 400.

aging a modicum of theological pluralism. The neo-scholasticism that had been dominant from *Aeterni Patris* until just before the council could now be complemented and, at times, surpassed by other methodologies.

One may legitimately object that the form/content distinction, if too positivistically or mechanistically understood, represents an immobile theory, disallowing true development and ignoring the necessary circum-incession between the two elements, a coinherence clearly illustrated from the worlds of literature, art, and music.[93] But few would argue that immobility is the fundamental intention of the context/content approach. It is lauded by Congar and Alberigo precisely because it represents a chance for theology to foster the "legitimate pluralism" endorsed by the council and to develop new concepts and formulations—which will themselves disclose unique theological perspectives—in order to express the Christian faith.[94]

Fides et ratio on the other hand, is very reserved about the form/content distinction. For example, the encyclical, unsurprisingly, invokes "certain and unchangeable doctrine"[95] and rejects the historicist claim that "what was true in one period [. . .] may not be true in another."[96] However, this expected emphasis on the identity and perpetuity of doctrine's truth is not balanced with earlier ecclesial accents on the possible variety of conceptual formulation. The crucial passages regarding pluralism, in *Gaudet mater ecclesia, Gaudium et spes,* and *Unitatis redintegratio,* are not cited by *Fides et ratio.*[97] Furthermore, the encyclical's sole reference to *Mysterium ecclesiae* cites that part of the declaration defending the claim that the meaning of

---

93 Rahner, for example, in two perceptive essays, notes the inadequacies of the form/content distinction if is not approached with subtlety and nuance, particularly with regard to the knotty question of determining the actual "substance" of a particular teaching. See Rahner, "*Mysterium Ecclesiae,*" trans. Margaret Kohl, in vol. 17 of *Theological Investigations,* 139–55 (Chestnut Ridge, NY: The Crossroad Publishing Company, 1981). Also, Rahner, "Yesterday's History of Dogma and Theology for Tomorrow," trans. Edward Quinn, in vol. 18 of *Theological Investigations,* 3–34 (Chestnut Ridge, NY: The Crossroad Publishing Company). An untenable positivistic understanding of form/content is also the gravamen of John Thiel's criticism of this distinction as found in Thiel, "Perspectives on Tradition," *Proceedings of the CTSA* 54 (1999): 11n12.

94 I have elsewhere argued that the context/content hermeneutical approach also allows for the organic and architectonic development of ecclesial teaching. See "Vincent of Lérins and the Hermeneutical Question," *Gregorianum* 75, no. 3 (1994): 491–523.

95 *Fides et ratio,* no. 92.

96 *Fides et ratio,* no. 87.

97 With regard to John XXIII's opening allocution, for example, the extract cited by *Fides et ratio* (no. 92) is found just before the overlooked but hermeneutically critical passage: "*Est enim aliud ipsum depositum Fidei, seu veritates, quae veneranda doctrina nostra continentur, aliud modus, quo eaedem enuntiantur, eodem tamen sensu eademque sententia.*"

dogmatic formulas remains constant,[98] while ignoring the significant passage pertaining to the possible plurality of conceptual expression.[99]

How should these omissions be understood? Is there an intentional brake placed on theological reconceptualization and the legitimate pluralism of expression? This does not seem to be the case inasmuch as the entire document is calling for pluralism, at least within certain limits. Perhaps the failure to cite the relevant conciliar and postconciliar passages is provoked by the encyclical's clear desire to preserve the ancient terminology, a language it is at pains to protect. For example, *Fides et ratio* rejects "disdain for the classical philosophy from which the terms of both the understanding of faith and the actual formulation of dogma have been drawn."[100] Or perhaps the encyclical has in mind that other sensible warning of *Humani generis* that the Church cannot tie itself to philosophical systems that have flourished for only a short period of time.

But the failure to cite the germane texts endorsing the context/content distinction is a significant omission and likely the result of excessive caution. Does not the very idea of historicity, of cultural plurality, demand new formulations that will, at the same time, protect the fundamental teaching of the Church? Is this not especially necessary as the Church in various parts of the world theologically matures? Does not the form/content distinction also protect the proper creativity of the theologian who, while always conserving the deposit of faith, must contribute to its proper development as well? Does not this distinction allow the theologian to reap the theological fruits of his or her dialogue with contemporary philosophy, anthropology, and the physical and social sciences? Does not the context/content distinction also recognize the ontological productivity of tradition as well as a proper understanding of the "fusion of horizons?" Does it not help solve the question of unity within multiplicity, of identity within the manifold?

---

98 *Fides et ratio*, no. 96, no. 113.

99 See note 38 above. *Fides et ratio* does briefly state (no. 95) that a question must be raised concerning the universality of truth and the historical and cultural conditioning of formulas. But instead of then invoking the conciliar distinction between the *depositum fidei* and the conceptual mode of expression, the encyclical immediately turns to the claim of *Humani generis* that it is wrong to depart from the traditional terms and notions (no. 96, note 112). It would perhaps have been better to state that the distinction between context and content is sanctioned by the Church and to encourage theologians to seek an intelligible language and appropriate methodology for their times, while concomitantly asserting that the tradition provides a theological terminology and conceptual framework of great nuance and sophistication not easily surpassed and often worthy of preservation.

100 *Fides et ratio*, no. 55, citing *Humani generis*.

One need only look at the Church's own ecumenical praxis to see how the form/content distinction has been employed. The Joint Declaration on the Doctrine of Justification, as already noted, sees the essential teaching on justification, which is doctrinally preserved for Catholics in the Aristotelian-Thomistic language of causality that dominates the Tridentine decree, as complemented by a Lutheran conceptual model that avoids classical and Scholastic frameworks. The same approach is used in the aforementioned document detailing the various modes, Catholic and Orthodox, of expressing the eternal procession of the Holy Spirit.

While one can understand that *Fides et ratio* takes a reserved approach on the form/content question because of a desire to see the traditional terminology preserved and an illegitimate pluralism avoided, nonetheless, the encyclical's comments on the hermeneutics of dogma remain flawed in that its emphasis on the proper plurality of theological expressions is not as vigorous as that of the council's itself.

CONCLUSIONS

Fides et ratio is an encyclical maintaining the traditional Catholic understanding that revelation is the epistemologically primary discourse, the *norma normans non normata*. No counter or opposing narrative, whether derived from sociology, anthropology, evolutionary psychology, sociobiology, or even philosophy itself, can ultimately rival the determinative truth-claims made by revelation.

The neuralgic question for *Fides et ratio* and for theology itself remains: how is revelation conceived? In the encyclical, God's self-manifestation is understood as an eternal and unchangeable word to humanity. It is a word that has been crystallized in the Church, under the divine guidance of the Holy Spirit, into various dogmatic and doctrinal statements. These assertions, although cast in imperfect human formulations and open to legitimate development, are fundamentally unchangeable. Any revelationally appropriate philosophy, capable of performing the *officium congruum*, must be able to defend the possibility of these universal, continuous, and objective truths. Hence, the encyclical's profound reliance on metaphysics.

But what if revelation is differently conceived? A different understanding of God's self-communication would place far greater weight on the historicity of truth, the perspective of the interpreting subject, and human embeddedness in particular socio-cultural-linguistic worlds; in other words, on all of the epistemological dimensions that received scant emphasis in the encyclical. In this view, revelation would be more Heideggerian and epiphanic in kind, moving, ultimately, within the fundamental horizon of immersed historicity rather than that of perduringly disclosed being. It would be a notion of revelation allowing for a more profound interplay between *lēthē* and *alētheia*, between presence and absence. It would also call into question—or at least significantly reinterpret in accordance with the strictures of historically situated thought—the traditional hallmarks of Catholic doctrine. Revelation would be seen less as an abiding word crystallized in certain doctrinal statements requiring universality and continuity as essential benchmarks and more as *Seinsgeschicke*, eruptive messages unveiled before humanity, distinctly differing from age to age and from culture to culture. Continuity of doctrine would not mean that the same doctrinal meaning could be found in every period. It would mean, rather, that the same text, in this case a doctrinal statement, would be subject to continuous interpretation in various epochs. There would certainly be continuity. But it would be a *formal* continuity provided by history and tradition, a continuity of the interpreting act in every generation rather than a *material* continuity, a continuous preservation of meaning, organically developed, from age to age. A particular interpretation of the "fusion of horizons" and the "ontological productivity of history" would subject the doctrinal tradition to rather clear, and, in its view, ontologically appropriate, revision. This protean hermeneutics of dogma would be, obviously, at some remove from the traditional understanding of the enduring quality of Catholic beliefs. Revelation would still require an appropriate philosophy, one that could fulfill the *officium congruum* and be *conveniens verbo Dei*, but this philosophy would now be very different from the "renewed metaphysics" that *Fides et ratio* envisions.

Is this different notion of revelation untenable?

The pope makes a very important statement in the encyclical when he says that theology can never "debase [*comprimere*] the discoveries and legitimate autonomy of reason."[101] Should reason, so praised by the encyclical, "compress" itself by subjecting itself to simply one, possibly outdated, notion of revelation? Did not Heidegger reject precisely this "compressed" notion of reason, and ultimately of revelation, when he rejected traditional "Catholic" metaphysics in order to seek a more primordial understanding of being and truth? And were not similar concerns, at least partially, behind Max

101 *Fides et ratio*, no. 79.

Scheler's final rejection of Catholicism?[102] So, when *Fides et ratio* says that it seeks to "emphasize the value of philosophy [. . .] as well as the limits which philosophy faces when it neglects or rejects the truths of Revelation"[103] is this not a *petitio principi* according to the encyclical's own norms? Certainly, then, holding that a proper understanding of revelation must itself conform to the legitimate and veridical demands of contemporary philosophy cannot be *a priori* ruled out of court as if it represents simply a deviant theological option.

On the other hand, to move in this direction, without absolute clarity regarding this direction's veracity, would be precipitous. For to understand revelation in a manner profoundly indebted to the Heidggerian notion of historicity (along with its various collateral dimensions) would result, rather clearly, in a significant departure from the traditional Catholic understanding of doctrine. It is one thing to use every possible element of theological epistemology: analogy, theological notes, the hierarchy of truths, the incomprehensibility of God, the surintelligibility of being, the apophatic tradition, the development of doctrine, and reversals of the ordinary magisterium, to establish the importance of legitimate pluralism and the possibility of methodological and conceptual diversity. It is quite another matter to call into question the idea that revelation is a self-communication of God that endures, essentially the same, but organically developed, in the Church's teachings. If revelation is indeed, tied to a perduringly, divinely communicated truth that is, at least in some fundamental sense, continuous and self-identical, then philosophies with a particular metaphysical range, with a particular notion of truth, and with a particular hermeneutical correlate, must be adduced as proper warrants. This is certainly neither to demand uniformity nor to diminish legitimate theological pluralism—on the contrary, too many factors, subjectivity and historicity included, inexorably give rise to such plurality. It is to say, however, that theological pluralism itself must move within certain circumscribed boundaries.

There is little doubt that an improved *Fides et ratio* would engage the ideas concerning truth and rationality stemming from a more culturally imbedded notion of humanity. It would accept, at least in a qualified sense, the historical and linguistic challenges to metaphysics issued by Heidegger

---

102 Scheler's philosophical reasons are noted in Herbert Spiegelberg, vol. 1 of *The Phenomenological Movement* (The Hague: Martinus Nijhoff, 1969), 237–38.

103 *Fides et ratio*, no. 100.

and Wittgenstein. It would move beyond a purely Scholastic notion of truth and explore other forms of philosophical realism. And it would more clearly affirm, with Vatican II, the distinction between the deposit of faith and the variety of conceptual expressions. But if the encyclical has inadequately faced some of the problems presented by contemporary thought, it has also properly indicated that pluralism itself must move within a certain scope and range ultimately bordered by the Church's faith.

Chapter Three

Introduction: Contemporary Lessons from the *Proslogion*

The mantra of much contemporary philosophy is that human beings are profoundly "situated," that is, we are indefeasibly embedded and immersed in history, society, culture, and language. This point of view, relentlessly hammered home by Heidegger, Wittgenstein, and others, has served to unmask the worldless subject of positivism which ignored the fact that humanity—and so human rationality—is inexorably conditioned and contextualized. Acknowledging these delimiting horizons has given birth to the popular maxim, "it's interpretation all the way down"—that is to say, there exist no *facta bruta*, no cold, hard, objective facts, apart from interpretation. It is precisely this idea that Nietzsche sought to capture with his well-known insight: there are no facts, only interpretations—and this too is an interpretation.

This emphasis on the culturally and linguistically conditioned subject—on the belief that "it's interpretation all the way down"—is often appropriated by theologians today, and for a specific reason: to show that Enlightenment assertions about "objective" knowledge are every bit as conditioned and "traditioned" as the claims made by the Christian faith. By displaying the contextual, embedded character of all knowing, theology can then legitimately argue that there exist no "higher" or more rigorous epistemic perspectives by which Christian statements can be judged. *Knowing of every kind*—not just religious knowing—emerges from the tight nexus of contingent circumstances and encircling webs of belief.

While one may understand this theological approach—especially its crucial insistence on preserving and protecting the epistemic primacy of Christian assertions—one may also ask if this is the best theoretical path for Catholic theology to pursue. Does this attempt to overcome Enlightenment imperialism, legitimate in its intentions, harbor its own dangers? One casualty of this approach may well be the loss of "universal natural realities." Does the very idea of "nature" not take a decided backseat if human beings are entirely enmeshed in history and culture? Would it then be possible to speak cogently of "natural law?" And what about warrants for arguments? Are all warrants merely internal to specific communities? If so, can natural theology exist as a discipline since it claims that some arguments are available, at least potentially, to all observers regardless of contingent circumstances?

St. Anselm's *Proslogion* helps to answer these questions. As is well known, the great Reformed theologian, Karl Barth, insisted that Anselm's famous argument for God's existence is understandable and convincing *if and only if* one shares his religious context and his full-bodied Christian faith. In other words, the warrants Anselm adduces in his celebrated argument are effective only for those who are already religious "insiders." But that conclusion is reflective more of Barth's thought than of Anselm's. While acknowledging the religious context of Anselm's work, I argue, to the contrary, that the monk of Bec insists that some arguments are available to all, at least in principle, on the basis of the universality of human nature. One need not be a member of the house of faith, or share Anselm's "thick" Christian culture, to see the validity of his argument. Indeed, Anselm envisages as his interlocutor a person who has never even heard about God, much less one who has conceptual fluency with the term. Why is this point significant?

It is important because Anselm's argument for God's existence (and philosophical reflection in general) has its own relative autonomy and integrity, even apart from intrasystemic Christian faith. The Anselmian proof (however one judges its validity) stands on its own, appealing to reason as it exists in all human beings. The proof has an integrity and logical structure that is intelligible based on a universal, trans-cultural *humanum*. The monk of Bec would disagree, then, with those holding that natural theology (or natural law) is unintelligible apart from the faith. His work clearly displays that philosophical argument possesses a natural visibility.

At the same time, St. Anselm is no rationalist. For him, the philosophical act comes to its full realization only within Christianity. Performative, participative knowledge is central for monk of Bec; however, it neither jeopardizes nor diminishes the relative autonomy of philosophical argument. Like Newman and Blondel centuries later, Anselm recognizes the crucial role of existential commitment in knowing—but without renouncing the appeal to universally available arguments. It is no surprise, then, that in the 1940s, theologians Hans Urs von Balthasar and Henri Bouillard explicitly appealed to Anselm's achievement in order to overcome both neo-Scholastic rationalism and Barthian fideism.

In Catholic theology, there exists a delicate balance between universal natural realities and socio-cultural embeddedness. Theology acknowledges philosophy's legitimate autonomy, while insisting that the philosophical act comes to fruition only in the light of revelation. Anselm's *Proslogion* can help us think with greater clarity about this intimate relationship that exists between the autonomy and visibility of the natural order and the participatory realm of history and grace.

Contemporary Lessons
from the *Proslogion*

The marked emphasis in contemporary philosophy and theology is squarely on the fact that, as human beings, we are deeply shaped and conditioned by the intricacies and practices of our societies, cultures, and languages. Human rationality is profoundly contextualized and circumscribed, rather than autonomous and neutral. As such, we only know ourselves and the world in and through antecedent norms and suppositions; there exist no pre-linguistic givens. We should avoid speaking, then, of "universal reason" or of "autonomous reason" as if there subsisted some pocket of reality not deeply defined by all of these interlacing emphases.

`This insistence on human embeddedness in culture, language, and tradition finds support in a broad variety of philosophical perspectives. For a long time now, Hans-Georg Gadamer and his disciples have been involved in unmasking the worldless, traditionless, Cartesian subject of the Enlightenment, with its truncated understanding of historicity and the nature of interpretation. Gadamer himself, of course, was hermeneutically developing many of the themes first broached by Heidegger in *Being and Time*, especially the latter's jeremiad against those ignoring our enmeshment in the "worldhood of the world," the profound embeddedness that *Dasein* is always tempted to bury in the unremitting search for absolute and unencumbered certitude and first principles. Wittgenstein, too, reacting against an untenable positivism, stressed our culturally constituted norms and language games, hoping to press the point that reality is linguistically and socially mediated, that is, meanings are determined by forms of life and particular practices rather than by neutral, autarkic, universal standards. Thomas Kuhn's influential manifesto, *The Structure of Scientific Revolutions*, introduced many of these same themes into the philosophy of science: we are profoundly theory laden; different standards lead inexorably to incommensurable paradigms; words are not attached to objects in ways that are

* This essay was originally published as "Contemporary Lessons from the *Proslogion*," *Nova et Vetera* English edition 7, no. 1 (2009): 125–52. Republished with permission.

unproblematic; and there is no neutral, sub-linguistic way of describing evidence.[1] All of these thinkers, of course, were responding to the pretensions of Enlightenment modernity, with its positivistic notion of rationality, with its imperious Cartesian/Kantian subject taken as the *fundamentum inconcussum* for knowing, and with its naïve and insolent claims to unsullied objectivity.

This view, deeply accenting our contingency and "situatedness," our immersion in tradition, culture, history, society, and language, has served to expose the inadequacies of positivism and radical empiricism, to overturn the Enlightenment notion of unconditioned reason and to dethrone the idea that human rationality is exercised "apart" from a world of historical contingencies. This stress on human embeddedness has also given rise to the now frequently encountered phrase: "it's interpretation all the way down."[2] By this is meant that one never has bare facts or *facta bruta*; reality, rather, is always interpreted reality, every seeing is an appropriative "seeing as," there exists no purely neutral level of observation, nor any unconditioned exercise of human rationality. Kuhn, one of the foremost proponents of the maxim, interpreted it in a very strong sense, arguing that, since every interpreter is deeply theory laden, we cannot know the world "in itself." The phrase "in itself" is, in fact, meaningless, Kuhn contended, because there is no "higher viewpoint" or neutral Archimedean platform surpassing the theory-ladenness and embedded status of actual observers.[3]

---

1 Thomas Kuhn, *The Structure of Scientific Revolutions*, 2nd ed. (Chicago: University of Chicago Press, 1970). Kuhn has also discussed many of these themes in *The Road since Structure*, ed. James Conant and John Haugeland (Chicago: University of Chicago Press, 2000).

2 For example, Brice Wachterhauser avers, "We seem to be in the uneasy position of having to admit that interpretation goes, as it were, 'all the way down.'" See "Getting it Right: Relativism, Realism, and Truth," in *The Cambridge Companion to Gadamer*, ed. Robert J. Dostal (Cambridge: Cambridge University Press, 2002), 52–78, at 53. Stanley Hauerwas says similarly, "It is contingency all the way down," taking this phrase as indicating that we cannot "secure truth against the contingency of our existence." *Performing the Faith* (Grand Rapids: Brazos, 2004), 21. Gianni Vattimo goes to the root of the maxim, eulogistically citing Nietzsche's well-known comment: There are no facts, only interpretations. See *After Christianity*, trans. Luca D'Isanto (New York: Columbia University Press, 2002), 49.

3 Since the phrase "in itself" is meaningless for Kuhn, he rejects the correspondence notion of truth as implausible. See *The Road since Structure*, 95, 99. Of course, there is a sense to the phrase "it's interpretation all the way down" that does not convey the idealistic connotations found in Kuhn's work. For the maxim can also mean that all knowing is inexorably exercised in determinate circumstances, that one indefeasibly sees the world "in and through" one's own language and culture and that knowing, therefore, is necessarily within a distinct visual angle, a particular perspective that allows a limited but actual grasp of states of affairs. The phrase, then, can be taken as equivalent to the unobjectionable position that all understanding involves

Insofar as the scientist has access only to interpretations, he or she is dealing with the world as a constructed entity, that is, the world as it appears rather than the noumenal world itself. It is no surprise, then, that Kuhn has referred to himself as a "dynamic Kantian," and, at times, approximates a position close to relativism, without committing himself to it.[4]

When *theologically* utilized and applied, these issues—the embedded-ness of reason, our sociocultural conditioning, our situated and "tradi-tioned" status, and the invocation of the phrase "it's interpretation all the way down"—has a determinate goal. With Kuhn, Gadamer, and others, this theological position wants to discredit the autonomous, worldless knowing championed by modernity. But it does this, often enough, in service to the affirmation that claims to scientific "objectivity," to "rigorous" rationality, are just as contingent, embedded, and "traditioned" as claims made by the Christian faith. There is, in other words, no "higher perspective" or, to use a different metaphor, no "fundamental ground" from which Christianity can be judged. There exist only different, culturally and linguistically con-stituted paradigms and points of view. One cannot apply Enlightenment criteria in judging truth and falsehood, as if they alone represent "objectiv-ity" while religious claims are "sectarian" because, in point of fact, all truth emerges from the tightly woven bonds of culture, history, and language. All claims to truth, then, reflect contingent perspectives; there exist no univer-sal, neutral, non-contextual warrants to which one may appeal. Any attempted imperialism by Enlightenment criteria is here exposed as philo-sophically unfounded, illusory, and even coercive. Varying theological approaches, even while differing among themselves, agree on several of these fundamental principles.

Now in this argument for human embeddedness, and in this legitimate reaction against a universal, neutral philosophy, there appear to be certain casualties or, at least, forgotten dimensions. Among these are ideas such as "nature" or, perhaps better, "universal natural realities." Does the idea of nature not take a backseat if we are deeply, if not entirely, embedded in and conditioned by history, culture, and tradition? How would one discern such a nature, even if it existed? One wonders, too, about warrants for arguments. Can there be any universal appeals, even in principle? Or must all appeals

---

interpretation. For a more extended discussion, see Thomas G. Guarino, *Foundations of System-atic Theology* (New York: T & T Clark, 2005), 176–79 and 188–90.

4 See Kuhn, *The Structure of Scientific Revolutions*, 206–7.

be offered within local, contextualized, "background" knowledge? Natural theology is also a likely casualty here because it contends that some arguments are available to all observers, at least potentially, regardless of their contingent circumstances. But given this strong emphasis on our "situated" milieux, can one adduce the kind of universal warrants that natural theology has traditionally needed? A reading of natural law, too, seems to be here impaired, since the norms it implies could only with great difficulty be accorded an integrity and relative autonomy beyond their particularized sociocultural context. If not proscribed entirely, these elements are at least considerably weakened or obscured precisely because they seem to imply a sphere of *universality*, a sphere common to all, or open to all even apart from, or better, even within, the enveloping dimensions of historical contingency and sociocultural embeddedness.

ANSELM'S ACHIEVEMENT: A RECENT VIEW

A good argument colligating several threads indicating the historical, cultural, social, and linguistic circumscription of human life and thought is offered by Brad Kallenberg's insightful reflections on Anselm's argument for God in the *Proslogion*.[5] Anselm is a good choice for this discussion because the Benedictine's work has sparked generations of controversy. Surely he must be one of the few thinkers simultaneously characterized as having both rationalist and fideist tendencies.[6] I would like first to discuss Kallenberg's article, itself representative of several recent theological trends, then offer an alternative reading of Anselm's work and, finally, show why Anselm's careful balancing of nature and embeddedness has been important to the Catholic tradition in the past and remains relevant for theology today.

I will briefly summarize Kallenberg's essay, hoping to do justice to his legitimate concerns. Kallenberg contends that Anselm is best read through Wittgenstein. By this he means that Anselm offers a good example of the Wittgensteinian claim that knowledge and practice are internally related. His brief, then, is that Anselm's proof for God, as proposed in the *Proslogion*,

---

5 Brad J. Kallenberg, "Praying for Understanding: Reading Anselm through Wittgenstein," *Modern Theology* 20, no. 4 (2004): 527–46. Page numbers in the text refer to this essay.

6 For the charge of rationalism, see Gilson's indictment of Anselm's "recklessness" in his attempt to give a rational demonstration for revealed truths (targeting Anselm's *rationes necessariae*). Etienne Gilson, *Reason and Revelation in the Middle Ages* (New York: Charles Scribner's Sons, 1938), 26. For Anselm as fideist, see the sustained argument in Karl Barth, *Anselm: Fides Quaerens Intellectum* (Richmond: John Knox Press, 1960).

"works," that is, is convincing, only if one shares something of Anselm's embeddedness, his religious context, that is to say, if one enters Anselm's prayerful circle.[7] The crucial point here is that rationality is deeply related to one's epistemic context, that is, one's embeddedness, one's practice, one's way of life, which will deeply condition, if not entirely determine, one's ability to grasp an argument, including the one tendered by the monk of Bec. Only those who share the practice of prayer can be rightly said to share the sense of Anselm's words[8] for knowing is a "rule ordered skill," that is, one knows from within a particular tradition, where one is already an "insider" in its linguistic conventions. Since meaning is deeply related to context and use, only those with a certain fluency in terminology can properly understand Anselm's discussion. Consequently, the warrants Anselm adduces in his well-known argument for God are only understandable by those who share something of his life, language, and practice. Claims to, and warrants for, knowledge are necessarily context specific. Our human socio-cultural-linguistic contingency necessarily militates against warrants that are universally applicable. It is for this reason that Kallenberg opens his article by noting that he found it "appalling" when an (unnamed) professor said he was interested only in "publicly accessible" arguments for God's existence.[9] Kallenberg wishes to make clear that this notion of "publicness" is philosophically naïve since we are deeply embedded observers. Appealing to public warrants, thereby bypassing particular forms of life, makes little sense since we cannot appeal to subjects in isolation from their lived contexts.

Kallenberg adduces the plentiful evidence offered by Anselm in order to buttress this strong emphasis on the interrelationship among practice, language, and knowledge. For example, Anselm says in the preface to the *Proslogion* that the title he originally gave to his argument was "Faith Seeking Understanding," a fit indication of the nature of the work.[10] Then, too, one must take account of the unmistakable context of Anselm's "proof": his asceticism, his regimen of prayer and fasting, his imploring God about his vices. To the claim that Anselm's argument is, indeed, meant to convince the "fool" of Psalm 53, Kallenberg responds by transforming Karl Barth's

7 Kallenberg, "Praying for Understanding," 527.

8 Kallenberg, 528.

9 Kallenberg, 527.

10 *"Proslogion,"* in *S. Anselmi Opera Omnia*, ed. Franciscus Salesius Schmitt (Edinburgh: Thomas Nelson and Sons, 1946), I, 94, 7. All citations will be given from Schmitt's critical edition of Anselm's works, citing volume, page, and line. Translations are my own.

earlier argument that Gaunilon is not, in fact, the *insipiens* of the psalm, but is, in actuality, *catholicus pro insipiente*, that is, a monk entirely fluent in Christian life, thought, and language.[11] Essential here is the claim that the particularity of Christian belief and practice determines one's understanding of the argument and thus, any knowledge of God that it may yield.

What may be concluded after briefly reviewing Kallenberg's perceptive discussion? The author is, from a theological point of view, clearly rejecting the modern project wherein faith needs to be legitimated by reason, particularly an imperious and autonomous reason. In this sense, Kallenberg is rejecting the project which has affinities with the medieval movement known as Radical Aristotelianism, one of the motivating forces for Gregory IX's letter to the theology masters at Paris in 1228 and for the condemnations by Etienne Tempier of 1277.[12] Reason cannot be a "wider" or "broader" context than faith itself, as if human rationality could see matters, to keep the spatial image, from a "higher" perspective. Christian faith does not need "alien" norms, or an "autonomous" reason (even if such existed) separated from the life of Scripture and the Church, to provide validation for its belief in God. Faith is under no obligation to meet foreign epistemic requirements which ultimately seek to tie the Church to an extrinsic bed of Procrustes. Trying to legitimate the truth of the biblical narrative by reason is especially futile now that universal and unconditioned rationality has itself been philosophically discredited. Here, we see a certain convergence between present-day philosophical themes on embeddedness and neo-Barthian concerns that philosophy not seek to colonize theology by means of an overarching, nonbiblical narrative.[13] Both currents of thought have reservations about universal dimensions of rationality and nature, with one emphasizing

---

11 Anselm himself notes that Gaunilon is no actual fool but *catholicus pro insipiente* in I, 130, 4–5. Kallenberg argues that while the psalm does indeed aver that the fool thinks there is no God, it does not necessarily mean the fool does not have conceptual fluency with the term "God" but only that he acts in such a way that bespeaks God's inexistence.

12 For a good commentary on Tempier's letter and the condemned propositions, see David Piché and Claude LaFleur, *La condemnation parisienne de 1277* (Paris; J. Vrin, 1999). For Gregory IX's letter, see *Enchiridion symbolorum*, ed. Heinrich Denzinger and Peter Hünermann, 37th ed. (Freiburg im Breisgau: Herder, 1991), no. 824. Also, John Wippel, *Mediaeval Reactions to the Encounter between Faith and Reason*, The Aquinas Lecture (Milwaukee: Marquette University Press, 1995), 14–28.

13 It is unsurprising that throughout Kallenberg's essay, one hears strong Barthian echoes. Barth, too, wants to discourage any reading of Anselm that allows for the knowability of God isolated from the specific context of faith. As he remarks, one cannot seek the *intellectus fidei* "anywhere outside of or apart from the revealed *Credo* of the Church and certainly not apart from or outside of Holy Scripture." See *Anselm: Fides Quaerens Intellectum*, 41.

human "situatedness," the other railing against "alien" warrants apart from the Church. The contemporary accent on the riveting influence of humanity's historical, sociocultural, and linguistic circumscription here licenses a *tu quoque* argument: all are situated and contextualized, both rationalists and Christians. There exists only faith-guided rationality (whatever that faith may be); participatory commitment is intrinsic to all understanding. So our holding onto validating norms specific to Christian faith is no more "sectarian" than the alleged "neutrality" of modernity.

Kallenberg, moreover, rightly calls attention to Wittgenstein's claim that knowledge and practice are internally related. One part of this assertion is that the anterior subjective disposition of the knower necessarily affects the known. Kallenberg wishes to overcome here, as Kuhn and Gadamer earlier had, Enlightenment positivism's obscuring of just this point. Surely a congeries of elements: education, prior tradition, personal interests, natural talent, cultural background, ideological predisposition, a life of sinfulness or holiness, all have some purchase on any knower, thereby entering the cognitive equation. John Henry Newman, for example, clearly recognized this in apologetics, claiming that any argument will necessarily be affected by the disposition of the one addressed.[14] But how far do we push this notion that the subjective disposition of the knower, the theory-laden subject, determines the known? Do we push it as far as Kuhn (whose affinities with Wittgenstein were self-noted) where one must make a distinction between the noumenal world in itself and the constructed world in which scientists (and by extension theologians) work? Are there not elements that are open to all rational observers, even if such observation will, necessarily, be accommodated within particular horizons? Are there not elements of "presentation" open to all?

Is there, then, in this reading of Anselm, something of a devaluation of the autonomy and integrity of human reason? It can legitimately be protested that there is no such devaluation. It is simply a matter of pointing to the *conditioned subject* as opposed to the neutral *Cartesian subject*. But Anselm is clearly not defending an autarkic, Cartesian being. He is defending a *humanum*, that is, a universal human nature and reason which, in

---

14 "A mutilated and defective evidence suffices for persuasion where the heart is alive; but dead evidences, however imperfect, can but create a dead faith." "Faith and Reason Contrasted," in *Fifteen Sermons Preached Before the University of Oxford*, sermon X, 200, cited in Avery Dulles, *Newman* (London: Continuum, 2002), 30. For a fuller discussion of the role of the anterior disposition in Newman, see Dulles, 48–63.

principle, is able to grasp his argument. Can we speak of such a nature, with certain formal dimensions of constancy across history and culture even in and through embeddedness? Or does Kallenberg's reading of Anselm eclipse the concept of a universal human nature, even if it rightly points to our contextualized existence?

Taking a cue from Kallenberg's study, I would like to examine certain aspects of Anselm's work, with an eye to the monk's understanding of how nature and practice are interlaced. While Kallenberg is surely correct to accent Anselm's religious context and so is legitimately attentive to the connections between his life and discourse, his practice and knowledge, I will argue that the monk of Bec subtly interweaves culture and nature so that the latter is not dissolved in the maw of socio-cultural-linguistic-religious particularity and practice.

ANSELM'S ARGUMENT

There is no need to recount Anselm's proof. It is well known to all and has been the subject of countless commentaries.[15] Further, what essentially interests us is not its validity as a general argument, but its approach or method which has direct relevance to contemporary debates on human nature and rationality. My contention is that Anselm carefully balances the relationship of knowledge to beliefs, practices, and prior commitments with the concomitant recognition that some arguments are available to all, at least in principle, on the basis of the universality of human nature.

Of the religious context of Anselm's proof, there can be little argument. Not only is the *Proslogion* entitled *Fides quaerens intellectum*, it begins with a long prayer to the living God, before whom Anselm prays in confidence, even while acutely aware of his sins. God is glowingly alive for Anselm, near to him in his immensity, even though the Benedictine is acutely conscious of both his own finitude and sinfulness. At the end of chapter one, Anselm utters his famous Augustinian plea, ultimately drawn from the *Vetus Latina* edition of Isaiah 7:9, part theological manifesto, part imploring prayer: "For I do not seek to understand that I may believe, but I believe that I may understand. For this I believe, that 'unless I believed, I would not understand.'"[16]

---

15 For classical and recent exegeses, see *The Cambridge Companion to Anselm*, ed. Brian Davies and Brian Leftow (Cambridge: Cambridge University Press, 2004). Also, Michel Corbin, *Prière et raison de la foi: Introduction à l'oeuvre de saint Anselme de Cantorbéry* (Paris: Cerf, 1992).

16 Anselm, *Proslogion*, I, 100, 18–19.

One cannot doubt, then, Anselm's situation: his immersion in Christian faith; his embeddedness in a monastic, contemplative setting; his ordered and rigorous life of prayer; his interlocutors who are fellow Benedictines sharing his easy fluency with Christian ideas and concepts. It is concrete Christian faith and life that clearly determines every aspect of Anselm's existence. He prays that God give him some knowledge, despite the smoke of vice that assails him. Anselm, we can fully agree, is reasoning *within*, not outside of the house of faith. He moves within a living tradition, indwells a thick culture of Christian life and discourse. And this heritage yields deeply fruitful knowledge. But can one conclude baldly, as Barth earlier insisted and as Kallenberg appears to concur, "When we consider the connection which Anselm held to be necessary between theology and prayer, we put our finger on the condition of the *intelligere*"?[17] For isn't it exactly Anselm's brief that some (formal) knowledge of God is possible by all, even those not engaged in the life of prayer? That some knowledge of God is available, at least potentially, to all inquirers, even to those unaware of the name "God"?[18]

Anselm's argument has an integrity and logical structure which, in principle, is available to those who share neither a life of prayer, nor faith itself. So while it is true that philosophy is not the foundation of Anselm's life, it is equally true that his faith gives rise to philosophical reflection, a reflection that has its own relative autonomy and integrity, that is, always ultimately related to God but meant to appeal to human reason apart from specific belief, apart from an "insider's" intrasystemic knowledge.[19] The proof arises from within faith, as virtually every proof for God does, but it seeks to stand on its own, *sola ratione*, on the basis of the relative autonomy of human nature.[20]

---

17 Barth, *Anselm*, 35.

18 In chapter one of the *Monologion*, for example, Anselm envisions a person who has never even heard about God, much less has conceptual fluency with the term, but is, nonetheless, able to convince himself or herself about many issues concerning the divine nature, even *sola ratione* (I, 13, 1–11).

19 John D. Caputo is surely right when he says that Anselm's argument does not move from "cognitive degree zero to infinity" and that Anselm offers his argument "on his knees"; however, by accenting only the circular movement of Anselm's thought, Caputo obscures the fact that the *Proslogion's* argument has an independent integrity intended to be available even to those without faith. See his *On Religion* (New York: Routledge, 2001), 39, and, with similar intent, his *Philosophy and Theology* (Nashville: Abingdon, 2006), 15.

20 The integrity of Anselm's argument was earlier defended by Henri Bouillard and by Hans Urs von Balthasar who were engaged with Barth's interpretation of the *Proslogion*. Both theologians were dissatisfied with Barth's exegesis of Anselm; at the same time, they wished to place a decided accent on what Balthasar calls "the full realization of the true philosophical act" which

It is true that the context of Anselm's argument is always faith. But it should not be forgotten that at the very outset of the *Proslogion* Anselm states,

> I began to ask myself if one could discover a single argument which is *ad se probandum*, i.e., an argument requiring no other proof than itself alone and which by itself would demonstrate that God truly is. (I, 93, 6–7)

The point of the proof is to demonstrate, as Anselm says, that *Deus vere est*, that God truly exists. He is seeking a single argument apart from Scripture and tradition, appealing to us on the basis of our common humanity.[21] The criteria of legitimation for Anselm's argument are meant to be universal; they are not to be restricted to a particular context or language game. Just here, one is reminded of Anselm's earlier comment in his prologue to the *Monologion*: his Benedictine confreres have asked for an argument which does not rely on the authority of Scripture, but only on the "necessity of reason."[22]

The fool, as Anselm observes in chapter two of the *Proslogion*, says in his heart there is no God, as Psalms 14 and 53 attest. But even the *insipiens* must understand the phrase "someone greater than which cannot be thought," even if he denies that such a being exists.[23] Of course, at just this point, Anselm makes his appeal for the necessary existence of *id quo maius cogitari nequit*.[24] However one judges the argument's validity, it is clearly meant to be available to all, even those not inducted into the particularities of Christian life, thought, and prayer. As Anselm says at the conclusion of chapter three: Why does the fool say in his heart that there is no God, when it is manifested to the rational mind that you are the greatest of all that

---

is found only in theology. This "realization" will be discussed below. See Balthasar, *The Glory of the Lord*, vol. 2, trans. Andrew Louth, et al. (San Francisco: Ignatius Press, 1984), 233. For Bouillard on the relative autonomy of the argument, see *Karl Barth: Parole de Dieu et Existence Humaine*, 2 vols. (Paris: Aubier, 1957), vol. 2, 152–54. In this essay, I try to advance and re-contextualize their analyses.

21 Of course, Anselm is not naïve about nature, as if it exists in a state of undiluted autonomy, for he says that the image of God, which has been effaced by vice and the smoke of sin, must be "renewed and reformed within me" (I, 100, 14–15). And in a striking chapter seventeen, he tells us that the "senses of his soul have become dulled and brittle by the weaknesses of sin" (I, 113, 14–15).

22 *Proslogion*, I, 7, 7–10.

23 *Proslogion*, I, 101, 7–9.

24 *Proslogion*, I, 102, 10.

exists? Why unless he is simple and a fool?[25] Later in the dialogue, Gaunilon, speaking on behalf of the *insipiens*, insists that he cannot form the idea of a being than which a greater cannot be conceived. To this objection Anselm sharply replies that the matter is clearly otherwise, appealing to participationist thought: Everyone can see that a lesser good is similar to a greater good, insofar as it is good. Indeed, *it is open to every rational mind* that by ascending from the lesser goods to the greater goods, we can form a notion of a being greater than which cannot be thought.[26] Anselm intends his argument to have a philosophical force clearly available to all. It is no surprise, then, that at the end of chapter four, Anselm concludes, "If I were unwilling to believe you exist, I would not be able not to understand that it is so."[27]

Anselm is transparently appealing to reason as it exists in all human beings. Even if reason is necessarily enveloped by particular circumstances, he thinks his argument addresses universal dimensions of human nature.[28] Anselm is not, let us hasten to add, legitimating faith by neutral or disengaged reason, in the sense that reason now sublates faith in a kind of philosophical *Aufhebung*. Though clearly proceeding from faith, he offers an argument that possesses its own integrity. He does not limit his proof to those who offer praise to the biblical God or even simply to those who are aware of him; he is saying that philosophy has a relative autonomy which exists even apart from belief. And Anselm is clearly citing warrants attainable, at least potentially, by all even if, as we shall see, specific contexts are not without considerable importance. Anselm's argument, then, occurs in a "second moment," reflecting in faith on what can be known without faith. There is an integrity, autonomy, and logical structure of the argument that is intelligible on the basis of universal realities with transcultural dimensions. One does not need the "insider" knowledge of Anselm's unique monastic context to see the structure of the proof; what holds the argument together, rather, is the very *humanum*, the nature of humanity. He refers to the formal structures of human existence, *remoto Christo* or *sola ratione*, not to deduce revealed truths, of course, but to provide an argument that is publicly and intersubjectively available.

---

25 *Proslogion*, I, 103, 9–11.

26 *Proslogion*, I, 137, 14–18.

27 *Proslogion*, I, 104, 5–7.

28 To the argument that reason itself is simply another language game, itself shaped by founding commitments and background beliefs, Anselm would answer, I believe, that there continue to exist discernable universal elements in and through human embeddedness.

Even though Anselm is insisting that his argument for the existence of *id quo maius cogitari nequit* is accessible to those who do not share intra-systemic Christian belief, who do not have conceptual fluency with Christian terms, who are not cultural-linguistic "insiders," nonetheless he *does* place a decided accent on experiential embeddedness, thus indicating the close relationship between knowledge and epistemic context. While Anselm would argue that there are formal dimensions of reasoning characteristic of human nature, he recognizes that these elements are deeply affected by contingent circumstances. In a well-known passage Anselm asserts that the one who does not believe will *not* understand, thereby indicating that social context and participated practice is intrinsically related to, deeply internal to, knowledge:

> Whoever does not believe will not understand. For the one who does not believe will have no experience and the one who has no experience will not know. For, indeed, just as experience surpasses the hearing about things so, in the same way, the knowledge of one who experiences surpasses the knowledge of one simply hearing about things.[29]

In this passage, we see Anselm's insistence on performative knowledge, a knowledge yielded by one immersed in a unique way of life. Experience, for Anselm, offers a vigorous, participated knowledge that enfleshes, enriches, and ripens the weaker knowledge available through argument alone. Appeals to natural human realities may offer a certain formal knowledge of God, but it is only within the house of faith, within the experience of concrete discipline, within the thick culture of Christian life, that one comes to know God in a vigorous and robust way. One recognizes here a self-involving knowing at work, a knowing understood as performance, practice, appropriation, and self-involvement superseding that which is available by way of arguments appealing to universal dimensions of rationality.

Henri Bouillard argued that this accent on experiential knowing in Anselm has affinities with observations made by Maurice Blondel. As Blondel says in his classic work, *L'Action*, "We cannot arrive at God, affirm him truly [. . .] have Him for ourselves, except by belonging to Him and by sac-

---

29 *Epistola de incarnatione Verbi* (II, 9, 5–8). This passage was important to the investigations of both Balthasar and Bouillard, particularly in their attempts to overcome, by accenting the cognitive significance of "living faith," a certain species of apologetical rationalism. For Balthasar, see *The Glory of the Lord*, vol. 2, 216–17. For Bouillard, see *Karl Barth: Parole de Dieu et Existence Humaine*, vol. 2, 166.

rificing all the rest to Him."[30] Here, Blondel wishes to accent the experiential, participative, performative dimensions of knowing. R. Garrigou-Lagrange denounced this as a noncognitive approach to knowledge, veering toward voluntarism and depriving truth of a sufficient foundation in the purely intellective order.[31] But Anselm (and perhaps Blondel as well) intends to protect a knowledge of God potentially open to all, however formal, together with a fuller moment that resonates more clearly with the claim that epistemic warrants for truth are answerable to particular forms of life. Anselm preserves, then, the moment of "nature," of universal, human realities, even while insisting that a "performative" and "vital" understanding of God requires something more than discursive argument. We may say that this embedded, experiential dimension "enfleshes" and renders "living" the formal autonomy of the proof itself. Natural theology is here brought to fruition in religious and even mystical experience.

The citation from Blondel makes us think, perforce, of the anterior disposition of the inquirer in knowing, raising again the knotty question of the relationship between practice and knowledge. This is the recognition that human rationality is necessarily shaped and tutored by many factors, that knowledge and experience have some internal relationship. It is the motivating force behind Pascal's well-known aphorism, "The heart has its reasons which reason does not know," his contrast between *l'esprit de finesse* and *l'esprit de géométrie* and his distinction, if not cleavage, between *le Dieu d'Abraham, d'Isaac, and de Jacob* and *le Dieu des philosophes*.[32] Newman, Pascal, and Blondel rightly found the prevailing tenets of modernity unable to account for the fullness of human experience. But while their insights helped to unmask an illegitimate rationalism, they do not overturn the Anselmian notion that all persons are potentially able to recognize an argument for God's existence *sola ratione*. I say potentially because subjective disposition, as noted earlier, will by necessity have some effect on the extent to which any argument is grasped as compelling; surely this is the case when we are speak-

---

30 Maurice Blondel, *Action (1893)*, trans. Oliva Blanchette (Notre Dame: University of Notre Dame Press, 1984), 404. The relationship between Anselm and Blondel was explored by Bouillard in *Blondel and Christianity*, trans. James M. Somerville (Washington, DC: Corpus Books, 1969), 196–201.

31 For an account of the exchange between Blondel and Garrigou-Lagrange on truth and knowledge, see Richard Peddicord, *The Sacred Monster of Thomism* (South Bend, IN: St. Augustine's Press, 2005), 61–79.

32 Blaise Pascal, *Pensées*, trans. W. F. Trotter (Mineola, NY: Dover Publications, 2003), no. 277.

ing of an argument for God's existence or a discussion of natural law. Is the intelligibility of arguments such as these necessarily tied, then, to performative, existential commitment? Anselm would surely hesitate before offering an unqualifiedly affirmative answer precisely because to do so would jeopardize the very notion of an argument theoretically available to all on the basis of a universal *humanum*. For Anselm insists that his argument is, indeed, open to all rational creatures, sternly rebuking Gaunilon for claiming he cannot see the logic of the proof. But Anselm would also recognize, with Newman and Blondel, that the efficacy of such arguments has some profound relationship with humanity's spiritual sensibility.

What is clearly evident here is the very tight nexus conjoining nature, culture, and history. There exists, undoubtedly, a web of suppositions, background beliefs, historical conditions, and ideological commitments that affect the noetic situation—what Kuhn short-handedly called theory-laden observation. But amidst this welter of contingencies, are we still able to have universal arguments open to all? Is some connaturality required between the warrant and the inquirer? And if so, does this entirely eviscerate Anselm's "public" claims? Arguments for God's existence, whether Anselmian, Thomistic, Cartesian, or Lonerganian seem not to be demonstrative in a mathematical sense. The same may be said of natural law reasoning. At the same time, these exercises in discursive logic are intended to be publicly available, possessing a legitimate, if relative, autonomy. I think it is correct to conclude that Anselm's proof, and others like it, while retaining a formal validity, have a "performative" dimension only within the circle of faith. In and of themselves, they lack the more efficacious and comprehensive knowledge yielded by experience, praxis, and action. This does not, however, denigrate the cognitive penetration which the arguments attain, but recognizes that their effectiveness may only be fully acknowledged by those exercising a reason tutored by practice and experience. Perhaps one finds something similar to this in Lonergan's own proof for God's existence. In chapter nineteen of *Insight*, he offers a finely proportioned argument for God's actuality based on the intelligibility of the existing real.[33] In a later work, Lonergan states that Vatican I's famous definition argues for a human potency rather than an actuality, a *quaestio juris* rather than a *quaestio facti*. He concludes, "I do not think that in this life people arrive at natural knowledge of God

33 Bernard Lonergan, *Insight: A Study of Human Understanding*, ed. Frederick E. Crowe and Robert M. Doran, Collected Works of Bernard Lonergan 3 (Toronto: University of Toronto Press, 1992), 692–99.

without God's grace, but what I do not doubt is that the knowledge they so attain is natural."[34] This seemingly enigmatic phrase resonates with the Anselmian insight that there is a structure of the argument that has its own integrity and autonomy, even if the argument only fully "lives" for those within the participated Christian life.

Because of this careful balance in Anselm, between the relative autonomy of the philosophical argument and the self-involving, "performative" knowledge gained by experience, we can say that Anselm would not likely endorse Stanley Hauerwas's strong Barthian claim that "natural theology is unintelligible divorced from a full doctrine of God."[35] Nor would Anselm agree with the claim that one needs insider, religious knowledge to know something of the divine existence. Of course, Hauerwas, with Barth, appears unwilling to make any commitment to "nature," fearful that this will introduce into theology a foreign, secular element determinative of revelation, sanctioning, in the process, a realm of religious truth "beyond" the one explicitly revealed by Christ and so, finally, marginalizing central Christian teachings.[36] But Anselm does not intend to ground Christianity in a neutral, autonomous reason. His project is clearly rooted in the *fides quaerens intellectum*, as he insists at the outset of the *Proslogion*. At the same time, he recognizes that there exists a relative autonomy of philosophical argument

34 Lonergan, "Natural Knowledge of God," in *A Second Collection*, ed. William F.J. Ryan and Bernard J. Tyrrell (Toronto: University of Toronto Press, 1996), 133.

35 Stanley Hauerwas, "Connections Created and Contingent," in *Grammar and Grace: Reformulations of Aquinas and Wittgenstein*, ed. Jeffrey Stout and Robert MacSwain (London: SCM Press, 2004), 75–102, at 75. See also Hauerwas, *With the Grain of the Universe* (Grand Rapids: Brazos, 2001), 15. At the same time, we can fully agree with Hauerwas's statement that those who have invoked Aquinas to argue that "'natural theology' is a necessary first step to sustain theology based on revelation have distorted Aquinas' understanding of Christian theology." Both Aquinas and Anselm begin with the *fides quaerens* even if their arguments are meant to have a *relative* autonomy and integrity. I am also sympathetic with Hauerwas's larger point that "natural" reasoning, improperly utilized, leads to a pale civic Deism and civic morality far from the vibrant faith of Israel and the Church. But can we conclude that deficiencies in cultural practice necessarily mean that the insights of natural theology and natural law offer only an *essential disparity* with revealed truth?

36 This, of course, is the Barthian objection that Catholic theology substitutes "being in general" for God's revelation, thereby offering knowledge of God otherwise than in faith. See, for example, Karl Barth, *Church Dogmatics* I/1, trans. G. T. Thomson (Edinburgh: T & T Clark, 1949), 39–44 and II/1, trans. T. H. L. Parker, et al. (Edinburgh: T & T Clark, 1957), 168–69 and 231. For a nuanced update of the Barthian position, see Colin E. Gunton, *Act and Being* (Grand Rapids: Eerdmans, 2002), 4–6. This hesitancy about nature extends, logically, to natural law. For a helpful analysis offering a positive account of the Protestant, and particularly Reformed, tradition on natural law reasoning (despite Barthian claims to the contrary) see Stephen J. Grabill, *Rediscovering the Natural Law in Reformed Theological Ethics* (Grand Rapids: Eerdmans Publishing, 2006).

which retains its integrity even when originally formulated within the context of explicit faith.[37]

What is clearly visible in Anselm, then, is the attempt to balance his prayerful context, his thick Christian and monastic tradition, with a publicly available argument. He neither reduces his argument to those who share his life of prayer and discourse, nor does he make Christian practice incidental to a living knowledge of God. I think one can safely say that Anselm is cautious on the relationship between practice and knowledge, without denying its importance. Anselm recognizes the relative autonomy of human reason, without turning reason into a neutral epistemological platform.

NATURE, RELATIVE AUTONOMY, AND THE TRADITION

Like Anselm, Catholic theology has held for the *possibility* of knowledge of God that is available to all inquirers apart from participation in the life of faith, apart from "insider" knowledge, even if this falls short of performative knowing.[38] Anselm's defense of this human potentiality is itself representative of a traditional Catholic emphasis on "nature" or natural human realities, on the relative autonomy of philosophy, and on the possibility of warrants that are publicly available. This customary accent has been simultaneously combined with the recognition that the life of embedded, participatory faith opens up a world of understanding that reason alone cannot penetrate. More recently, the traditional approach has also become cognizant of the profound effects of society, culture, and history on human life, being, and knowing. Let us hasten to add, therefore, that a distinction between nature and culture

---

37 Hauerwas does say, "Like Anselm, Aquinas knew that revelation comes first and that provability and the insights gained from the proofs only second." This statement indicates that Hauerwas is well aware of the primacy of revelation in the medieval construal of the faith/reason relationship; it is not clear to me, however, that Hauerwas recognizes that the proofs are intended to possess a relative autonomy and integrity even apart from explicit Christian faith. See *With the Grain of the Universe*, 165.

38 On the difficulty of *actually* knowing something of God by way of human reasoning, one need only consult the comments of Aquinas in *Summa contra gentiles* I, chapter 4 and *Summa theologiae* I, 1, c. The precise affirmation of Vatican I on this question has long been the subject of debate. Still important is Hermann Pottmeyer's classic exegesis of the conciliar definition, *Der Glaube vor dem Anspruch der Wissenschaft* (Freiburg: Herder, 1968). The *relator* of *Dei Filius*, Vinzenz Gasser, emphasized that the definition regarded a human potency (*posse*), not an actuality, although Gasser himself claimed it would be difficult to identify a human possibility that had never been actualized (*Mansi*, 51, 278D). Denys Turner has also offered an exegesis of Vatican I, arguing that it is a matter of Christian faith that God's existence is rationally demonstrable, although he, too, accents possibility over actuality. See *Faith, Reason, and the Existence of God* (Cambridge: Cambridge University Press, 2004).

or nature and grace is not intended to inscribe two easily separable tiers. One finds, rather, tightly entwined strands of history, nature, culture, and grace. Examples of this relationship between universal realities and human embeddedness are drawn in a pointed way in several statements of John Paul II. In the encyclical *Fides et ratio*, for example, the pope argues that philosophy and reason have an autonomy that cannot be suppressed (*comprimere*) by the content of revelation.[39] His intention here is transparent: the philosophical order has a relative autonomy in and of itself, even "apart from" revelation. So ardently does the pope defend this position that he eschews, at least theoretically, the traditional term for philosophy as the *ancilla theologiae*, not because it is mistaken, but lest it give the impression that nature and philosophy do not have a legitimate sovereignty within their own estate.[40] Reason, even as wounded, has an authentic, if not total, independence. The pope strongly defends this position, I think, because he wants to uphold the capabilities of human nature, precisely in recognition of the universal *humanum* which characterizes the being of men and women. The implications of this defense become clear in the encyclical *Veritatis splendor* wherein the pope insists that the person, while embedded in various dimensions of society and culture, is not exhausted by those elements. There is, in fact, a universal *humanum* which is distinct from sociocultural mores or customs:

> It must certainly be admitted that the person always exists in a particular culture, but it must also be admitted that he or she is not exhaustively defined by that same culture. Moreover, the very progress of cultures demonstrates that there is something in humanity which transcends those cultures. This "something" is precisely human nature: this nature is itself the measure of culture and the condition ensuring that human beings do not become the prisoner of any culture, but asserts their personal dignity by living in accordance with the profound truth of their being.[41]

---

39 John Paul II, Encyclical Letter *Fides et ratio* (September 14, 1998), no. 79. In *Acta apostolicae sedis* 91 (1999), 5–88. An English translation may be found in *Origins* 28 (October 22, 1998), 317–47. See the supporting comments found at nos. 48 and 67. Of course, John Paul II also makes clear that philosophy has no *ultimate* "self-sufficiency" and must itself undergo "profound transformations" in light of the truths of faith (nos. 75, 77). This is why one most fittingly refers to philosophy's *real but relative autonomy*.

40 John Paul II, *Fides et ratio*, no. 77.

41 John Paul II, Encyclical Letter *Veritatis splendor* (August 6, 1993), no. 53. In *AAS* 85 (1993), 1133–1228, at 1176. An English translation may be found in *Origins* 23 (Oct. 14, 1993): 297–334, at 314.

The universality and relative autonomy of nature, of a metaphysical dimension of humanity, is here clearly affirmed without denying, of course, our historically conditioned existence. A similar point may be found in the pope's 1995 encyclical *Evangelium vitae*. This document teaches that the Gospel of Jesus Christ is intrinsically linked to certain conclusions in the moral order even if many of the same conclusions may be reached on the basis of arguments disengaged from the context of faith. So the encyclical states that the Gospel of life "despite the negative consequences of sin . . . *can also be known in its essential traits by human reason.*"[42] This is not to make the untenable claim that reason subsists within a *natura pura* outside of the domain of grace (or culture); it is to affirm that arguments may be made regarding the moral order which have a rational validity even apart from full-blooded, intrasystemic Christian belief. Of course, these arguments would surely be strengthened by belief, but they are neither unintelligible nor lacking in cogency without them. In other words, we may affirm that there exists only one supernatural order of grace. But within this order, "natural" arguments can be made on the basis of reason alone, that is, arguments having a logical structure, a universal value and a rational validity independent of faith, even though never independent, ultimately, of the estate of grace.

Evangelium vitae, of course, is relying on aspects of natural law reasoning. Just here, however, we must acknowledge the careful symbiosis between universal human realities and "participatory" thought. Natural law cannot be reduced to a kind of rationalism that fails to take account of either the embeddedness of the inquirer or the anterior subjective disposition and inclinations of the knowing person. As noted earlier, these elements will necessarily have some purchase on the success of any argument, including those concerning God's existence and natural law. Faith itself will serve to strengthen, concentrate, and illuminate one's grip on what is provided on the basis of natural human reason.[43] The Anselmian oscillation between

---

42 John Paul II, Encyclical Letter *Evangelium vitae* (March 25, 1995), no. 29. In *AAS* 87 (1995), 401–522, at 434 (emphasis in the original). An English translation may be found in *Origins* 24 (April 6, 1995): 689–727, at 700. The *Origins* translation, however, does not italicize the remarks found in the authentic Latin text.

43 It is no surprise that in his encyclical *Deus caritas est*, Benedict XVI affirms that the Church "argues on the basis of reason and natural law," that is, on the basis "of what is in accord with the nature of every human being." See Encyclical Letter *Deus caritas est* (December 25, 2005), no. 28. In *AAS* 98 (2006), 217–52, at 239. An English translation may be found in *Origins* 35 (Feb. 2, 2006): 541–57. Serge-Thomas Bonino, in his fine analysis of the encyclical,

universal natural realities and human circumscription offers a model, perhaps, of what *Evangelium vitae* intends. For the *Proslogion* is elaborated within a robustly theological context, but presents an argument having its own integrity in the natural order, apart from explicit faith. It is intended to have a universal validity, without relying upon "insider" knowledge. It is on the basis of natural human realities that one can invoke arguments that are, in principle, available to all even while realizing, to mark the essential Anselmian caveat, that experience, that is, embeddedness in Christian life and faith, will offer a performative, enfleshed knowledge surpassing what is attained on the basis of nature alone. [44] The encyclical then, like Anselm, is saying that epistemic warrants for particular moral teachings are not limited only to specific forms of life, even if the "traditioned" life of grace and Christian practice would surely strengthen one's grasp on its teaching.

This entire Anselmian dynamic between the universality of human nature and context-laden existence brings to mind the theological dialogue between Karl Barth and Hans Urs von Balthasar, a dialogue whose lessons remain instructive today. The core issue was the balancing of natural human realities with historical embeddedness which played itself out under the rubric of nature and grace. To summarize briefly: Barth severely criticized the entire Schleiermacher-Ritschl-Hermann axis of liberal Protestantism, as well as the *analogia entis* of Catholicism because both, he alleged, seek to establish a philosophical starting point outside of faith that, in turn, becomes determinative of the content of faith.[45] The fear was that some "universal idea," broader and deeper—to use spatial metaphors—than the faith itself was being preliminarily established. The perceived danger was that a philosophical concept of nature constituted a general prolegomenon into which "faith" was inserted at just the proper point. Church teaching,

---

argues persuasively that the entire document reflects an attempt to balance properly the interrelated spheres of nature and grace, of *eros* and *agape*, justice and charity, state and Church. See "'Nature et grâce' dans l'encyclique *Deus caritas est,*" *Revue Thomiste* 105, no. 4 (2005): 531–49.

44 Robert Sokolowski subtly expresses the kind of relative autonomy that is proper to natural law reasoning: "We might also tend to look to revelation for the more definitive communication of the true ends of things [. . .] . [. . .] [And] it is true, of course, that revelation will often declare certain natural human practices to be good and others to be bad, but these things also have their *natural visibility,* and one can argue more persuasively about them if one brings out their *intrinsic* nobility or unworthiness, their *intrinsic* rightness or wrongness, as well as the confirmation they receive from revelation." See "What is Natural Law? Human Purposes and Natural Ends," *The Thomist* 68, no. 4 (2004), 507–29 at 524, (emphases added).

45 Karl Barth, *Church Dogmatics* I/1, x.

in this instance, becomes secondary to philosophical positions that now imperiously claim to warrant the legitimacy of Christian beliefs. The transparent concern here is that a generic "common nature" becomes the properly "foundational" idea with revelation taken simply as a subset of a pre-existing philosophical category. Athens, then, is taken as normative while Jerusalem is simply a religious manifestation of a wider "Athenian" culture. Barth's fear is of an alien, philosophical *a priori* setting the agenda, so to speak, for Christian faith.

Balthasar answered Barth by conceding to him every point about the priority of grace; there exists only the *unicus ordo supernaturalis*, the one and only supernatural order of sin and grace in which humanity is embedded. At the same time, Balthasar defended at length the *relative autonomy* of the natural order, meaning by this phrase that inscribed within the supernatural sphere is the order of creation. It is only "relatively" autonomous because it always exists within the one estate of God's graciousness; but it is, indeed, autonomous because it possesses a certain freedom, a certain "nature" in and of itself and distinct from God. Balthasar conceded that nature is always, to some extent, a theological concept because the beatific vision is the goal of creation and all nature is oriented towards this *telos*. Further, there exists no surgical procedure for "removing" the order of creation from its embeddedness in the singular, concrete order of grace. But a certain autonomy of nature is necessary in order to protect the realm of creatureliness, which itself is the baseline concept for the very possibility of revelation. It is true, Balthasar agreed, that theology is always a *scientia de singularis*, a reflection on the concrete events of salvation history. But within this concrete order we find room for universal concepts, categories, and being itself.[46] Natural human realities constitute one of these concepts, even if nature must always be thought of as a "second moment" within the *fides quaerens intellectum*, but which nonetheless possesses its own comparative autonomy. It is no surprise that Balthasar defended the universality and integrity of nature even while reserving particular venom for Hegel and Idealism, with their attempts to overcome speculatively the *concretissimum* of salvation history. For Balthasar saw clearly that the emphasis on nature is not, as Barth feared, an attempt at the conceptual integration of Christianity by something other than revelation itself. It is hardly the philosophical

---

46 Hans Urs von Balthasar, *The Theology of Karl Barth*, trans. Edward T. Oakes (San Francisco: Ignatius Press, 1991), 384.

imperialism reminiscent of an earlier Radical Aristotelianism, which Balthasar strongly opposed in its later philosophical incarnations.[47]

But if both popes and theologians have emphasized, with Anselm, the relative autonomy of philosophy and nature, as well as the integrity of argumentation not requiring specific induction into the Christian community, then why, we may ask, has this defense been so important to Catholicism? One significant reason for this advocacy of universal human realities is the necessary convergence of philosophy with theological truth. Christian doctrine, in its most authoritative statements, is understood by the Church as universally, transculturally, and trans-generationally true. But if, in fact, Christian affirmations are enduringly true amidst very different societies, cultures, worldviews, and perspectives, then what notion philosophically supports this doctrinal constancy and meaning invariance over the course of cultures and centuries? How, in other words, does one find in the "natural" order a proper resonance with what the Church holds by faith, namely, the substantial continuity of Christian teaching in and through historicity, change, difference, and sociocultural "otherness"? It is precisely because of the Church's belief that faith and reason are deeply conjunctive realities that John Paul II in *Fides et ratio* argued that theology needs philosophy to "confirm the intelligibility and universal truth of its claims."[48] Such philosophies are required because they must substantiate in the *philosophical* order (such as the very *possibility* of the universally and abidingly true and the very *possibility* of meaning invariance) the logic of Catholicism's doctrinal affirmations by way of revelation. This is to suggest that reason, in its own relatively autonomous domain, must be able to confirm certain aspects of the universal truth of revelation. If it were unable to do so, then Christian doctrine and theology would appear irrational, thereby violating nature and transforming faith into merely authoritarian belief.[49] It is no surprise, then, that

---

47 Balthasar argues, for example, that God can never be assigned a place within a pre-existing system as he is with Hegel's *Geist*, Schopenhauer's *Wille*, or Schelling's *intellektuelle Anschauung*. Revelation, on the contrary, in the words of Mary's *Magnificat*, "*deposuit potentes de sede.*" See *Love Alone*, trans. A. Dru (New York: Herder and Herder, 1969), 34.

48 *Fides et ratio*, no. 77.

49 In other words, one cannot simply argue for the substantial continuity of Christian truth on the basis of the gospel of grace, absent confirming philosophical warrants, without lapsing into an untenable fideism. The other option, intelligible on its own grounds but a significant departure from the prior tradition, is to claim that the teachings of the Church are in fact, limited in their sociocultural scope and necessarily have wide meaning-variance over the course of times and cultures.

the pope called for a philosophy with a commodious "metaphysical horizon," one that is able to fulfill its *officium congruum* or "proper stewardship," precisely because this kind of philosophy has at its center an ability to account for unity within multiplicity, identity within difference, continuity within change. How else to explain, in the philosophical order, doctrinal constancy, universality, and perdurance (which stand at the very heart of Catholicism) in a world of incommensurable and highly variable customs, norms, and mores?

This traditional defense of the relative autonomy of philosophy and nature helps to explain Benedict XVI's direct and sustained attack on "dehellenization" in his Regensburg Lecture of September 12, 2006. Against a certain anti-metaphysical sentiment emerging from the Reformation and against an Hebraic/Hellenistic split championed by Adolf von Harnack in *Das Wesen des Christentums*, the pope strongly insists that Christianity cannot be severed from the heritage of Hellenistic inquiry. Benedict wishes to argue, like Anselm, that reason retains something of its independence and autonomy, precisely as a faculty of human nature, apart from explicit Christian belief. How else could there exist, as he states, "mutual enrichment" between the Christian faith and philosophy?[50] How else could he so ardently insist on the conjunctive confluence between the language of being of ancient philosophy and the language of faith and revelation?[51] The legitimate assertion of human embeddedness in sociocultural networks, as well as within the *unicus ordo supernaturalis*, does not mean the loss of the autonomy and integrity of nature, even if universal natural realities participate in this tightly knit web of human and divine dimensions. As earlier

---

50 See *Regensburg Lecture* (September 12, 2016). An English translation may be found in *Origins* 36 (September 28, 2006), 248–52, at 250. Benedict's comment recalls the claim of *Fides et ratio* that faith and reason offer each other mutual support as well as mutually purifying critiques (no. 100).

51 One finds this confluence in the Regensburg lecture and even more transparently in Ratzinger's earlier work *Introduction to Christianity*, trans. J. R. Foster (London: Search Press, 1969), 94–104 (which appears in the footnotes of the redacted Regensburg text). In this earlier work, Ratzinger speaks of belief as "wedded to ontology." The "I am" of Exodus 3:13 finds resonance in the "I am" texts of the Gospel of John (8:24; 8:58); here, the primacy of the existing real, of being itself, so prized by ancient philosophy comes to fulfillment in Christ. Ratzinger, then, would have little interest in a facile condemnation of "ontotheology" if this term is understood simply as the invocation of being-language within theological reflection. Ontotheology *is* properly condemned if the philosophical notion of being is taken as an *a priori* and univocal horizon which limits the appearance of God. But Ratzinger is arguing here, as much of the tradition before him, for a proper reciprocity between *ontos* and *theos*, with revelation, of course, as the leading partner and with God understood as analogically related to created being.

noted, to recognize the relative autonomy of philosophy and nature is not to assert that the truth of the Gospel is now "secured" by an "alien" philosophical integration, the secular *Aufhebung* that neo-Barthians fear. Anselm's emphasis is on the "second moment" of philosophical integrity *within* the *fides quaerens*. It recognizes, as John Paul II insists in *Fides et ratio*, the legitimate autonomy of philosophy even while indicating that such thinking has no ultimate self-sufficiency.[52] This lack of self-sufficiency means that philosophy must, in the last analysis, be theologically measured. Insofar as theology is a *scientia de singularis* (and surely the Incarnation is preeminently illustrative of this), then Christian revelation always has priority in the order of truth. Jerusalem, indeed, takes precedence over Athens. But there needs to be ancillary scaffolding in the philosophical order to ensure that there exists a conjunctive coherence between faith and reason.[53] For philosophy, in its own order, must offer support for theological conclusions lest theology appear simply to be a free-floating act of faith, unrelated to human reason and dependent, therefore, on authority alone. To say this is to recognize that knowledge and practice are related, but without undermining the kind of understanding available to nature, precisely as Anselm had argued. George Lindbeck, for example, speaks of the world absorbed into the biblical narrative, rather than the Bible being absorbed by the heteronomous standards of secular thought. In one sense this is surely true for philosophy cannot seek to be the aggressively hegemonic partner in the

---

52 See *Fides et ratio*, no. 75. Bruce Marshall has written, "When Aquinas speaks as a teacher of Catholic truth, which is to say all the time, he rejects the very idea of an autonomous philosophy." See Marshall, "In Search of an Analytic Aquinas," *Grammar and Grace*, 55–74, at 55. With this we can agree but with a few further words of explanation. It is undeniable that Aquinas begins from the *auditus fidei* and so from the *fides quaerens*. But he also thinks that philosophy has a certain *real but relative autonomy* (paralleling the kind of quasi-autonomy found in the *Proslogion*) as indicated by his strong respect for philosophy in its own order and his concern that Christian faith not be *repugnans ad rationem*. Thus, while Aquinas is undoubtedly always a teacher of Catholic truth, he believes that philosophy may marshal arguments for God's existence on the basis of causal and participationist metaphysics, absent any "insider" knowledge of Christian faith.

53 One thinks, in just this regard, of Aquinas's campaign against Radical Aristotelianism on the question of the nature of the intellect (which dispute centers, ultimately, on the faith/reason issue). Against the monopsychism of Siger of Brabant, Aquinas intends to show that there is a diversity of intellect in diverse beings. In his forward to the work, Thomas states that this could easily be shown simply by relying on the truth of the Christian faith (which is always normative). But he will display the nature of the error by arguing on philosophical grounds alone. Here we have a strict parallel with Anselm: the context is surely Christian belief, but the argument has a philosophical integrity and quasi-autonomy in and of itself. See *On the Unity of the Intellect Against the Averroists*, trans. Beatrice H. Zedler (Milwaukee: Marquette University Press, 1968), 22.

faith/reason relationship.[54] But neither can philosophy lose its proper autonomy by being absorbed into theology—just as nature cannot be entirely absorbed into culture.

Another issue importantly related to the defense of natural human realities and the integrity of philosophical reasoning is the existence of an area which may be shared by Christians, by people of other faiths, and by those of no faith at all, an area that we may call the relatively autonomous secular sphere. By this is meant the *agora* in which natural virtue is cultivated, in which publicly available arguments may be made from natural law as well as from natural theology. Anselm himself, of course, is quick to call attention to how vice obscures his own intellect and leads to faulty reasoning. Even here, however, he offers a discourse with its own integrity, an argument intended to be accessible to all reasonable inquirers, even if those with experience, that is, with participatory knowledge, walk in a brighter light. But the secular can only exist as a comparatively autonomous arena of shared theory and science, if, in fact, philosophy and nature themselves have a quasi-autonomy. The vitality of situated faith cannot exclude the realm of the secular, even if it enfleshes and supersedes it. Jürgen Habermas recognized this aspect of Catholic thought when he noted that Catholic theologians have traditionally had a less troubled relationship with the *lumen naturale*.[55] And it is precisely because of this "natural light" of reason that Catholics have been able to offer arguments in the public square for the intelligibility of God and for the natural visibility of universal moral principles. Insofar as we live in a society far more pluralistic and multivalent than that of Anselm, we need to ask if arguments that are not context specific, that have public, intersubjective warrants, are not even more necessary today.[56]

---

54 George Lindbeck, *The Nature of Doctrine* (Philadelphia: The Westminster Press, 1984), 135. I have discussed how faith must "measure" philosophy in "'Spoils from Egypt' Yesterday and Today," *Pro Ecclesia* 15, no. 4 (2006): 403–17.

55 See Jürgen Habermas, "Transcendence from Within, Transcendence in this World," in *Habermas, Modernity, and Public Theology*, ed. Don S. Browning and Francis Schüssler Fiorenza (Chestnut Ridge, NY: The Crossroad Publishing Company, 1992), 231.

56 Of course, Habermas, too, is a great defender of public reason. But inasmuch as Habermas wants all validity claims to be cognitively redeemed by public warrant, he would have little use for Anselm's attempt both on the grounds that religious discourse (even when speaking philosophically) has an *a priori* teleological view and arguments resting on elements of a universal *humanum* (which Habermas generally associates with the untenable Kantian being deconstructed by Heidegger) do not adequately account for the historically, culturally, and linguistically embedded subject of our post-transcendental, post-metaphysical age.

As noted at the outset of this essay, many contemporary thinkers wish to emphasize that meaning is mediated by one's participation in a cultural-linguistic community. All knowledge gained by individuals, therefore, is deeply informed by social practice and local custom. Further, the criteria by which such knowledge is judged, the epistemic warrants for truth, are internal to the communities themselves. Since modes of social life and discourse possess an internal logic, they are not subject to external criteria and verification. It is a deep affinity with just these themes that one sees in the interpretation of Anselm tendered by Kallenberg and one detects throughout Hauerwas's thought. For both, the accent is on the meaning and identity given within the *practices* of the robust, engaged, and participated life of the Christian Church. This approach has the significant merit of repairing some of the damage caused by the bloodless subject of modernity. The danger, however, is that it obscures the relative autonomy of nature and of philosophy; it also appears to abandon the notion of a *humanum*, of a universal human nature, and of arguments that appeal, in principle, to all human beings. The tension that Anselm keeps alive in his own thought and that is defended in the later tradition (even if this devolves, at times, into a strict disjunction) between the ontological constancy of nature and the specificity of embeddedness is thereby impaired. Anselm recognizes that the fullness of meaning and knowledge is mediated through experience, through the life and practices of the community, but he also argues that there is a prior givenness of meaning available through the *humanum* itself. The universal order of natural human realities and the historical orders of salvation and culture are thereby kept in delicate balance and strict tension. By arguing on the basis of evidence available to all inquirers, even while speaking of the vital, enfleshed knowledge available through experience, Anselm is acknowledging the relative autonomy of the natural order; reason has an integrity and universality in its own sphere. Does this mean reason and nature are "unconditioned"? Surely this cannot be the case insofar as every person is necessarily enfolded in socio-cultural-linguistic traditions. But can there be universals that are operative in and through perspective and situatedness? Anselm is an example of one who seeks to appeal to a universal *humanum* even while his careful approach is far distant from the Enlightenment subject of absolute autonomy.

CONCLUSION

There is a legitimate attempt on the part of many thinkers today to redeem reason from Enlightenment rationalism, to repair the damage wrought by modernity with its misguided defense of a neutral, autarkic subject, a subject existing apart from human traditions and sociocultural conditions, what Charles Taylor has described as the "ontologizing of the disengaged perspective."[57] In actual fact, there is no irreducible ahistorical rationality, no Archimedean platform outside time and history; there exists neither life nor consciousness without protention and retention, without presuppositions and anticipations. Much contemporary philosophy, then, is a therapeutic attempt to unmask this neutral subject of modernity, thereby recognizing the conditioned, situated, embedded, traditioned nature of human existence. Postmodern and hermeneutical thought (both philosophical and theological) have rebelled against this rationalist, Enlightenment point of view. It is reflected, for example, in John Milbank's representative comment that one cannot now contrast the alleged "particularist obscurantism of religion" with the universality of the human.[58] One cannot do so because postmodernity has exposed *this* kind of universality as nothing more than the allegedly unconditioned subject of modernity.

But should this legitimate exposure of the implausible worldless subject of the Enlightenment, hammered home by Heidegger's insistence that history cannot be buried under the cloak of immutability and by Wittgenstein's accent on the subject who participates in a cultural-linguistic community, demand a flight from the kind of metaphysical reasoning that accents a universal *humanum* or *physis* characteristic of Anselm and a significant part of the tradition? Should the emphasis on participatory reasoning exclude a common essence or eidetic (*eidos*) form? Should the excesses of modernity mean that Catholicism abandons universal natural human realities? And does jettisoning the Enlightenment subject mean we should also jettison the relative autonomy of philosophy?

Anselm seeks to circumvent the Scylla and Charybdis that threaten to overcome the proper balance between nature and culture, between nature and grace by avoiding, on the one hand, a devaluation of the relative autonomy of philosophy and natural human realities and, on the other, a ration-

---

57 Charles Taylor, "Engaged Agency and Background in Heidegger," in *The Cambridge Companion to Heidegger*, ed. Charles B. Guignon (Cambridge: Cambridge University Press, 1993), 317–36, at 323.

58 John Milbank, *Theology and Social Theory* (Oxford: Blackwell, 1990), 260.

alism that fails to understand the intimate relationship between knowledge and practice. While recognizing the unique knowledge given through the life and culture of the Church, Anselm holds that the Church herself is not the only locus of meaning and intelligibility. He suggests that there is some (formal) knowledge of God potentially available to all rational observers (even if this lacks the performative vigor of experience) beyond explicitly Christian sources. Warrants for the truth about God (and, in the case of natural law, for the intrinsic worthiness of actions) are available on the basis of reason as well as through the participated life of the Church. This is not to say, it bears repeating, that one seeks warrants outside faith to justify faith. It is to say that some knowledge of God is, in principle, available to all, even if the practices of the Church enflesh this knowledge, making it vital, robust, and performative. One states this even while acknowledging the profound interlacing of nature and culture, of natural human realities with their conditioned and situated character. *Gaudium et spes* recognized this when teaching that "wherever human life is involved [. . .] nature and culture are quite intimately connected."[59] A distinction is possible between the two even if one may also legitimately speak of an ontological reciprocity.

I address this question, a traditional one in Catholic theology, because of the contemporary emphasis, displayed in writers such as Hauerwas, Kallenberg, and many others, of the strong relationship between knowledge and practice, fueled, often enough, by the contemporary philosophical accent on the embedded, traditioned subject. Surely what is right in this is the vigorous reclamation of Christian identity as opposed to the pallid universalism of modernity. But this decided accent has brought a reaction against the traditional Catholic stress on a universal *humanum* as well as the relative autonomy of philosophy. The reaction is understandable. For if hermeneutical and postmodern thought (in its manifold variations) has taught one lesson well, it is the danger of a rationalist, conceptualizing objectivism that devalues the heteromorphous nature of life and discourse, the enveloping dimensions of historicity and culture, of alterity and difference.

But the correlative danger is a lapse into a contemporary either/or: Either universalist modernity or situated postmodernity. But such an antinomy is too starkly posed. As everyone knows, Catholic theology cast off a wooden neo-scholasticism that too-sharply divided nature/grace, reason/faith, and philosophy/theology, a thinking itself abducted by Enlightenment themes, strictly separating the two spheres. Theology eventually rebelled

59 Vatican Council II, *Gaudium et spes* (December 7, 1965), no. 53.

against this modality which ignored not only the congeries of elements involved in human knowing, but also the circuminsession of nature and grace. This is the stream of thought represented by Pascal, Newman, and Blondel (and later de Lubac) who reacted against an untenable rationalism by displaying dimensions and horizons of human being and knowing that modernity (and its theological *Doppelgänger*) overlooked and devalued. But if, at one time, theology needed to be rescued from manualist rationalism, evacuated of ideas such as theory-laden interpretation and situated reason, the danger today may be that by accenting just these dimensions, the truth offered by reason to all inquirers, available on the basis of a shared nature, is obscured. In jettisoning the excesses of modernity, then, we must beware the danger of jettisoning universal natural realities whose defense long predates the Enlightenment. Anselm may stand on the precipice between the early Church and the High Middle Ages, but he can hardly be understood as a harbinger of modernity or of Cartesian rationality except in the most attenuated sense. As with many therapeutic remedies in theology, a reparative counter-narrative may list too far in the other direction. Does the contemporary accent on human embeddedness, at least in some of its formulations, eclipse a proper understanding of natural human realities?

The rationality proper to Catholic theology is a careful interweaving of universal and contingent elements, of nature and grace, of reason and revelation, of human potentiality and participatory knowing. Anselm's argument in the *Proslogion* is a model of balance and proportion on just these matters. Does this contemporary invocation of Anselm constitute another flight to the premodern, a flight (and recovery) visible, for example, in the keen interest in Pseudo-Dionysius found in thinkers such as John Milbank and Jean-Luc Marion, and discernible in the return to patristic exegesis championed by various present-day projects? Does offering a medieval thinker's reflections as a significant model for understanding the relationship between the universal *humanum* and historical contextualization not also smack of antiquarianism? I do not think this is the case. It is, rather, the recognition that there has been in the tradition of Catholic theology a great respect for the *relative* autonomy of nature, creation and reason, an autonomy that, properly understood, protects the proper integrity of natural human knowledge as well as the distinctions between philosophy and theology, nature and grace, nature and culture. Anselm, I suggest, offers substantial theological lessons on these points, even (and perhaps especially) today.

Chapter Four

Introduction: Postmodernity and Five Fundamental Theological Issues

What is the relationship between postmodern philosophy and Catholic theology? Can theology reap any benefits from the postmodern understanding of ontology, of truth, of hermeneutics, and of language? Can the philosophical insights of Heidegger, Habermas, Gadamer, and Derrida be productively "despoiled" by Christian theologians? These are the questions that animate this essay on postmodern thought and foundational theological issues.

Important to this chapter is the distinction between "strong" and "moderate" postmodernism. The latter, while rejecting metaphysics and its veridical, hermeneutical, and linguistic correlates, does not demonize, in Nietzschean fashion, rationality itself. Rather, moderate postmodern thinkers, and I include in this group theologically influential authors such as Hans-Georg Gadamer and Jürgen Habermas, seek to develop "ontologically appropriate" notions of reason, truth, and interpretation—notions, that is to say, which are congruent with our actual historical situation and lived experience.

They insist that ontologically appropriate understandings of foundational philosophical ideas mean acknowledging, in a way that traditional Western philosophy (and theology) has not, that we are profoundly embedded in socio-cultural-temporal webs which necessarily determine all our theoretical constructions. Given this historical and cultural embeddedness, postmodern thinkers argue that one cannot defend traditional or modern (transcendental) metaphysics (which is often derided as ontological foundationalism). Neither can one cogently defend the idea of a common human nature which remains substantially the same over time.

This philosophical challenge to classical metaphysical ideas has significant theological ramifications. One major problem, of course, is that Catholic theology upholds the material continuity of the faith over the course of centuries and cultures. But how is such meaning-invariance defended? How can transtemporal and transcultural truth and meaning be supported if metaphysics is now ruled out of court as intellectually dishonest?

One approach—clearly influenced by Karl Barth, and adopted by both the Lutheran theologian George Lindbeck and the Catholic thinker Jean-Luc Marion—has been to assert the biblical and doctrinal truth of Christianity. But is such assertion possible absent philosophical warrants that support and buttress these doctrinal claims? Or does such assertion smack of an unacceptable fideism which reeks of an overweening *sola gratia* position? The other option, represented by David Tracy and other theologians, is to argue that significant dimensions of postmodern thought must be integrated into Catholic theology, otherwise Christianity itself becomes academically marginalized, idiosyncratically insisting on its private truth.

Of course, some kind of "integration" of philosophy into theology has been sanctioned by the Church from the beginning. However, this assimilation or correlation has never been envisioned as an equal partnership. Orthodox Christian belief must always be the standard against which any philosophy is measured. Fully integrating postmodernity into theology—with its rejection of metaphysics, its reduction of truth to practical reason, and its repudiation of traditional hermeneutics—results in a deeply historicized understanding of the Christian faith.

I propose here a theological alternative which allows for a qualified use of postmodern thought, but one that must ultimately conform to Christian truth.

Postmodernity and Five Fundamental Theological Issues

P ostmodernity is a word one finds now with some frequency in both scholarly and casual literature. It is a "movement" that has inspired raging debates about the "cult of theory" across the arts and sciences. My intention in this article is to examine several central themes of postmodernity and the manner in which they affect critical theological issues. I contend that individuals grappling with many of the major disputed questions in theology today—truth, hermeneutics, language, and correlation— have much to learn from postmodern theory, but must do so without abandoning the legitimate achievements of previous epochs.

All have some familiarity with the term postmodernity and its logical contrast with modernity. In brief, postmodernity is that type of thought that rebels against any totalizing understanding of reality. It rejects various attempts to "stop the show," "freeze the flux," or "release the truth-police."[1] Postmodernity accuses its predecessor, modernity, of having sacralized human rationality. In the quest of the Enlightenment to uncover the basic and essential structures of human thought and discourse, modernity leveled and homogenized reality. The Enlightenment's concern with methodology as the path to truth caused it to veil historicity and to ignore the nuances, complexities, and ambiguities of being and knowing. This truncated notion of humanity led, in science, to an excessive Baconism that ignored the historical-hermeneutical elements of thought and inappropriately canonized the foundationalisms of positivism and empiricism. Particular postmodern invective is reserved for this kind of rationalism that deified algorithmic positivism, leading ineluctably to technocracy and even

* This essay was originally published as "Postmodernity and Five Fundamental Theological Issues," *Theological Studies* 57, no. 4 (2001): 654–89. Republished under terms of SAGE author re-use policy.

1 Several works are useful for examining the relevant postmodern literature, e.g., James Marsh, John Caputo, and Merold Westphal, eds. *Modernity and Its Discontents* (New York: Fordham University Press, 1992); David Lyon, *Postmodernity* (Minneapolis: University of Minnesota Press, 1994) and Louis Dupré, "Postmodernity or Late Modernity?" *Review of Metaphysics* 47, no. 2 (1993): 277–95.

totalitarianism. This is the meaning of Adorno's suggestive and provocative phrase, that modernity is the primitive "belly turned mind."[2] It is the mind of modernity that now represents the atavistic rage of instrumental reason against the Other.

Postmodernity, on the other hand, seeks to put an end to the manipulable domination of instrumental reason, of the reificatory thinking of positivism and rationalism. It strives to overcome the pathology of the identity principle with its nostalgia for presence and its romance with totalities. It fulfills this goal by exalting the heteromorphous nature of life, thought, and speech. It exhumes from the obsequies of the Enlightenment alterity, *différe(a)nce*, rupture, and breach. In place of pallid universalism, postmodernity celebrates the opacity and sovereignty of the Other, the "apologetics of the accidental," and the deracinated and anamorphous nature of thought. By unmasking horizons rooted in our factical situatedness—social location, ideological determination, cultural embeddedness, saturated reason, paradigm-bound rationality, contextualized knowledge, and the ontological productivity of history—postmodernity has become a militant protest and call to arms against universalizing tendencies.[3]

What is the effect of postmodernity on theology? Does it mean that Dionysus is now invading the City of God? Or, as others have it, is God now

---

2 Theodore Adorno, *Negative Dialectics*, trans. E. B. Ashton (New York: Seabury Press, 1973), 23. With his "negative dialectics" Adorno attempted to redeem the Enlightenment aesthetically. Art is here a glimmer of messianic light avoiding dominative reason and the conceptual truncation of reality. With similar intentions, see Helmut Peukert, "Enlightenment and Theology as Unfinished Projects," in *Habermas, Modernity, and Public Theology*, ed. Don S. Browning and Francis Schüssler Fiorenza, 43–65 (Chestnut Ridge, NY: The Crossroad Publishing Company, 1992).

3 In an earlier article, I distinguished between "strong" and "moderate" postmodernity: "Between Foundationalism and Nihilism: Is *Phronēsis* the *Via Media* for Theology?" *Theological Studies* 54, no. 1 (1993): 37–54. The essential difference between the two is that those adopting the "moderate" position will not reject rationality per se, nor will they necessarily reject the political and intellectual achievements of modernity. So, for example, New Left thinkers like Terry Eagleton, who wish to preserve aspects of critical theory, call the "stronger," more deconstructive type of postmodernity a "jejune brand of anti-totalizing thought." For Eagleton, such attempts at post-political discourse are wrong because they conflate all attempts at social change "in Nietzschean fashion with a craven conformity." See Eagleton, *The Ideology of the Aesthetic* (Cambridge, MA: Blackwell, 1990), 354. Similarly, Albrecht Wellmer argues that while the pathologies of the Enlightenment must be opposed, many of its aspects, e.g., liberal democracy and critical consciousness, should be positively redeemed. Postmodernity rightly resists transcendental deductions, but it must likewise avoid the temptation to demonize reason. See Wellmer, *The Persistence of Modernity*, trans. David Midgley (Cambridge, MA: The MIT Press, 1991). In this article, I focus largely on the moderate group of postmodernists (e.g., Habermas and Gadamer), those interested in adjusting rather than abandoning our notions of truth and rationality. It is the moderate group which has had significant influence on contemporary theology.

wakening us to Otherness by a kind of theological entropy, or, at least, an eclipse of classical thought? The purpose of this chapter will be to examine the influence of postmodernity on theology across five fundamental issues: foundationalist ontology, theological truth, hermeneutics, language, and correlation. What can postmodernity teach us about those issues? And what unresolved problems remain?

FOUNDATIONALIST ONTOLOGY

As has been amply documented, Heidegger and Wittgenstein constitute the dual-headed Zeus from whom postmodernity springs.[4] The works of those thinkers have given rise to the thought of Gadamer, Derrida, Foucault, Lyotard, Kristeva, Baudrillard, and Irigaray. Although each of these differs in important and even essential ways, their fundamental goal and task has been to "present the absent," to uncover the world that *Dasein* has epistemologically buried, to put an end to ontologically inappropriate norms and standards. Postmodern thinkers argue that the newly presenced horizons of finitude, socio-cultural embeddedness, and contextualized reason present a conclusive and destructive argument against foundationalism of any kind. Metaphysics, whether of the classical type, more recent transcendental ontologies, or empirical-positivistic approaches have all been exposed as inappropriate and untenable.[5]

---

4 Works on these thinkers vis-à-vis the critique of foundationalism include Gertrude Conway, *Wittgenstein on Foundations* (Atlantic Highlands, NJ: Humanities Press, 1989); Jacques Taminiaux, *Heidegger and the Project of Fundamental Ontology*, trans. and ed. M. Gendre (Albany: SUNY Press, 1991); Fred Dallmyer, *Between Freiburg and Frankfurt: Toward a Critical Ontology* (Amherst: University of Massachusetts Press, 1991); Brice Wachterhauser, ed., *Hermeneutics and Truth* (Evanston, IL: Northwestern University Press, 1994); Susan Brill, *Wittgenstein and Critical Theory* (Athens, OH: Ohio University Press, 1995).

5 It will be helpful to clear up a terminological issue. In some authors, "foundationalism" is connected uniquely with Cartesian thought and modern epistemic justification, that is, with an apodictic certainty only acquired through methodical doubt and evidential warrants. Other contemporary postmodern thinkers, Richard Rorty for example, condemn the entire classical, medieval, and modern axis with the "foundationalist" label (including Plato, Aristotle, Aquinas, Kant, Hegel, and Husserl), widening the original epistemic critique to an ontological critique as well. See *Philosophy and the Mirror of Nature* (Princeton: Princeton University Press, 1979). Here, I use foundationalism in this latter sense. Given this usage, one can oppose the isolated ego of Descartes—or the notion that one achieves rational justification only through evidential certainty—without opposing foundationalism itself. Useful works on nonfoundationalist thought include John Thiel, *Nonfoundationalism* (Minneapolis: Fortress, 1994), which stresses the postpositivist empiricism of Sellars and Quine, and Tom Rockmore and Beth J. Singer, eds., *Antifoundationalism Old and New* (Philadelphia: Temple University Press, 1992), which examines various attempts at "foundations" in the history of philosophy.

Postmodern thinkers reject foundationalist ontologies of all types because these philosophies seek to "close down" effective history, to end historical consciousness. What postmodernity has shown, however, is that historicity is not merely a casing for transcendental subjectivity, nor for any of the classical or modern attempts to "nail down" or finally "name" Being.[6] Philosophy can give us no final answers, nor can it outline ultimate structures, metaphysical, transcendental, or empirical. The postmodern philosopher's task is, rather, to foster civilized discourse, to "keep the conversation going."[7] This fostering of civilized speech serves as a legitimate replacement for philosophy's former goal: determining the deepest structures of reality and the transcendental conditions allowing for knowledge of them. The radical temporality saturating every aspect of being and thought has forced the ancient discipline to rethink its object and task.

Given this fresh understanding, it is logical that postmodern thinkers subject to particular invective ontological mainstays such as a common human nature or a universal notion of rationality. Such ideas seek to establish and embed a solid rock, an immovable object, within the river of historicity. Richard Campbell, for example, is representative of current trends when he says, "In assuming the timelessness of truth, the traditional view assumed a human capacity to know that truth and thus a human nature that, if only in virtue of that decisive capacity, is unchanging."[8] Rather than speak of a stable and universal human nature, postmodern thinkers are much more likely to refer to a culturally constituted human rationality emerging from the tight web of history, society, and language. Precisely as *post*modernity, this represents a new moment in the history of philosophy.[9]

---

6 One cannot "freeze the flux" with *eidos, ousia, esse, essentia, res cogitans*, the transcendental ego, or any other foundation. The event character of Being is such that it is given differently in each epoch. The Heideggerian *es gibt* confounds every attempt, in John Caputo's words, to "out-flux the flux."

7 In Heidegger's wake, this is the goal of philosophy envisioned by, among others, Rorty, Bernstein, and Caputo. Rorty's position may be found in *Philosophy and the Mirror of Nature*, 389–94, Bernstein's in *Beyond Objectivism and Relativism* (Philadelphia: University of Pennsylvania Press, 1983), 223–31, and Caputo's in *Radical Hermeneutics* (Bloomington: Indiana University Press, 1987), 257–64.

8 Richard Campbell, *Truth and Historicity* (Oxford: Clarendon, 1992), 398. He continues, "But what if there is no permanent human nature? What if [. . .] man's very being is historical? These suggestions encapsulate the concept of historicity."

9 Louis Dupré makes much of the rise of medieval nominalism in the passage to modernity. For the ancient realists, nature was communicative of reality; truth was mediated by the cosmos. Dupré argues that the ancients were constructivists only to the extent that culture represented

What are the theological implications when one deconstructs the foundations of ontology, when history and culture are placed in dialectical opposition to nature? More pointedly, what becomes of the truth status of Christian doctrine?

In order to sharpen the issue, it should first be noted that contemporary postmodern thought and Protestant theology display a clearer confluence than does Catholicism. At the root of this inner congruence is the traditional and well-known difference between Catholic and Protestant theology in their classical ways of understanding the nature-grace or creation-salvation distinction. For Catholics, the two orders, ontological and soteriological, are distinct (at least notionally) but in fundamental continuity. For traditional Protestantism, on the other hand, a wedge has been driven between fallen and corrupted nature and the work of the Redeemer. Protestantism finds the call of postmodernity for a meta-onto-theology legitimate and useful precisely because Protestant theology has resisted the notion of the Form of the cosmos and of the *logos* structure of reality intelligible in itself, even apart (again, notionally) from Jesus Christ and the gospel of grace. Protestant thinkers find in postmodernity's deconstruction of ontology a connatural convergence with their own suspicion of the inner intelligibility of nature and being.

Of course, the roots of the Protestant protest against theological ontology go back to the Pauline imagination undergirding the Reformation. The *logos* structure of reality that Catholicism adopted from the ancient world, further fueled by the rebirth of pagan learning begun by the late medieval Italians, gave rise to the suspicion that the glory of the world was now confused with the glory of God. The Reformation protest was precisely against a semi-Pelagian analogizing imagination that tended to overlook God's

---

a further molding of a given nature. For the nominalists, on the contrary, form belongs not to nature but to the mind. With Descartes and Kant, the form-giving principle of the subject is intensified. There is a gradual loss of cosmic intelligibility, of the truth mediated by *physis* and *nomos*, of the link between God and creatures. For post-Kantian voluntarism, nature is an enemy of freedom precisely because it tries to mold the subject *a priori*. But only the idealizing synthesis of the person is truly mediative of meaning. See *Passage to Modernity: An Essay in the Hermeneutics of Nature and Culture* (New Haven: Yale University Press, 1993). Both the classical tradition and modernity, in different ways, sought to preserve the notion of form, one by means of nature, the other by synthetic interiority. Postmodernity, in its "strong" form, seeks to overcome any ontology of either cosmos or subjectivity. Moderate postmodernity does not reject all form, only the classical foundationalist form of nature and the foundationalist subject of modern transcendental thought. Gadamer and Habermas, for example, defend form, but now in a highly protean manner—in the case of Gadamer, tradition and history; for Habermas, the discourse community.

judgment on the world rendered dramatically in the cross of Christ. This movement challenged a too-easy medieval and Renaissance elision of the majesty of nature with grandeur of the Revealed God.[10] The evangelical objection was aimed at every attempt to collapse the unique and undeducible Form of the Crucified God into the form of inner-worldly or subjective beauty. Even apart from the influence of postmodernity, then, classical Protestantism has strong lethic and decentering currents born of its understanding of the gospel.

One indication of the theoretical confluence between Protestantism and elements of postmodern philosophy may be seen in the exchange between Gadamer and Leo Strauss on the publication of *Wahrheit und Methode*. In one part of the dialogue, Strauss protests against Gadamer's hermeneutical theory, especially its overthrow of the stability of textual meaning. Gadamer responds, "What I believe to have understood through Heidegger (and what I can testify to from my Protestant background) is, above all, that philosophy must learn to do without the idea of an infinite intellect. I have attempted to draw up a corresponding hermeneutics."[11] For Gadamer, both hermeneutical phenomenology and the Reformation teach humanity about finitude. And finitude is what Protestantism, by its early deconstruction of theological ontology, by its exaltation of the theology of the Cross, by its intense apophaticism, and by its emphasis on eschatological rather than present realization, clearly understands. Fixed meanings and dogmas are ill suited to handle human historicity and human limitations.

Under the penetrating influence of Heidegger, Wittegenstein, and Gadamer, Catholic thinkers, too, have moved in the direction of deconstructing theological ontology. Jean-Luc Marion, for example, has argued that only the dismantling of traditional thought will allow an apposite notion of the Christian God to emerge, for the "idolic imagination" to be replaced by the truly iconic vision. Marion's project is to establish the limits of the being question, discarding, in the process, the classical and transcendental metaphysical baggage that has led to a distorted image of divine

---

10 Hans Urs von Balthasar has pointed out that the iconoclasm of Luther remains important because it "keeps the transcendental beauty of revelation from slipping back into equality with an inner-worldly natural beauty." See vol. 1 of *The Glory of the Lord: Seeing the Form*, trans. Erasmo Leiva-Merikakis (San Francisco: Ignatius Press, 1982), 41.

11 Hans-Georg Gadamer, "Correspondence concerning *Wahrheit und Methode*," *Independent Journal of Philosophy* 2 (1978): 10.

12 Marion's position will be discussed more fully below.

life.[12] Framing his arguments somewhat differently, David Tracy represents another type of Catholic postmodernity; he, too, argues that in light of our newly-presenced situation, theology must honestly evaluate its classical self-understanding, particularly its notion of ontology.[13] The traditional assessment, notably with regard to doctrine, seeks to freeze the flux, to deaden historical consciousness, to finish the conversation. By so doing, theology leaves itself open to Habermas's charge that it must be sealed off from the ideal-speech situation and from the communicative praxis of egalitarian society. Theology is already committed *apriori*; it is not fully "open" to effective history nor to the serious rethinking demanded by radical temporality.

Perduring questions remain in the wake of postmodern thought. Are the traditional approaches now simply wrong, that is, ontologically inappropriate given our newly-presenced cultural and linguistic horizons? Does foundationalist ontology paper over the ruptures and breaches within life and thought? Does it ignore the Cross? If so, what meta-onto-theological discourse should we create as a replacement? Some Catholic thinkers have turned to mysticism and doxology. This is the move made by Marion, curiously approximating the nonreligious esthetic and poetic mysticism of Adorno and Heidegger.[14] But does this solve the persistent systematic issues? More specifically, when one turns toward postmodernity (even in its moderate genre) how is the continuity and identity of the deposit of faith established? And how is the truth-status of doctrine to be understood? Obviously, a move towards nonfoundationalist ontology means either a turn toward significant mutability and flexibility in fundamental Christian teachings or, conversely, a fideistic assertion of the immutable truth of the gospel, prescinding for any attempt to establish this immutability reasonably. Without a foundationalist ontology of some sort, there is no possibility for logically sustaining the stability of textual meaning or a referential notion of truth, essential principles for traditional understandings of doctrine.

Of course, several postmodern concerns have already been addressed by Catholic theology. Bernard Lonergan, for example, has been one of the most balanced thinkers on this issue, again and again seeking to show the

---

13 I have treated Tracy's reception of hermeneutical phenomenology and his consequent non-foundationalism in *Revelation and Truth: Unity and Plurality in Contemporary Theology* (Scranton: University of Scranton Press, 1993), 68–71.

14 Others have moved in the direction of Gadamer and Habermas, as I discuss below.

extent to which historical consciousness and its attendant horizons have affected the traditional understanding. Lonergan argues that classical culture was right in assuming there was a universal human nature, but it misunderstood the extent to which this essential nature was open. In conjunction with this premise, Lonergan developed a transcendental philosophy outlining the invariant structures of human consciousness while concomitantly championing changing worlds of meaning and tirelessly defending, against neo-scholasticism, the mutability of conceptual constructs.[15] Karl Rahner, too, even while defending his transcendental gnoseology, ceaselessly sought to show the extent to which historical and hermeneutical consciousness had a deep and lasting effect on meaning and interpretation. As his thought progressed, Rahner argued with increasing vigor for the influence of postmodern horizons on the formulations of doctrine, without ever abandoning the theological ontology of his critical starting point.[16] A more recent phenomenological defense of foundationalism is offered by Robert Sokolowski, who justifies both the possibility of knowing "essentials" and the constructive dimension of noetic acts intrinsically connected with historicity. Seeking to illumine the complementarity rather than opposition between nature and culture, he writes, "We never have sheer nature without convention, or sheer convention without nature; the two are always tangled. Nature is displayed to us only as refracted through custom and custom always mixes with the natural. The interweaving of the two is what makes it so apparently plausible to say that there is no nature, but only convention."[17]

Catholic "foundationalist" thinkers like Rahner and Lonergan were certainly not interested in defending any form of theological Cartesianism. On the contrary, they fought an Enlightenment concept of nature which gradually led to anthropologies fraught with extrinsicism. On the other hand, they thought that some foundationalist ontology is necessary if one is

15 "[Classicism] [. . .] is not mistaken in its assumption that there is something substantial and common to human nature and human activity. Its oversight is its failure to grasp that that something substantial and common also is something quite open." See *Doctrinal Pluralism* (Milwaukee: Marquette University Press, 1971), 8.

16 For Rahner's later position, see, for example, *"Mysterium Ecclesiae,"* in vol. 17 of *Theological Investigations*, trans. Margaret Kohl, 139–55 (Chestnut Ridge, NY: The Crossroad Publishing Company, 1981) and "Yesterday's History of Dogma and Theology for Tomorrow," in vol 18 of *Theological Investigations*, trans. Edward Quinn, 3–34 (Chestnut Ridge, NY: The Crossroad Publishing Company, 1983).

17 Sokolowski, "Knowing Essentials," *Review of Metaphysics* 47, no. 4 (1994): 697.

adequately to defend fundamental Catholic positions on doctrine.[18] If one accepts postmodernity more fully, thereby abandoning some form of foundationalist ontology, one's entire understanding of revelation, especially the role of Christian doctrine, is deeply affected. Either the truth of the gospel must be simply asserted, breaking its link with a rationally elaborated infrastructure. Or, by opening a fissure between ontology and theology, one develops a quite different understanding of what the deposit of faith is, how it develops, and the type of continuity and identity proper to it. Particularly affected is the type of truth mediated by it.

THEOLOGICAL TRUTH

At the beginning of the *De consolatione philosophiae*, Lady Philosophy visits the imprisoned Boethius to comfort him. Inscribed on the lower part of her robe is the Greek letter *pi*, standing for practical philosophy, while on the upper section is embroidered the letter *theta*, for theoretical philosophy.[19] One suspects that in any postmodern version of the *De consolatione*, however, Lady Philosophy would be forced to undergo a serious fashion makeover. This is so because postmodernity holds that the deconstruction of classical and modern ontologies, of substance and transcendental subject, means likewise the logical deconstruction of classical and modern notions of truth. The failure of traditional foundationalist systems to recognize the sociocultural embeddedness of rationality and the historical facticity of discourse has led, inevitably, to atomistic and ontologically inappropriate ideas about what truth is.[20] The depth of the postmodern critique has occasioned one commentator to claim that the current battle against the Enlightenment is, at base, a rebellion against truth.[21] But surely this is only partially true. It *is* a rebellion against truth as traditionally understood; in this sense, it does amount to an abandonment of the theoretical notion of truth which was formerly philosophy's domain. But this abandonment is done consciously

---

18 I have discussed the "foundationalisms" of these thinkers in *Revelation and Truth*, 38–56. It is important to remember that the positions of Rahner and Lonergan (and Kasper as well) are not defenses of Platonic forms or Cartesian substances; they do amount to vindications of theological ontologies which ultimately resist a total acceptance of Heidegger's notion of historicity.

19 Boethius, *The Consolation of Philosophy*, trans. Richard Green (Indianapolis: Bobbs-Merrill, 1962), 4.

20 Our primary concern is not with "strong" postmodernists who bid "farewell to reason" but with the moderates who seek notions of truth appropriate to our new situation.

21 Stanley Rosen, *Hermeneutics as Politics* (Oxford: Oxford University Press, 1987), 138.

and in the interest of adjusting to further knowledge about our historical limitations. Under the forceful influence of Heidegger and Wittgenstein, postmodernity argues that truth is entirely mediated by historical flux, societal norms, and cultural warrants. To speak of truth as a grasping of actual states of affairs is naïve precisely because it fails to take account of an ever-mutable humanity and society. To the extent that the solid earth of human nature (with its ontological constancy) has been abandoned, to this same measure must our notion of truth be adjusted. An appropriate understanding of ontology has, necessarily, veridical effects. In Campbell's words, "If man's very humanity differs from age to age, from culture to culture [. . .] [then] our own being varies relative to differing historical situations; in turn, that seems to imply that what is appropriated, the truths we claim to grasp, are likewise relative."[22]

While the end of foundationalism should not be confused with the end of philosophy, it should awaken us to the fact that claims to truth are largely, if not exclusively, culturally constituted frameworks. But if it is true that knowledge arises only within a web of contingent, finite, sociocultural situations (and not only arises within but is likewise totally delimited by them), then the present and continuing philosophical task is to develop new understandings of truth and rationality consonant with our rethinking of ontology. In accord with this goal, several notions of truth have been advanced as appropriate to our postmetaphysical, posttranscendental, postpositivist world. The ideas common to many contemporary philosophers and theologians include variations on the ethical pragmatism of James, Dewey, and Peirce, the rehabilitation of Aristotle's *phronēsis* or "practical reason" by Gadamer, and the neopragmatic communicative discourse theory of Habermas. Each of these is congruent with our more recent understanding.[23]

Practical reason, for example, as classically understood, is that dimension of reason that deals with mutable, changing circumstances; it was normally opposed to epistemic or theoretical reason which grasped unchanging truth or essentials.[24] Yves Simon is representative of the traditional distinc-

---

22 Campbell, *Truth and Historicity*, 402.

23 Both classical pragmatic thought, as well as its contemporary renascence in Rorty and Habermas, are clearly treated by John Patrick Diggins, *The Promise of Pragmatism* (Chicago: University of Chicago Press, 1994).

24 Aristotle, *Ethics*, Book 6, 1139A, 6–14. I have discussed the use of *phronēsis* in "Between Foundationalism and Nihilism," 44–51.

tion when he argues that practical reason is proper to contingent circumstances and does not have the universality proper to essences. Along the same lines, C. D. C. Reeve notes that *"phronēsis* is more concerned with particulars than with universals" for *"phronēsis* studies *endechomena*, things that admit of being otherwise."[25] Postmodern thinkers argue that practical reason is the proper mode of all truth precisely because of finitude and historicity; these horizons have taught us that truth is necessarily contingent, is always reversible, is capable of being otherwise.

One postmodern understanding of truth which is gaining wide currency is that proposed by Jürgen Habermas. Many contemporary thinkers acknowledge him as successfully advancing a notion that fully recognizes the historicized, saturated, and embedded character of reason, while maintaining a proper appreciation for the legitimate achievements of modernity. Habermas develops his theory of communicative praxis in order to establish an understanding of truth congruent with our lived situation. To that end, Habermas accepts much of Heidegger's critique of modernity and his censure of the Western onto-theological tradition. With Heidegger, he argues that Husserl's "thing itself" always slips away in the cultural constructivism of speech acts and truth claims: "Historicism and *Lebensphilosophie* have attributed an epistemological significance to the transmission of tradition, to aesthetic experience, and to the bodily, social, and historical existence of the individual; this significance had to explode the classical concept of the transcendental subject."[26]

Habermas, however, is fearful that society cannot properly function within the poetic mysticism of Heidegger's understanding of human existence. If we are to avoid the aporias of esoterism and privatism, we must have the means to adjudicate claims to truth within contemporary society, the *polis*. It is one thing to stipulate that radical historicity and the assimilation of rationality to conventionally accepted language games demonstrates the inappropriateness of metaphysics. It is quite another task, however, to provide democratic societies with political and philosophical guidance on the proper functioning of the marketplace of human ideas, the *agora*, in postfoundationalist society. Against those championing completely

25 Yves Simon, *The Tradition of Natural Law* (New York: Fordham University Press, 1965), 23–27; *Practical Knowledge* (New York: Fordham University Press, 1991), 100–5; C. D. C. Reeve, *Practices of Reason: Aristotle's Nicomachean Ethics* (Oxford: Clarendon, 1992), 68n2, 74.

26 Jürgen Habermas, *Postmetaphysical Thinking*, trans. William Mark Hohengarten (Cambridge, MA: The MIT Press, 1992), 40.

incompatible standards and languages, Habermas defends the importance of the public redemption of warrants for the substantiation and validation of truth-claims. Without such publicly redeemable warrants, even if these are deeply embedded within the community, society cannot function. There is, then, no denial of rationality, but a recognition that communicative reason is "a rocking hull—but it does not go under in the sea of contingencies, even if shuddering in the high seas is the only mode in which it 'copes' with these contingencies."[27]

What type of truth is characteristic of the "rocking hull" of communicative rationality? It is, of course, the truth of practical reason, now strengthened and fortified by means of a universal neopragmatics. Truth is reached by the community of inquirers through free, rational, and undistorted appeal, not by coercion through the stipulation of first principles. It is true that reason is thoroughly historical and functions within highly delimited circumstances; nonetheless, historical, situated reason must redeem its assertions by public warrants. Only public redemption adequately allows the distinction between warranted claims and acts of ideological consciousness. This view does not provide us with the inappropriate security of transcendental metaphysics and of referentialism, but neither does it lapse into anarchism or Gnosticism. The pragmatic understanding of truth, subtly structured as communicative praxis, has the further advantage of fundamental congruency with the aims of egalitarian liberal democracies increasingly heterogeneous in population, views, customs, and mores. Defenders of neopragmatism appear to foster the creation of multivalent cultures of tolerance, while those expressing doubt about practical forms of truth seem to be *a priori* opposed to the inclusive ideals of liberal democracy itself.

What are the theological implications of this move toward pragmatic and praxis-oriented models of truth? Why have many theologians found them useful?[28] One reason for the attraction to Habermas's discourse theory is that it may be marshaled to heal the split between the public and private domains. Religion, it is argued, should not be excluded from the marketplace, the sphere of public interchange. Ghettoizing religion serves neither

---

27 Habermas, *Postmetaphysical Thinking*, 144.

28 Essays illustrating the influence of Habermas include David Tracy, "Beyond Foundationalism and Relativism," in *On Naming the Present*, 131–39 (Maryknoll, NY: Orbis, 1994), and Paul Lakeland, *Theology and Critical Theory: The Discourse of the Church* (Nashville: Abingdon, 1990). Other theologians strongly influenced by Habermas may be found in *Habermas, Modernity, and Public Theology* and in *Habermas et la théologie*, ed. E. Arens, trans. D. Trierweiler (Paris: Cerf, 1993).

believers nor the societies in which they are citizens. How can religion remain part of the public conversation without demanding that it alone is true and all other "secular" philosophies must yield before it?[29] Can Habermas's communicative praxis give theology a significant role in wider society? Can it help provide a public validation of theology's claims? At first glance, Habermas seems an unlikely ally. Truth, in the ideal-speech situation, amounts to those validity claims that can be cognitively redeemed by public warrants. And there's the rub. To what extent can religion provide public warrants for its claims? Habermas says it cannot do so at all, ironically arguing that it might harm its very essence if it sought this goal.[30] The unavoidable consequence, however, is that religion must be excluded from communal discourse. Religion, with its *a priori* teleological view, cannot be allowed as a player in this discussion because (from the start and according to its very essence) it violates the rules of the game by limiting communicative freedom. This is why, for Habermas, the authority of consensus ethics must now replace the authority of the sacred: "The legitimizing function of religious views of the world is replaced by rationally motivated agreement."[31]

Despite this Habermasian refusal, some theologians seek to show that theology can become a viable player in the larger community of discourse according to neopragmatic rules. David Tracy and Helmut Peukert, for

29 This issue concerns both David Tracy and Richard John Neuhaus. Each seeks to mend the rift between "secular" and "sacred" realms. Tracy does it by adopting *phronēsis* and mutually critical correlation. Only such mutuality (and the abandonment of *a priori* truth claims) allows religion to be taken seriously by the democratic publics of the academy and society. Neuhaus, on the contrary, thinks that religious citizens of the American republic must insist on a public voice and are under no necessity to relinquish their unique truth-claims. Such relinquishment would continue the relegation of religion outside of the "public square" begun in the Enlightenment. Both Tracy and Neuhaus are close to the classical Catholic position of validating at least some of Christianity's truth-claims on the basis of public warrants. For Neuhaus, this involves a turn to the natural law tradition; for Tracy, a turn to discourse theory.

30 "In the Federal Republic of Germany [. . .] it was primarily a group of Catholic theologians who, having always maintained a less troubled relation to the *lumen naturale*, were able to draw upon this tradition [of conversation with the discourses of the humanities and social sciences]. Yet, the more that theology opens itself in general to the discourses of the human sciences, the greater is the danger that its own status will be lost in the network of alternating takeover attempts." See Jürgen Habermas, "Transcendence from Within, Transcendence in this World," in *Habermas, Modernity, and Public Theology*, ed. Browning and Fiorenza, 231.

31 Francis Schüssler Fiorenza, "The Church as a Community of Interpretation," in *Habermas, Modernity, and Public Theology*, ed. Browning and Fiorenza, 70. This point has also been made by William Meyer who concludes that, while Habermas has made some concessions to the existential usefulness of religion, he continues to deny that religion has any cognitive dimension. See "Private Faith or Public Religion? An Assessment of Habermas's Changing View of Religion," *Journal of Religion* 75, no. 3 (1995): 371–91.

example, argue that the critical transformation of society may serve as a public warrant and criterion, validating and redeeming, to some extent, the truth-claims of Christianity. Habermas's theological conversation partners "argue that theology as a critical, practical and public theology is self-confidently theology when it is not authoritarian [. . .] when it is not sectarian but engaged in discursive deliberation about its ethical content and when it advocates a method of critical correlation."[32] Religious and moral traditions are not simply warranted by authoritarian norms, but are validated by their continuing publicly illuminative value. Tracy most clearly represents this position when he argues, like Adorno, for the public and imaginative character of theological truth, claiming that "The truth of religion is, like the truth of its nearest cousin, art, primordially the truth of manifestation."[33] Tracy and others are seeking ontologically appropriate understandings of truth, and compellingly argue that theology cannot remain wedded to veridical notions intrinsically conjoined to discredited and untenable foundationalist ontologies. Christianity, just as existence and thought itself, is radically historical, and it simply excludes itself from democratic, public discourse when it insists on certain first principles that are posited rather than effectively argued for.

On the other hand, it is clear that the turn toward pragmatic notions of truth creates certain tensions. The tradition, as emphasized by Boethius's *Consolation*, distinguished practical from theoretical truth. As Aquinas was to say seven centuries later,

> Truth in the practical intellect is not the same as truth in the speculative intellect as is said in *Ethics* VI (1139A 26). For the true in the speculative intellect arises from the conformity of the intellect with the thing [. . .]. The true in the practical intellect arises from conformity with rectified appetite, a conformity which has no place in necessary things which do

---

32 Francis Schüssler Fiorenza, "Introduction: A Critical Reception for Practical Public Theology," in *Habermas, Modernity, and Public Theology*, ed. Browning and Fiorenza, 15.

33 Tracy, *Dialogue with the Other* (Grand Rapids: Eerdmans Publishing; Leuven: Peeters, 1990), 43. Stanley Rosen disapprovingly notes (in a nontheological context) that "there can be no doubt that the thesis that art is worth more than the truth is the dominant principle of our time." See *Hermeneutics as Politics*, 138. But this, I think, is to miss the point. What is being argued is that the truth of art illuminates and reveals an *appropriate* understanding of what truth is. Of course, the enduring theological issue is the potential reduction of truth to its imaginative, creative, and symbolic dimensions. Adorno sought to redeem the modern pathologies of positivism and dominative reason by turning toward art. But is esthetic redemption appropriate for theology? Is there necessarily in theology a representative and referential dimension which is not intrinsic to art? And must all non-artistic notions of truth lead to instrumental and reificatory thinking?

not come about because of the human will, but only in contingent things [. . .]. Therefore, only a virtue of practical intellect is concerned with contingent things.[34]

Of course, postmodern thinkers will logically argue that Aquinas, like Aristotle on whom he is commenting, is working with an inappropriate understanding of ontology, one virtually ignorant of the radical contingencies of historicity, leading inexorably to an inappropriate understanding of truth. For theology, however, the crucial issues remain: Is revealed truth given to us? To what extent is it a human construction? Can revelation be justified by the process of public and practical argumentation? Can its truth-claims be validated by universal consensus? Habermas's own words should give theologians pause: "As seen by [. . .] metaphysics, the procedural concept of communicative reason is too weak because it discharges everything that has to do with content into the realm of the contingent and even allows one to think of reason itself as having contingently arisen."[35] Certainly, most theologians would claim that theology involves both construction and constraint; it is work of imagination and description. But how are the two conjoined? As noted above, practical reason deals with things that admit of being otherwise. Are all elements of revelation to be placed in this category? Are all matters of content now discharged, as Habermas says, into the realm of the contingent? Can the turn to communicative praxis and practical reason sustain the referential dimension of Christian truth?

It is no surprise that Catholic thinkers have generally allied themselves philosophically with some form of foundationalism and referentialism, even when not adhering to the conceptual apparatus of the Aristotelian-Thomistic tradition. This can be said of Kuhn and Möhler, Newman and Blondel, Rousselot and Maréchal. More recently, Robert Sokolowski avoids Thomistic notions of abstraction and conceptualization while arguing phenomenologically for our ability to "know essentials." Sokolowski advances the position, taken by several nuanced realist thinkers, that the subject *is* an essential player in noetic acts and necessarily affects the known by virtue of an entire preunderstanding, a welter of suppositions, background beliefs,

---

34 *Summa theologiae*, I-II, q. 57, a.5, ad 3, cited by Ralph McInerny, *Aquinas on Human Action* (Washington, DC: The Catholic University of America Press, 1992), 155. This recognition of absolute historical contingency fuels Gadamer's universalization of *phronēsis* as the truth proper to all knowing.

35 *Postmetaphysical Thinking*, 116.

and ideological commitments. The subject is anything but a *tabula rasa* who, in Lonergan's terms, naively "takes a look" at the world. Rather, "natural wholes [essentials] are displayed to us in the *thick of human custom, making and culture*."[36] But this is simply to note that the world as known is always already mediated by the knower.

This echoes what Chenu, Bouillard, de Lubac, and others argued at the time of the *nouvelle théologie*, that the truth of revelation inexorably follows the law of the Incarnation. God's truth comes to us in the midst of, and embedded within, sociological, anthropological, and cultural horizons; all truth, human and divine, is mediated by historical norms. Still, the fundamental question persists: Amid this web of beliefs and network of contingencies, are essences still displayed to us? The answer to this question separates the two notions of truth under discussion. For one, historicity is so determinative of both knower and known that knowledge is fundamentally, if not entirely, a human construct. The agent is the grasper, molder, shaper, former, and creator. For the other, a constructive dimension of knowing is acknowledged (and not simply admitted but welcomed as ontologically productive), but it is further claimed that the human noetic faculty is connaturally proportioned to the *logos* structure of the world. Inasmuch as the intellect is *capax mundi*, it can and does represent existing states of affairs accurately.

The theological concern raised by theories of communicative praxis is that revelation is now seemingly discovered by the consensual community of discourse, attenuating at least to some extent the idea that revelation is primarily the Word of God, the gift of God to the Church. More seriously, emphasis is no longer placed on the substantial continuity of God's revelatory Word because such material continuity can only be sustained by a referential notion of perduring truth.[37] Of course, in theories resting on practical rationality, a new understanding of revelation emerges, one that is deeply informed by contingency and historicity. Jack Bonsor offers a good example of this understanding of revelation and the truth proper to

---

36 Sokolowski, "Knowing Essentials," 696 (emphasis added).

37 On this issue of perduring truth, note the words of Adolf von Harnack: "A dogma without infallibility means nothing. This was already settled by Luther's position at the Leipzig Disputation, although Luther himself never fully realized the implication of his assertions [. . .]. This is why already in the first edition of my *History of Dogma* I set the fall of dogma in the sixteenth century." Harnack clearly recognizes here that without the Church's ability to teach truth infallibly, dogma always belongs to the reversible matters. See "Erik Peterson's Correspondence with Adolf von Harnack," trans. Michael J. Hollerich, *Pro Ecclesia* 2, no. 3 (1993): 337.

it.[38] Revelation is now highly epiphanic, strongly influenced by Heidegger's dialectic of absence and presence, veiling and unveiling (the etymological meaning of "apocalypse"). The revealed truth emerging is not enduringly descriptive and representational; it is not meant to provide an ontologically truncated immutable Word. One may say that revelation offers insight, but it is insight that always appears in a moment of the historical flux; it cannot be captured or stake a permanent claim to normativity. There is a sense here in which revelation perdures, but the perdurance is of a unique type, formal rather than material in kind. Humanity continues to receive flashes of unveiledness, glimmers of presence. One would be entirely mistaken, however, to insist on historical identity or to reject conflicting claims or descriptions as illogical. Such an approach, once again, is trapped in onto-theology and its parallel misunderstandings.[39] For postmodern theologians, Christians possess texts and symbols that continue to make claims on them and on which they continue to reflect. Different truths and different understandings reveal themselves successively. It is essential to note that one is decidedly not speaking of complementary perspectives, or of simple changes in angle, but of possibly conflicting statements that appear over the course of time.

In this understanding of revelation and the truth proper to it, one clearly sees the influence of Heidegger, with his notion of the "givenness" of Being and the "event" from which it emerges. In the continuing dialectic of presence and absence, of disclosure and hiddenness, the truth of Being is variously given in different epochs. This is precisely what it means to take temporality seriously. The process of giving and withdrawing, mediated by history, does not allow for the kind of material continuity that has been traditionally associated with doctrine. Such continuity relies on discredited notions of both being and truth, with their forgetfulness of historicity and its deeply lethic dimensions. Postmodern theologians argue that an appropriate ontology now demands an apposite theology of revelation. It demands as well a proper understanding of interpretative theory.

---

38 Jack Bonsor, "History, Dogma, and Nature: Further Reflections on Postmodernism and Theology," *Theological Studies* 55, no. 2 (1994): 295–313.

39 One sees here the convergence between the epiphanic understanding of truth and the assertion that the truth proper to art is paradigmatic for the truth status of religious claims.

HERMENEUTICS

If postmodernity affects one's understanding of truth, then it also affects, necessarily and forcefully, one's understanding of textual interpretation. For any hermeneutical theory is a logical corollary of one's (non)foundationalist option. The crux of the matter involves determining interpretative appropriateness in light of our contemporary situation.

The neuralgic issue in the current debate is the status of reconstructive hermeneutical theories. The hallmark of such theories is the claim that texts have a stable and determinate meaning that may be recovered and re-presented by an interpreter (even centuries or millennia later) after proper philological and sociocultural analysis. Traditionally, this understanding was based, even if not always explicitly, on the fundamental unity of human nature perduring across history. A shared ontology or common nature, however understood, grounded a recoverable and representable textual meaning. If, however, as postmodernity claims, there is no fundamental human nature, shared essence, transcendental consciousness, or invariant structure of knowing, then one cannot speak of a common matrix for reconstructive thought. Without some universal nature "rooting" objectivist hermeneutics, one cannot logically defend a stable and recoverable textual meaning.

Reconstructive understanding is the basis of the form/content or context/content distinction so popular in theology and in other disciplines. This approach holds that one may distinguish the meaning or content of a text from its particular context or form. It is to recognize that authors may say the same things (with nuances, of course) within a variety of expressions, systems, and schemas. It is not to claim that language is simply a shell; it is to recognize a distinction between meaning and expression.[40] The form/content distinction rests on the ability of the interpreter to understand an "alien" text, to reproduce its meaning (with the help of proper tools), and then to recast the meaning in another form or context. A determinate meaning will be preserved, even if this meaning is re-expressed in another notional system.

Theologically, the context/meaning distinction has its roots in Gardeil, Bouillard, Chenu, de Lubac, and Balthasar. It was particularly helpful in trying to free theology from the univocal method imposed by *Aeterni Patris.*

---

40 As William Hill remarks, "Truth and its form (*vêtement*) or expression can never be separated— as if one could peel away the outer appearance and discover a disembodied and transcultural truth at its core. But the impossibility of a real separation is no denial of grounds for a *distinction.*" See *The Three-Personed God* (Washington, DC: The Catholic University of America Press, 1982), 246.

By emphasizing a stability of content within a variety of conceptual forms, theologians could legitimately argue for the material transmission of the selfsame deposit of faith while simultaneously pressing the case for a new dialogue with phenomenology, Marxism, and transcendental thought. A stable and perduring doctrinal meaning was combined with some degree of fluidity and flexibility in formulation and expression. Ultimately, this viewpoint was officially sanctioned by Vatican II and by subsequent magisterial documents. It has been equally endorsed by Lonergan, Rahner, Kasper, and Dulles.[41]

Postmodern hermeneutics, of course, finds fault with all of the foregoing. Reconstructive interpretation, like the realist and referential notion of truth, is inexorably linked to a discredited and truncated ontology.[42] Heidegger has deconstructed any notion of enduring nature or transcendental structure by unveiling the epistemologically buried horizon of historicity enveloping all being and thought. He has revealed the depths to which *Dasein* is always already constituted and constructed by preunderstanding, linguisticality, thrownness, and finitude. Gadamer has extended the Heideggerian project to interpretative theory, showing how the previously forgotten "worldhood of the world" and the fundamental matrix of temporality are now essentially constitutive of all textual readings. A different kind of continuity than the type established by "Romantic" hermeneutics must now be found.[43]

[41] Bernard Lonergan, *Doctrinal Pluralism*, 10–11, 44–45; *Method in Theology* (London: Darton, Longman, and Todd, 1971), 324–26; Walter Kasper, *Theology and Church*, trans. Margaret Kohl (Chestnut Ridge, NY: The Crossroad Publishing Company, 1989), 144–45; Avery Dulles, *The Craft of Theology* (Chestnut Ridge, NY: The Crossroad Publishing Company, 1992), 108. For Karl Rahner, see the essays cited in note 16. Rahner is extremely nuanced when endorsing the form/content distinction, emphasizing its epistemological difficulties and the friction likely to occur when new formulas are advanced.

[42] Joseph Dunne rightly identifies the basis of the criticism: "But this critical assumption [of reconstructive hermeneutics] was usually buttressed by another more affirmative one which provided an escape from the flux of history onto the *terra firma* of a kind of metaphysical psychology. This psychological element in nineteenth-century hermeneutics postulated 'human nature as the unhistorical substratum of its theory of understanding.'" See Dunne, *Back to the Rough Ground: "Phronesis" and "Techne" in Modern Philosophy and in Aristotle* (Notre Dame: University of Notre Dame Press, 1993), 108. Dunne is citing Gadamer, *Truth and Method*, trans. and ed. Garrett Barden and John Cumming (New York: Seabury Press, 1975), 258.

[43] So Gadamer says that "Romantic hermeneutics had taken homogeneous human nature as the unhistorical substratum of its theory of understanding and hence had freed the con-genial interpreter from all historical conditions." See *Truth and Method*, 2nd rev. ed., trans. Joel Weinsheimer and Donald G. Marshall (New York: Continuum, 1993), 290. Gadamer, and now others in his wake, repeatedly use the label "Romantic" in order to identify certain nineteenth century

Building on Heidegger's insights, Gadamer rejects both the form/content and understanding/application distinctions of traditional hermeneutical theory. Both distinctions assume the possibility of reconstructive interpretation, a strategy necessarily rooted in some type of foundationalist ontology. But such an interpretative theory fails woefully to understand the deep lethic consequences of historicity. This is one reason why "tradition" is so central to Gadamer's thought. Having rejected foundationalist ontology, he must now uncover some other form of continuity that successfully avoids random pluralism and hermeneutical anarchy. He turns to the Hegelian ontologization of history and the "fusion of horizons" as a way of rescuing historical identity. The unity now established is quite different from any classical and inappropriate notion of material identity; it is rather a formal, historical continuity which allows Gadamer simultaneously to defend the importance of tradition and a wide plurality of textual readings.[44]

The triumph of Gadamerian hermeneutics in philosophical and theological circles has been so thorough and convincing that today hermeneutics is frequently spoken of as a replacement for metaphysics and epistemology. What is attractive about Gadamer's hermeneutical theory? In the first place, he properly centralizes Heidegger's attempt to exhume the *Lebenswelt* from the obsequies pronounced by neo-Kantian transcendental philosophy. No naïve positivism, bloodless transcendentalism, or abstract conceptualism could obstruct Heidegger's retrieval of the starkly tenebrous dimensions of historicity. Gadamer brought the full weight of Heidegger's ideas to interpretative theory, properly employing them to unmask hermeneutical positivism, with its exaltation of subjective self-annihilation. Second, Gadamer exposed in a new way the impossibility of reconstructing and interpreting texts apart from the mediation of personal subjectivity. The interpreting agent emerges from the nexus of history and language with a contextual rationality, an embedded subjectivity, and an ideologically saturated perspective. Interpretation, then, is never simply repetition; it is always and everywhere production and creation. Third, Gadamer maintains the axial

---

theories accenting psychological empathy with the author. But "Romantic" is a misleading term and unnecessarily limits the scope of the tradition that Gadamer seeks to overturn. This wider reality might better be named "reconstructive" or "objectivist."

44 This turn to Hegel undergirds John Caputo's argument that Gadamer has domesticated Heidegger, burying the latter's most radical insights. See Caputo, "Gadamer's Closet Essentialism," in *Dialogue and Deconstruction: The Gadamer-Derrida Encounter*, ed. Diane P. Michelfelder and Richard E. Palmer (Albany: SUNY Press, 1989), 258–64.

nature of tradition, but the kind of tradition affirmed superseded a stolid traditionalism that forestalls growth, change, and development.

To classical theological thought, postmodern hermeneutics presents a persistent and troubling challenge. Once the deconstruction of foundationalist ontology is accepted as demonstrated, certain conclusions inevitably follow. One such conclusion is the denial of the intelligibility of the form/content distinction, the interpretative path undergirding the magisterium's view of theological pluralism, inculturation, and bilateral ecumenical agreements.[45] In all cases, it is claimed, there is an identity of content that may be reconstructed, transmitted from age to age, and then re-contextualized and re-expressed in a way that, while certainly allowing for new insights, formulas, and perspectives, also preserves the essential content of the original meaning. Postmodern thought, of course, regards such an approach as philosophically naïve. The context/meaning distinction, with its corollaries of reconstruction and preservative re-expression, is only viable within the presumption of a foundationalist ontology. But if such an ontology is unsustainable, what hermeneutical theory is now appropriate?

Postmodern theologians do not speak of an identity of meaning that persists through the ages; they speak rather of an identity of classical texts and symbols that, in their polyvalent and historical character, open themselves to reflection and interpretation from epoch to epoch. Bonsor, for example, rejects the form/content distinction, in which Christians affirm the same content (although expressed in a variety of forms and theologies), in favor of an identity of the enduring gospel symbols that open themselves to fresh readings in every age.[46] The classical Christological dogmas are reflections on Jesus and on gospel texts. The Nicene and Chalcedonian definitions present Christ in a particular way, and this way may still make an enduring claim on us. The meaning of the dogma, however, is not irreversible, nor does it preclude other meanings, even contradictory ones. To say otherwise would be to misunderstand the hermeneutical enterprise by

---

45 I have argued elsewhere that a study of the *Acta Synodalia* of Vatican II shows clearly that the form/content approach undergirds the type of theological pluralism sanctioned by the council. See *Revelation and Truth*, 166–78.

46 Jack Bonsor, *Athens and Jerusalem* (New York: Paulist Press, 1993), 169. On the issue of enduring symbols giving rise to a plurality of readings, see also David Tracy, *The Analogical Imagination* (Chestnut Ridge, NY: The Crossroad Publishing Company, 1981), 319–29; 372–86. The inadequacy of the form/content distinction is also alluded to by Tracy in his "Evil, Suffering, Hope: The Search for New Forms of Contemporary Theodicy," *Proceedings of the Catholic Theological Society of America* 50 (1995): 26.

ignoring the consequences of temporality that have enmeshed the notions of truth and interpretation. Bonsor can conclude logically that the dogmas of the early Church do not grasp reality itself.[47] Such a position displays, with absolute seriousness, the consequences of radical historicity and the web of contingencies and beliefs in which human life, thinking, and discourse arise. As such, it allows for a much greater plurality in terms of textual meanings and the truths arising from them.

One may legitimately harbor reservations about the theological hermeneutics of postmodernity. Does its rejection of the form/content distinction issue in such wide pluralism that the unity and identity of the evangelical and creedal structure of the Church is now untracked? Does its tendency toward unlimited pluralism make it difficult, if not impossible ultimately, to defend the uniqueness of the salvific mission of Jesus Christ? At the same time, postmodern thought applies appropriate theoretical pressure to any facile understanding of the context/meaning distinction. Rahner has argued elegantly and convincingly that both the magisterium and theologians make things too easy for themselves when they invoke this distinction apart from the deep epistemological problems attending it.[48] What is the form and what is the content? How are these known? Is the distinction surgically precise? Any subtle and refined sense of interpretation knows how difficult these questions are. One certainly cannot speak of a stable content as a kind of ideal form residing apart from the deep and creative influences of theological authorship, of the social location and the varying cultural spheres that profoundly and productively influence all thought.

True theological authorship, as well as authentic pluralism, necessarily results in new insights and allows for the organic and architectonic growth of tradition. Reconstructive hermeneutics need not and should not result in unimaginative immobilism. Properly understood, it sanctions a true surplus of textual meaning, a legitimate "undecideability," for fresh perspectives always permit (indeed, demand) Christian symbols to yield features and dimensions not previously seen. Objectivist hermeneutics should not be understood, then, as iterative repetition, even if such were possible.[49] Rec-

---

47 Bonsor, "History, Dogma, and Nature," 308.

48 See, for example, "*Mysterium Ecclesiae*," 151.

49 One may examine with interest the debates at Vatican I as that council gradually became aware of the development of doctrine. The council turned to Vincent of Lérins who escapes the antiquarianism mistakenly assigned to him by the *semper, ubique et ab omnibus*. To the question of his opponents, *Nullusne progressus in ecclesia Christi?*, Vincent answers, *Habeatur plane*

ognizing the ontologically productive effects of historicity means affirming unhesitatingly not only the ministerial task of the interpreter, but the creative mission as well.[50] Can the form/content approach, with its decided emphasis on congruency with tradition, sustain the notion of doctrinal development and unfolding revelation demanded by temporality? Postmodernity doubts that it can and sees it as entailing not only an outdated ontology but an outmoded semiotics as well.

LANGUAGE

The influence of postmodern thought on contemporary theories of language finds paradigmatic expression in the work of Jacques Derrida.[51] For Derrida and postmodernity generally, the central linguistic issue is this: What is the status of signifiers? Implicitly questioned here is the classical claim that the meaningfulness of representational language is guaranteed by the intelligibility of the cosmos, a cosmos that is proportioned to and graspable by the human intellect. Traditionally, the semiotic sign has been understood as the sensible representation of the intelligible, the sign now presencing the absent. Derrida's entire project amounts to reversing this understanding by loosening the space between the representable and linguistic signification. He argues that the conventional view of language is ultimately undergirded by an untenable presumption: the *logos* structure of reality. But this supposition fails to realize that the architecture of the cosmos is beyond us, that the world always escapes the text. The supersession of linguistic representationalism and ostensive definition is demanded by the "chaotic" dimen-

---

et maximus. Invoking his "second rule," Vincent notes that true progress must always be *in eodem sensu eademque sententia* with what the Church has believed. Johann E. Kuhn, Möhler's colleague at Tübingen, presciently saw in Vincent the resources to begin meeting the challenges of history, calling Vincent's *Commonitorium* a *goldenes Büchlein*. See Josef R. Geiselmann, *Die lebendige Überlieferung als Norm des christlichen Glaubens* (Freiburg: Herder, 1959). For conciliar and postconciliar discussions about Vincent's hermeneutics in service to pluralism, see Thomas G. Guarino, "Vincent of Lérins and the Hermeneutical Question," *Gregorianum* 75, no. 3 (1994): 491–523.

50 The proper goal of theological hermeneutics should approximate Blaise Pascal's maxim: A pluralism that cannot be integrated into unity is chaos; unity unrelated to pluralism is tyranny. See *Pensées* (Paris: Charpentier, 1861), 388–89.

51 Although Gadamer and Habermas have written extensively on language, Derrida's work remains exemplary. An excellent summary of his thought and its theological implications may be found in Walter Lowe, *Theology and Difference: The Wound of Reason* (Bloomington: Indiana University Press, 1993); also useful is John Caputo, "The Good News about Alterity: Derrida and Theology," *Faith and Philosophy* 10, no. 4 (1993): 453–70.

sion of life, its otherness. Traditional semiotic systems, like instrumental rationality, serve to level the heteronomous Other. Countering this tendency, Derrida speaks of the "play of the signifiers" that simultaneously "refer and defer." The world cannot be captured; it defies homogenization by the flattening conceptualism of representational language.[52]

In some ways, all of Derrida's work should be seen as a rhetorical trick with a deadly serious philosophical point. He champions the deconstruction of classical semiotics because linguistic entropy is necessary to allow an ontologically appropriate understanding of language to appear. The world's otherness and *différe(a)nce* will only emerge when we acknowledge the limits of representational thought. Conceptualization is "the first falsehood" for Derrida precisely because it seeks to marginalize the Other; it falsifies and excludes the particular, the different, the "accidental." Postmodernity, on the other hand, searches for rupture and breach; it shows that our semiotic systems fail to see the polyvalence of the world beyond the logocentrism of the text. In place of representation, the playful character of language is lionized. Difference, rather than unity, is raised to the prime hermeneutical principle.

Derrida's understanding of language has a determinate logic. If the representational force of linguistic and semiotic systems can be deconstructed, then the *logos* structure of reality, and ultimately the one who undergirds this cosmos, the Transcendental Signified, may be deconstructed as well. For Derrida, God has become the ultimate totalizing agent, the Signified who unites the metaphysical idea of cosmic intelligibility with the ostensive view of language. It is the Transcendental Signified, especially as exemplified by the Logos, that weds Western representational thought to signifiers. The Logos becomes *the* signifier of the Absent (now) Present because in the Incarnate Logos we have the presenced absence of God himself. In Christ, the signified is perfectly expressed in the signifier, divinely undergirding of course the idea of semiotic representation.[53] Derrida can only overcome

---

52 This point is argued, implicitly or explicitly, in all of Derrida's works. His comments on language are very clear in *Positions*, trans. Alan Bass (Chicago: University of Chicago Press, 1981) and in *The Post Card: From Socrates to Freud and Beyond*, trans. Alan Bass (Chicago: University of Chicago Press, 1987).

53 As Dupré says, "Jacques Derrida has pointed out how a systematic and historical link exists between a theology of the Logos and the intrinsic meaningfulness of language. Only when spoken words partake in that divine Word through which the Creator secures the essential intelligibility of his creation can we safely presume that they intrinsically correspond to the very nature of the real." See *Passage to Modernity*, 104, citing Derrida, *Of Grammatology*, trans. G. Chakravorty (Baltimore: Johns Hopkins University Press, 1976), 13–14.

this tradition by denying that the sign is a signifier for the absent present. Linguistic deconstruction will release texts from any vestige of logocentric reproduction and authorial control. The metaphysical link between the intelligible and the sensible (the signified of the absent now present) will be severed. This will free language from its metaphysical prison of mechanistic representation. Heidegger's original philosophical project is now extended to the deconstruction of onto/semio-theo-logy.

From a theological viewpoint, postmodernity's desire to deconstruct linguistic imagism has a robust affinity with several central themes. Has not twentieth-century theology sought to recover much of the apophatic tradition that was lost in the conceptualizing Thomism hegemonic since the days of Cajetan and Suarez? Does not the theologian, on reading Derrida, naturally recall the entire apophatic tradition pervading Catholic thought and spirituality? Is it not true that Catholicism has been very guarded about the rigidity of semiotic systems in the matter of language about God?[54] Insofar as postmodernity seeks to relieve us from pallid universalism and monistic conceptualism, theology should be grateful. For Christianity announces as true that there can be no language about God without qualifications, no reference without difference.

Of course, questions about the postmodern view of language are equally apparent. If the *logos* structure of reality is undermined or denied, then how does theology exist at all? How far can the difference between the signified and the signifier be stretched without abandoning referentialism in its entirety? Is theology served by the linguistic entropy that signals the end of representation? Derrida, naturally, does not see those questions as problems; he rejoices in the concerns they raise. But what of Catholic theology? The notable work of Jean-Luc Marion helps to outline the crucial issues regarding postmodernity and theological language. Marion's clearly stated goal is to out-difference Heidegger's ontological difference, to show that "being" language has no place whatsoever in the question of God. The celebrated Heideggerian distinction between Being and beings serves simply as a negative propaedeutic to thinking about divine life. In service to protecting transcendent Otherness, Marion's major work, *God Without Being*, is largely

---

54 Feminist theologians have further explored this apophaticism in order to rethink the kind of names properly predicated of the Godhead. See Elizabeth A. Johnson, *She Who Is: The Mystery of God in Theological Feminist Discourse* (Chestnut Ridge, NY: The Crossroad Publishing Company, 1992), and Gail Ramshaw, *God Beyond Gender: Feminist Christian God-Language* (Minneapolis: Fortress, 1995).

devoted to a screed against the screen of Being. He illustrates the problem of "being" language by invoking the difference between the idol and the icon. Borrowing from Husserl's intentionality analysis, Marion argues that the idol fills the breadth of our gaze, offering us pure presence without the transparency of absence. The icon, however, masks and obscures as well as "presences;" it challenges the viewer but is never exhausted by the viewer's subjectivity.[55] Marion's sensitivity to postmodern concerns naturally influences his understanding of theological language. The traditional language of Being, in reference to God, he calls idolic, not iconic. Such discourse allows God, but not Gxd (the truly Other) to appear. The thought of Being cannot properly mediate the heteronomy of Gxd. It keeps him tethered to the conceptual idolatry of the onto-theo-logical tradition that seeks to take God in its grasp, defining and measuring him. The classical tradition has, unwittingly, made God the "divine prisoner of Being." But Gxd is the Giver beyond the ontological difference. He gives the Being/beings distinction, but he himself cannot be dominated by Being or placed within its framework.[56] It is no surprise, then, that Marion expresses Derrida-like reservations about signifiers, especially when applied to God. Not wanting to follow Derrida entirely, however, Marion turns to Pseudo-Dionysius, Meister Eckhard, and the mystical tradition in order to explain the type of intelligibility proper to theology. The inadequacy of the language of Being forces a cathartic turn to the more poetic forms of agapic love. Such a shift successfully subverts the enclosing dimensions of ontology. Rather than freezing the idolic gaze, the agapic turn yields an iconic attitude, recognizing the Gxd who is both ungraspable and unknowable.

What Marion ultimately offers is a kind of deconstruction of attempts to name God, a project undertaken precisely in service to God's Otherness. We move very close to the heart of his central theological concern when he says that true theology "will submit all of its concepts [. . .] to a 'destruction' by the doctrine of divine names, at the risk of having to renounce any status as a conceptual 'science' in order, *decidedly nonobjectivating, to praise by infinite petitions.*"[57] Marion logically roots theology in mysticism rather than

---

55 Marion, *God Without Being*, trans. Thomas Carlson (Chicago: University of Chicago Press, 1991), 17, 27.

56 Marion, *God Without Being*, 104–6.

57 Marion, *God Without Being*, 81 (emphasis added). This move ultimately portends the "reduction" of analogical predication, as well as the cognitive penetration offered by it, to doxology. But once theology cuts its ties to referential language theory, two possible choices emerge:

in any kind of conceptual logic. Such a move is necessary inasmuch as theology has "nothing like an *object*, theology having none of the characteristics of scientificity, and especially not its objectivity."[58]

From one point of view, Marion's rich work reminds us, unceasingly, of God's alterity. He consistently "presences" the "hidden God," the God beyond all representations. He deconstructs the provincial God captured by determinate logic. The Derrida-inspired neologism "Gxd" is meant to alert us precisely to the irreducible divine heteronomy beyond human control. Marion rightly states that "Revelation [. . .] can neither be confused with nor subjected to the philosophical thought of 'God' as being."[59] His project, of course, is to defend and advance the deep apophaticism of the tradition; the "divine mysteries" cannot be captured and encompassed by any conceptual system. With Heidegger, then, Marion condemns any attitude of theological "objectification" as particularly inappropriate when speaking of the "hidden things

---

either an infinite play of ideas on which there can be no limits, or a Barthian-like, nominalistic assertion of the Scriptures (or, on the Catholic side, of the formal authority of Scripture and tradition as interpreted by the Church). Marion has no interest in the first, Derridean option. Necessarily, then, he veers toward the second possibility as illustrated by his claim that only the bishop properly merits the title of theologian (153). Of course, in one sense this is true, for bishops are indeed the paradigmatic teachers of the faith. But this spills over into a fideistic assertion of episcopal authority, severed from the right-reason tradition, when the intelligible infrastructure is removed from properly theological statements.

58 Marion, *God Without Being*, 163. Marion is here emphasizing the gift-like nature of revelation, its otherness, the fact that humanity does not control or measure it. This he clearly opposes to a kind of "anthropological" theology dominant since Schleiermacher. Such emphasis explains why David Tracy, in his laudatory "Foreword" to *God without Being*, says that Marion is more clearly a *Communio*-oriented Catholic rather than a *Concilium*-oriented one (xv). To a certain extent this is true; however, it should be remembered that Balthasar (the paradigmatic *Communio* Catholic) criticized Barth for failing to see that Catholicism's interest in philosophy, especially the analogy of being, was for the sake of maintaining the rational infrastructure of revelation. Consequently, Balthasar, despite clear and deep sympathies with Barth, resisted the kind of fideism characteristic of Barth's (and now Marion's) thought. In fact, Balthasar comes much closer to Tracy's correlationist option, but with a clearer priority extended to the *fides quaerens intellectum*.

59 Marion, *God Without Being*, 52. Of course, for most theologians, this is a truism, and its wide acceptance is the basis for the severe critiques Marion received, largely emanating from French Thomists (see note 62). When Marion continues, "The Gxd who reveals himself has nothing in common [. . .] with the 'God' of the philosophers, of the learned and, eventually, of the poet," he comes very close to positing a chasm between the two orders of creation and salvation. But is this disjunction between reason and faith needed to protect God's otherness? Marion's skewing of the nature-grace distinction is further cemented by his benign appraisal of Heidegger's comment that "each concept, in order to appear authentically theological, must measure its essential disparity with the 'pre-Christian *Dasein*'" (67, citing *Phänomenologie und Theologie*, 63). Is an *essential* disparity needed in fact? Or has Rahner taught us something about the universality of transcendental revelation?

of God." Such condemnation is ironically lurking behind Marion's positive comments on transubstantiation, which, for all of its Aristotelian apparatus, nonetheless properly protects the "otherness" of God's presence in the Eucharistic elements. Divine alterity is far better guarded by the medieval synthesis than, for example, by the Hegelian understanding of God residing in the consciousness of the community. One approach allows the full heteronomy of God, the Giver of the Gift to appear; the other quickly descends to an idolic anthropocentrism. Only the medieval achievement allows the "shock" of revelation to appear in all its uniqueness.[60]

Marion's bold effort to introduce dimensions of postmodernity into reflection on theological language also raises problems. Most importantly, Marion underestimates, to a significant degree, the extent to which the tradition was on guard about excessive presence. All are aware of theology's long history of attempts (not always successful) to avoid monism, univocity, and conceptual idolatry, to shun reference without difference when speaking of God. One may clearly identify a palpable "idoloclastic" fervor in the tradition that Marion does not acknowledge. Examples of the classical negative way are easy to multiply. One need only note the stringent apophaticism of the Greek Fathers, perhaps paradigmatically represented by the *Theological Orations* of Gregory Nazianzen, who seeks to undermine the semirationalism of the Eunomians while still maintaining a positive cognitive content to revelation. Or recall the guarded reserve of St. Thomas who opens the *Summa* by questioning his entire project with a citation from Ecclesiasticus 3:22: *Altiora te ne quaesieris*.[61] Further, the tradition vigorously affirmed, in a way overlooked by *God without Being*, the claim that God is beyond common being. Several commentators on Marion's book were rankled by his misplaced charges regarding the "conceptualism" of the tradition, pointing out that Aquinas claimed that no created form can represent the divine essence for God cannot be circumscribed by a determinate

---

60 Marion, *God Without Being*, 168–69.

61 Further examples may be found in Deirdre Carabine, "*Apophasis* East and West," *Recherches de théologie ancienne et medievale* 55 (1988): 5–29; also in G. L. C. Frank, "The Incomprehensibility of God in the Theological Orations of St. Gregory the Theologian," *Greek Orthodox Theological Review* 39 (1994): 95–107. The apophaticism of the tradition is vigorously defended by Yves Floucat, "L'être de Dieu et l'onto-théo-logie," *Revue thomiste* 95, no. 3 (1995): 437–84. Derrida, unsurprisingly, argues that the *via negativa* remains entirely within the confines of the ontotheological tradition. See "How to Avoid Speaking: Denials," in *Languages of the Unsayable: The Play of Negativity in Literature and Literary Theory*, ed. S. Budick and W. Iser, 3–70 (New York: Columbia University Press, 1989).

perfection.[62] Of course, a major task of Thomistic studies in this century has been to recover the grand apophatic strategies of Aquinas: the *res/modus* distinction; the *per prius* predication of perfections to the Godhead; and the polemic against the *plura ad unum* type of analogy. All serve to avoid the subordination of the divine essence to the transcendentals.[63]

It should also be noted that the apophatic dimensions of theology have been well represented in the official statements of the Church. Lateran IV's famous sentence on analogy is well known,[64] but the insistently apophatic features of Vatican I, especially in the conciliar response to the perceived semirationalism of Frohschammer and Günther, have not always been fully appreciated.[65] The Church's traditional understanding of "noematic" apophaticism (the radical incomprehensibility of God occasioned by the infinity of the divine essence) has been complemented by the "noetic" apophaticism of more recent statements. *Mysterium ecclesiae*, of course, acknowledges the historical, sociocultural, and constructive elements affecting the formulation and transmission of revealed truth. The International Theological Commission statement of 1989 made additional progress on this issue, vigorously arguing both for the historical conditioning of doctrinal formulations and for the cognitive limitations imposed by all finite perspectives.

At the same time, the tradition does not wish to loosen the tie between language and God to such an extent that theology descends into equivocity

---

62 *Summa theologiae* I, q. 12, art. 2. This is argued by J. H. Nicolas, "La suprême logique de l'amour et la théologie," *Revue thomiste* 83 (1983): 639–59; also, R. Virgoulay, "Dieu ou l'Être," *Recherches de science religieuse* 72, no. 2 (1984): 163–98. Aquinas himself repeatedly says that we cannot have *quid est* knowledge of God, even in revelation: *per revelationem gratiae in hac vita non cognoscamus de Deo quid est, et sic ei quasi ignoto conjungamur* (*Summa theologiae* I, q. 12, a. 13, ad 1). Since the concept can never yield full quidditative knowledge of God (in Maritain's words, "quidditatively quidditative"), then Aquinas must insist that we are joined to God *quasi ignoto*. At the same time, the judgment attributes created concepts to God by way of the *via negativa et via eminentia*, and these truly give us some insight into the divine essence.

63 For Aquinas's apophatic strategies, see Gregory P. Rocca, "The Distinction between the *Res Significata* and *Modus Significandi* in Aquinas's Theological Epistemology," *The Thomist* 55, no. 2 (1991): 173–97, and "Aquinas on God-Talk: Hovering over the Abyss," *Theological Studies* 54, no. 4 (1993): 641–61. Marion, it should be noted, has started to take the apophaticism of the tradition more seriously subsequent to *God Without Being*, e.g., "Saint Thomas d'Aquin et l'onto-théo-logie," *Revue thomiste* 95, no. 1 (1995): 31–66.

64 *DS* 806.

65 One should note, for example, the firmly apophatic passage of Dei Filius, chapter four: *Divina enim mysteria* [. . .] *ut etiam revelatione tradita et fide suscepta ipsius tamen fidei velamine contecta et quadam quasi caligine obvoluta maneant* [. . .] (*DS* 3016). Several bishops, in fact, were alarmed by this strong emphasis on divine hiddenness. See Thomas G. Guarino, "Vatican I and Dogmatic *Apophasis*," *Irish Theological Quarterly* 61, no. 1 (1995): 70–82.

or agnosticism. Aquinas, for example, argued that names are not only causal, as with Maimonides, but may be predicated of God formally and substantially.[66] Thomas agreed with Pseudo-Dionysius on the priority of the apophatic, given the radical incommensurability between our cognitive capacity and the goal of our quest. But while borrowing from this line of reasoning, Aquinas significantly tempered its excesses. One author notes that

> Aquinas rejects [. . .] an outright negativism or agnostic attitude. The aim and intention of his negative theology is eminently positive and requires a positive foundation [citing *De potentia*, 7.5]. [. . .] So, referring to the *Mystical Theology* where Dionysius states that we are united to God *to pantelos de agnosto*—translated by Eriugena and Sarracenus as *OMNINO autem ignoto*—Aquinas modifies the negative tone: *QUASI ignoto coniungimur*. A similar correction is introduced in the *Summa Theologiae* [citing *Summa theologiae* I, q. 12, a. 13]. Such a modification indicates an important reappraisal of the role of negative theology and presents a more balanced theory of our knowledge of God.[67]

Jean-Luc Marion, with his concern for the conceptual reification and idolic tendencies within the tradition, invites us to examine carefully our linguistic usage. He offers a salutary warning that deserves repeating: To write theology is to deal with the Other, not the same. Theology has a natural congruency with postmodern anxiety about naively referential semiotic systems. Willingly it speaks of the "deferring" character of theological signs and the "undecideability" of language. At the same time, only a qualified appropriation of postmodern thought on the nature and function of signifiers seems called for. Marion minimizes the extent to which the tradition has already understood and defended the surplus of intelligibility proper to the Godhead, while still preserving a positive moment within revelation. Must language be completely nonobjectifying to protect God's otherness? To claim that predication must yield to praise appears to limit theological

---

66 In *Summa theologiae* I, q. 12, a. 1, ad 3, for example, Thomas says, "It does not follow that God cannot in any way be known, but that he exceeds all knowledge; there cannot be a comprehensive knowledge of him;" see also *Summa theologiae* I, q. 13, a. 6, c. Further references and commentary may be found in William Hill, *Knowing the Unknown God* (New York: Philosophical Library, 1971), 111–44.

67 Fran O'Rourke, *Pseudo-Dionysius and the Metaphysics of Aquinas* (Leiden: Brill, 1992), 55. He adds that Aquinas writes that God is *super omnia existentia*, not *super omne esse*, for "although God surpasses all existing things, he cannot be said without qualification to transcend *esse* as such, as Dionysius holds, because it is his nature to be *ESSE* itself" (95).

language to its doxological and anagogical dimensions, thereby enervating its cognitive spine. Of course, if one's understanding of revelation is epiphanic, then the status of theological language will be largely symbolic, in the sense of allegorical and suggestive rather than analogical, in the sense of predicable and referential. Such an approach allows a much wider berth for constructive theology than has been the case classically, but it moves in a very different direction than the tradition on the issue of the intelligible yield of theological statements.

CORRELATION

Unlike the four subjects discussed above, postmodern thought has no independent position on the question of correlation. Yet correlation is a good illustration of how postmodern themes affect an important dimension of fundamental theology.[68] I take as prime analogues two schools prominent in contemporary American thought, postliberalism and revisionism, or as they are sometimes called, Yale and Chicago. I argue that, although these schools have been widely perceived as opposed or as taking very different approaches to theology, they are in fact much closer than is usually supposed. The reason for this is that both positions rely heavily on nonfoundationalist themes. The differences between them result from the type of nonfoundationalism each espouses.[69] I will briefly outline these two styles, then offer what I consider a possible third form of correlation.

The term "postliberalism" has been widely associated with the work of George Lindbeck, Ronald Thiemann, and various other representatives of the Yale School. Strongly influenced by nonfoundationalist thinkers such as Quine, Sellars, Geertz, and Wittgenstein, postliberals accept the position that each of us is initiated into a unique form of life and world of discourse. We are largely, perhaps entirely, determined by particular cultural-linguistic

---

68 For an excellent summary of correlational theologies, see Francis Schüssler Fiorenza, "Systematic Theology: Task and Methods," in vol. 1 of *Systematic Theology: Roman Catholic Perspectives*, ed. F. S. Fiorenza and John P. Galvin, 55–61 (Minneapolis: Fortress, 1991). Once again, it will be clear that I am using postmodernity in its "moderate" rather than its "strong" sense.

69 In his fine article "The Postpositivist Choice: Tracy or Lindbeck?" *Journal of the American Academy of Religion* 61, no. 4 (1993): 655–77, Richard Lints says that both authors reject Enlightenment modernity. This is true. However, it should be added that, for different reasons, both reject any foundationalism whatsoever, epistemological or ontological, of classical, medieval, or modern thought. Lindbeck's rejection is based on a concern that Christianity is now judged by external warrants. Tracy rejects foundationalism because he connects it with a metaphysical and transcendental desire to avoid the impact of historicity.

societies. Criteria, warrants, and standards used to judge one community are inapplicable to another. This is precisely the reason we have moved past rationalist modernity to postliberal postmodernity. The result of this kind of nonfoundationalism, with its accent on the regional determination of thought, is the rejection of universals of any kind. The overarching circumscription by socio-cultural-linguistic worlds demands that postliberalism reject the claims of transcendental thinkers (even if they are truly historicized metaphysicians) like Lonergan and Rahner, as well as those advanced by Schleiermacher and all "experiential-expressive" reactions to neo-Kantianism. These different brands of universalism are both philosophically and theologically inappropriate.[70]

Postliberals resist foundationalist, universalizing thought because they see it as a secular Archimedean lever, a purely philosophical warrant by which some thinkers, entirely unconnected with the house of faith, seek to judge Christian beliefs. The gospel now becomes secondary to some prior unity, some foundation, some epistemological or ontological standard to which the Christian message must submit its truth-claims. But cultural-linguistic systems are incommunicable; modes of verification are proper and unique to specific forms of life. Therefore, Christianity is under no obligation to offer public warrants for its claims or to defer to any kind of extra-biblical adjudication.

Questions have quickly arisen: Does the avoidance of public standards of truth and rationality limit theology merely to intrasystemic coherence? Does "intratextual consistency" smack of a fideistic assertion of the truth of Christianity over and against other forms of life and discourse?[71] If cultural webs and networks of belief are such delimiting horizons, how does one find truth or, more accurately, to what kind of truth does one attain?[72] Lindbeck and other postliberals are clear in asserting that Christianity does

---

70 See *The Nature of Doctrine* (Philadelphia: The Westminster Press, 1984), 16–25. A good summary of postliberal theology generally and Lindbeck in particular may be found in John Thiel, *Nonfoundationalism*, 57–63.

71 David Bryant thinks postliberalism inconsistently seeks to affirm both cultural-linguistic determinacy and "an enduring and unchanging structure within the Christian tradition that can anchor Christian identity." Such an assertion of unchanging truth becomes anomalous once the nonfoundationalist move is made. See "Christian Identity and Historical Change: Postliberals and Historicity," *Journal of Religion* 73, no. 1 (1993): 31–41.

72 Lindbeck's palpable hesitancy on the referential character of Christian doctrine has been noted by Alister McGrath, *The Genesis of Doctrine* (Oxford: Blackwell, 1990), 26–32. Along similar lines, Brian Hebblethwaithe criticizes Lindbeck for following too closely the tradition of Kant's constructivism. See "God and Truth," *Kerygma und Dogma* 40, no. 1 (1994): 2–19.

not attain certitude by means of foundationalist first principles nor by consensus arising from the ideal-speech situation. It does so by its proclamation of the truth of the gospel. And Lindbeck and the postliberals see this not as a difficulty, but precisely as a continuation of the classical Protestant project, an extension of Barth's revelational positivism with its disdain for common religious experience and metaphysics. In consequence of these nonfoundationalist principles, postliberalism thinks that Chicago, in search for "common ground" between religion and culture, is "foundationalist." It is so because revisionism submits religious truth claims for redemption and validation by alien and public warrants. But these attempts at mutually critical correlation between the gospel and the world are unacceptable. They represent a capitulation to secular, extrabiblical norms outside of faith, now used inappropriately to justify and adjudicate faith's claims.

Seemingly opposed to postliberalism is revisionist theology, a label widely associated with David Tracy and various other thinkers of the Chicago school. Tracy and the revisionists, as documented in several works, accept the criticisms that postmodernity has leveled at the foundationalist tradition.[73] Like Yale, the Chicago school accepts the nonfoundationalist ontology outlined above, especially the priority of the historical flux and the illusion of searching out immutable first principles or Archimedean points whether metaphysical, transcendental, phenomenological, or empirical. In this respect, revisionist theology is comparable to its postliberal counterpart. The distinction between the two schools is to be found in the fact that revisionist theology thinks all validity claims, including theological ones, must have public attestation; in Habermasian terms, truth claims must be redeemed by publicly available warrants rather than by authoritarian assertion. Such an approach is fueled by the revisionist desire to justify theology in the educational marketplace, to establish the discipline as a legitimate academic and therefore public enterprise. But what must be clearly understood is that this public redemption of truth claims must be nonfoundationalist in kind. It is not a matter of seeking unshakeable foundations or principles, but of pursuing, even if asymptotically, the consensual norms yielded by the ideal-speech situation. In this type of nonfoundationalism, the shuddering contingencies of Habermas's "rocking hull" are not abandoned.

---

73 Such acceptance is clearly stated in Tracy, *Plurality and Ambiguity: Hermeneutics, Religion, Hope* (San Francisco: Harper and Row, 1987), 43, 59, and in "Beyond Foundationalism and Relativism," in *On Naming the Present*. Revisionist theology is discussed by William Placher in *Unapologetic Theology* (Louisville: Westminster/John Knox, 1989), 154–60.

Revisionism further speaks of intertextuality, of a "mutually critical correlation" between Christian theology and other disciplines. Here Tracy and others introduce into the ancient notion of interpenetrative mutuality a deeply apophatic sense. One cannot now take the truth-claims of Christianity to be normative *a priori* as understood by the traditional "faith seeking understanding." If all narratives must be justified by publicly available warrants, then one must argue in the marketplace for the warranted assertability of the Christian faith. Theological truth-claims can only be defended through the consensus arising from the community of inquirers on the basis of publicly adduced and adequately redeemed warrants. Any other approach is simply regarded as untenable special pleading.

One may see here, as with Habermas himself, a true universalism, but a universalism of a very specific type. There is no defense of classical or Enlightenment standards of rationality. Revisionists recognize that all of us are gathered in the rocking hull of contingencies and no one, not even those on the ship of faith, has a secure and privileged position amid the tides of history. Against the accusation that it has abandoned the clarion purity of the gospel for the golden calf of dialogue and mutuality, Chicago counters that the mere assertion of Christianity's truth ghettoizes the faith, excluding it from the larger world of scholarly and humane discourse. In some ways of course, the revisionist school is clearly echoing classical Catholic themes. Its concern with "publicness," for example, with the idea that some evidence for faith is available to all reasonable inquirers, strikes a deeply resonant chord in the Christian tradition. The endorsement of true interchange between theology and the disciplines is firmly rooted in the Catholic understanding of the relationship between faith and reason. In seeking this common language of discourse between Christianity and other narratives, revisionist thought avoids a privatization of faith antithetical to the deepest instincts of Catholic theology.

On the other hand, the reflections of the Chicago school raise questions. To what extent can Christianity justify its truth claims publicly, apart from faith? If revelation and its *a priori* authority is eschewed, or if it can only be redeemed by the community of inquirers, by which criteria are theological claims now authenticated? By liberative praxis? Emancipatory transformation? Reception by the community? Consensus? While one might insist that there is an important and legitimate place for each of these criteria, can any of them be taken as an ultimately justifying warrant? Then, too, what becomes of revelation when one supports the equality of metanarratives in service to mutually critical correlation? If we cannot stipulate that the faith that seeks understanding extends a certain priority to the revealed truth of Christianity, can we ever make any determination about Christianity's ultimate content, message, and final truth? If one may speak typologically (and cautiously) of the postliberal school as tending toward fideism, then Chicago courts the danger of its traditional dyadic counterpart, semirationalism. Such a description finds justification in Habermas's claim that the "good" of religion (its concern with social justice) is cognitively redeemed through discourse ethics. The sacral part of religion (revelation and faith) is either abandoned as meaningless or relegated to the private sphere and thereby disallowed from making public truth claims. Needless to add, Tracy (and Peukert) do not accept Habermas's conclusions, but one wonders if, by allowing him to establish the rules of discussion, they have not already ceded too much ground.

In distinction from both postliberalism and revisionism, I would like to offer a third understanding of correlation. For want of a better term, I have called this position historically conscious foundationalism. With the neo-Barthians, this approach too rejects the "secular" foundationalism that seeks to provide a universally available option outside of faith now serving as the norm for faith's claims. Lindbeck is quite right in saying that Christianity cannot endorse a profane Archimedean norm that judges its truthclaims and acts as an epistemological standard to which Christian faith must adhere. One must equally recognize the palpable dangers of mutually critical correlation. The gospel cannot be understood as simply one voice within a mixture of narratives; nor is the primacy of Christianity based ultimately on its publicly verifiable warrants. At the same time, the revisionists rightly criticize an assertive postliberal fideism divorced from any interchange with secular ideas. By championing critical correlation, they creatively develop and advance the classical interpenetration and cross-fertilization of faith and reason, of theology and the disciplines. Revisionists helpfully resist a mere formal assertion of the truth of Christianity. Such assertion, if unjustified by supplementary public warrants, can easily degenerate into fundamentalism and ideological authoritarianism.

Both schools, then, offer significant insights. However, in their qualified typological reprise of Kierkegaard and Hegel, each misses the third option largely operative in the Christian tradition. In the historically conscious foundationalism proposed here, one must applaud the interdisciplinary approach of the revisionists. A certain critical correlation between Christianity and "secular" wisdom, based on the integrity of nature, even wounded nature, before God, has been classically sanctioned in Catholic theology.

The entire tradition witnesses to this understanding of intertextual mutuality that, at the same time, is always also a symbolic "despoiling of the Egyptians."[74] Secular narratives may, indeed, offer truths that sharpen and illuminate some aspect of Christianity; however, any notion of correlation must proceed from the *a priori* truth of Christian faith.[75] So there cannot be a capitulation to the Habermasian demands of discourse-ethics, thereby implying a complete equality among narratives and a publicly warranted redemption of all truth-claims. This approach violates the primacy of faith and the uniqueness of the knowledge yielded by it.

In this third understanding of correlation, theology is not captive to Enlightenment modernity, either in its foundationalist form or in its contemporary metamorphosis as communicative rationality; nor is it bound to assert fideistically Christianity's truth-claims without the benefit of philosophical supports.[76] With Yale, the normativity of the gospel is proclaimed. However, it is hardly essential that correlation be repudiated to achieve this, or that the primacy of the gospel demand concomitantly a strident either/or. On the contrary, theology and the Church choose and absorb as they wish. In the words of de Lubac, "In the Church, the work of assimilation never ceases and it is never too soon to undertake it!"[77] With revisionism, then, the importance of correlation is championed. However, there is an option in the act of faith such that sheer interpenetrative mutuality between theology and the disciplines is excluded. Historically conscious foundationalism, while always seeking truth from new sources,

---

74 I have treated this theme in "Spoils from Egypt: Contemporary Theology and Nonfoundationalist Thought," *Laval théologique et philosophique* 51, no. 3 (1995): 573–87.

75 Balthasar peerlessly expressed this in a 1946 essay, without shrinking from criticizing the blinkered narrowness of some theologians and church authorities in their allegiance to neoscholasticism. See "On the Tasks of Catholic Philosophy in Our Time," trans. Brian McNeil, *Communio: International Catholic Review*, no. 1 (1993): 147–87.

76 Such is the truth of Adorno's statement: The great Scholastics neither ostracized reason, nor did they absolutize it. What Adorno says of Scholasticism is better said of Catholic theology at large. See *Vernunft und Offenbarung*, cited by Matthew Lamb in "Praxis communicationnelle et théologie par-delá le nihilisme et le dogmatism," in *Habermas et la théologie*, ed. Edmund Arens (Paris: Les Éditions du Cerf, 1993), 123. Ghislain Lafont notes that Catholicism is not easily at home with either of the contemporary tendencies, modernity triumphant or modernity suspected; exaggerated reason and exaggerated doubt are both foreign to it. See his *Histoire théologique de l'Église catholique* (Paris: Cerf, 1994), 382.

77 De Lubac, *The Drama of Atheist Humanism*, trans. E. Riley (London: Sheed and Ward, 1949), vi.

recognizes the ascendancy of the revelatory narrative. And if revelation requires some form of ontological foundationalism for the sake of protecting the continuity and material identity of the gospel message, this too must be reasonably defended. This third form of correlation supersedes the positions of Yale and Chicago by recognizing both the primacy of the gospel and the importance of mutual fertilization. At the same time, it calls into question the accepted presuppositions informing the thought of both Lindbeck and Tracy.[78]

CONCLUSION

In conclusion, we may assess the suitability of postmodern themes for contemporary theological discourse. Does postmodernity, even in its moderate variety, simply open the gates of the City of God to Dionysus? Does it chain theology to Nietzsche, or at least to Heidegger?

Before specifying some problems, I would like to emphasize all that theology can and should learn from postmodern thought. Perhaps most importantly, postmodernity evinces a sense of openness toward the unfamiliar and the Other. It calls into question claims of absolute truth and closed systems. It demands that we listen to other narratives, other stories, other histories. Postmodernity forces traditional theology "to think not," awakening us again to the Otherness of God, rescuing us from rationalism and theological Cartesianism. It helps us to live with contingencies and differences, correcting a provincial monism and warning against a lapse into univocity. Tillich traces Christianity's desire to "kill off" the Other to the growth of Islam in the seventh century leading ultimately to the Crusades and to intolerance toward Judaism.[79] And Pannenberg has asked: Why does the passion for religious truth so often degenerate into a narrow dogmatism?[80] Postmodernity cautions us about facile claims regarding divine and natural law; it alerts us to systemic distortions, ideo-

---

78 De Lubac, citing what Augustine had said in another context (*Conf.* VII, 16), properly encapsulated Christian correlation: *Non in te me mutabis, sed tu mutaberis in me.* See *A Brief Catechesis on Nature and Grace*, trans. R. Arnandez (San Francisco: Ignatius Press, 1984), 69. De Lubac himself is following in the train of the classical tradition. One well-documented example is that of the Cappadocian thinkers. See Jaroslav Pelikan, *Christianity and Classical Culture* (New Haven: Yale University Press, 1993).

79 Paul Tillich, *Christianity and the Encounter of the World Religions* (New York: Columbia University Press, 1963), 36–39.

80 Wolfhart Pannenberg, "Christianity and the West: Ambiguous Past, Uncertain Future," *First Things* 48 (December 1994): 19.

logies, and pathologies. It exposes the misery of identity-thinking and uniformity; it unveils the economic and cultural bases and biases of any theoretical formulation.

At the same time, postmodernity itself is a totalizing discipline with an (a)systematic view of reality. As such the questions it raises are clear: Does its large-scale abandonment of universal first principles erect barriers among peoples? Does such abandonment call into question the theoretical foundations of liberal democracy? Is not the Western European lineage of democratic government founded on unshakeable axioms about nature, truth, and personhood? Can such language be dismissed as mere Enlightenment homogeneity and naïveté? If it is so dismissed, by what rational warrants should we continue the civil conversation among men and women? More apposite to our discussion, of course, are the central theological issues. Primary among these is the notion of revelation and the theological demand for a revelationally appropriate ontology. All of the issues examined above turn, ultimately, on this subject. The enduring genius of Heidegger is that he saw with unparalleled clarity the absolute centrality of this fundamental question. From the outset, he recognized that philosophical change could only be initiated by a radical deconstruction of the tradition, a new "fundamental ontology."[81]

The theologically neuralgic question is this: Is Heidegger's deconstruction of classical ontology, given its nonfoundationalist turn and the pulsating implications this has for truth, hermeneutics, and allied issues, *revelationally appropriate*, that is, can it clarify, sustain, and illuminate the theology of revelation undergirding the Catholic Church? It is clearly not revelationally appropriate, in any ultimate and final way, if revelation is understood in the classical sense of a *locutio Dei* that is, in some substantive manner, continuous, identical, perpetual, universal, and self-same. Traditionally, there is a material continuity of faith and belief, classically denominated as the deposit of faith, that survives from age to age. This perpetuity, of course, is highly nuanced and qualified, but unmistakably contains an element of unchangeability.[82] This is what is ultimately behind the theolog-

---

81 *Being and Time*, 34.

82 For a clear analysis of the material content of faith, see Avery Dulles, *The Assurance of Things Hoped For* (Oxford: Oxford University Press, 1994), 141–42, 185–92. I am affirming this continuity with all of the essential nuances, e.g., the possibility of errors and reversals on the level of the ordinary magisterium, the importance of the 1968 statement by the German bishops, the epistemological significance of both the hierarchy of truths and the *sensus fidelium*, as well as the

ical use of "adequation," "correspondence," and "analogy." It is behind the concern for reconstructive hermeneutics. If revelation means, in one sense, that there is an identity of fundamental affirmations from generation to generation, then Heidegger's approach is unacceptable because it is simply unable to maintain this understanding.

On the other hand, it is legitimate and essential to invert the question: Does the tradition provide an ontologically appropriate understanding of revelation? A particular understanding of revelation—with its veridical, hermeneutical, and linguistic corollaries—would need to be abandoned if it were unquestionably proven to be philosophically unsustainable. No view of revelation, however deeply rooted in tradition, can finally stand if it is repugnant to reason.[83] So the question currently asked across the disciplines—literary criticism, philosophy of science, cultural anthropology, and critical legal studies—must necessarily be addressed to theology. Is the traditional understanding of revelation, with its corollaries of truth, hermeneutics, and language, now linked to a discredited and truncated ontology? Must not theology, too, properly adapt itself to the illuminating work of Heidegger and postmodernity? The Catholic conjunction of faith and reason, as well as an authentic understanding of correlation, demands answers to such questions. Of course, several theologians have already concluded that the traditional ontology and its allied theses are inappropriate, that one must rethink the entire tradition in order to meet this new situation honestly. If classical ontology is now inappropriate, leading to intractable aporias in the face of radical historicity, then one must seek an understanding of revelation that properly befits a newly presenced ontology. When Bonsor asks, for example, whether there is an epistemology inherent in revelation, his negative response is predicated on the conclu-

---

danger of systemic distortions within the Church. Further, the material continuity of the deposit of faith cannot be confused with the theological mummification properly decried by Rahner as "sacrosanct immobility." See Karl Rahner, "Theology and the Roman Magisterium," in vol. 22 of *Theological Investigations*, trans. J. Donceel, 176–90 (Chestnut Ridge, NY: The Crossroad Publishing Company, 1991).

83 This is the true meaning of the traditional axiom describing philosophy's relationship to theology: *ancilla theologiae sed non ancilla nisi libera.* This relationship between reason and revelation represents the concern I have with Lindbeck and postliberalism generally. Lindbeck wishes to defend, in a broad sense, and with cultural-linguistic differences, the material continuity of Christianity. He escapes, then, from the highly protean understanding of revelation at work in more explicitly Heideggerian-influenced thinkers. But he does this by positing divine agency alone, without any further ontological or hermeneutical warrants. From the viewpoint of Catholic theology, this position appears fideistic.

sion that traditional epistemology and the view of revelation it undergirds simply must be superseded.[84]

There is certainly a highly defensible logic in this view. One cannot simply posit a theory of revelation and assert that this must be maintained at all costs and in the face of all evidence. As Kuhn, Hanson, and others have shown, this kind of theoretical myopia has been fully operative in the scientific tradition. Rather than adapt to evolving evidence and the accumulating weight of facts, scientists have frequently complicated older theories in order to avoid entirely new paradigms. Most infamously, this was the case with the addition of epicycles to the Ptolemaic model in order to avoid the conclusions of Copernicus. Is theology doing this as well? Are apodictic and ideology-driven minds protecting fanciful interstices of truth not saturated by enveloping change? Is the current admission of the influence upon doctrine of historical limitations, finite perspectives, sociocultural horizons, and ideological conditioning simply a "Ptolemaic" strategy to avoid conceding the triumph of historicity and consequently of postmodernity? Does theological resistance to postmodernity not bring to mind the observation of Lord Radnor to de Tocqueville that Catholicism's dogmas are unreasonable, but they are precise, offering a haven for tired minds?[85]

Of course, it is true that if revelation is patient of nonfoundationalist ontologies, then our understanding of it must be reconceived as highly epiphanic and dialectical. Revelation must now be understood as profoundly changeable and protean, not simply in form (an advance already demanded by history), but even in fundamental content.[86] In this instance, revelation has the "givenness" characteristic of Being itself. Revelation is conceived along the Heideggerian notion of event, with its constant oscillation between presence and absence. Even if there are material contradictions from age to age, these should not be understood pejoratively but as newly revelatory of the elusive character of being and truth. What continues in the Church is not the same content held from age to age (even as devel-

---

84 Bonsor, *Athens and Jerusalem*, 158, 168–71.

85 Alexis de Tocqueville, *Journeys to England and Ireland*, trans. G. Lawrence and K. P. Mayer (London: Faber and Faber, 1957), 58.

86 It is precisely because of the alleged mutability of revelation that Gordon Kaufman says, "Theological work grounded principally on what is claimed to be authoritative 'revelation' is simply not appropriate today. The concept of revelation is itself a part of the conceptual scheme which has become questionable, and it is the overall scheme, therefore, which now must be carefully examined and possibly reconstructed." See Kaufman, *In the Face of Mystery* (Cambridge, MA: Harvard University Press, 1993), 21.

oped and nuanced); what survives is Christian reflection on the same texts and symbols, elements that have been handed down in the community and that continue to make claims on believers. Interpretations of the texts will (and must) vary even widely from age to age. A certain normativity belongs to the texts themselves, as witnesses to an originary event. But the understanding of them will always be reflective of varying and incommunicable forms of life; changes in interpretation and meaning will reflect the inexorable tides of historicity and mutability characteristic of all humanity, including the Christian community.

Catholic theology has adopted much from postmodernity and will continue to do so. Our theology has rightly become post-rationalist, post-Enlightenment, and post-positivist. The march of Catholic thought in the twentieth century has incorporated the principles of historical and ideological sensitivity. It has abandoned a naïve and wooden referentialism, dismissed the phantom of naked conceptualism, and accepted the difficulties attendant upon hermeneutical events. It has intensified the apophaticism inherent in understanding the divine. The best of this theology has perceived these changes not as grudging concessions, but as ontologically enriching and productive. At the same time, many questions remain vibrant: Can Catholic theology avoid the referentialism traditionally associated with its understanding of the mysteries of faith without betraying its identity? Can the metaphysics that undergirds the logic of realism, presence, and continuity be thought of dyslogistically? Is there a surplus of intelligibility in divine truth that allows for material continuity without any claim of exhaustion? Can theology defend unity without lapsing into a simple-minded claim of absolute luminosity and presence?

The answers to these questions, I think, force a departure from postmodernity and its nonfoundationalism in favor an historically and ideologically sophisticated foundationalism. This is a legitimate alternative to Heidegger's postmodernity, to the fideism of Lindbeck and Marion, and to the polycentrism of Tracy. It is not simply a restatement of ontotheology, but an attempt to understand the faith within the broad contours of both tradition and contemporary thought.

Chapter Five

Introduction:
The Return of Religion in Europe?
The Postmodern Christianity
of Gianni Vattimo

The Italian philosopher, Gianteresio (Gianni) Vattimo, is well known throughout Continental Europe, and increasingly so elsewhere, thanks to the many translations of his works into English, such as the impressive translation project of his numerous works undertaken by Columbia University Press. He has served in the European parliament and is recognized as a public intellectual who frequently engages in general cultural commentary. In 2010 he was invited to deliver the prestigious Gifford Lectures in Scotland, a kind of Nobel Prize for philosophers. Not that Vattimo has gone entirely unnoticed in the United States. The American philosopher Richard Rorty has said that Vattimo's "writings are among the most imaginative contributions to the tradition of philosophical thought that flows from Nietzsche and Heidegger."[1]

Why, it may be asked, is Vattimo's work significant for contemporary Catholic philosophy and theology?

One reason is because the Torinese philosopher continually writes about Catholic themes—although Catholicism now viewed through the postmodern lenses of Heidegger and Nietzsche. It is precisely postmodern philosophy—discussed at length in the prior essay—that most accurately characterizes Vattimo's mode of thinking. How is postmodernity best described? As we have seen, this school of thought has grave doubts about modern rationality, with its aggressive insistence on objectivity, finality, and

---

1 See Richard Rorty, "Heideggerianism and Leftist Politics," in *Weakening Philosophy: Essays in Honour of Gianni Vattimo,* ed. Santiago Zabala (Montreal and Kingston: McGill-Queens University Press, 2007) , 149–58, at 149.

certainty. It opposes modernity's celebration of scientism, its devaluation of the truth of art and tradition, and its marginalization of religion.

Creatively appropriating postmodern themes, Vattimo assails the excesses of modernity, and trumpets the significance of *il pensiero debole* or "weak thought." By this he means the profound provisionality and contingency that attends all assertions and interpretations. As the internet bears witness, we live in an infinitely interpretable world, one without clearly attested first principles or ultimate grounds, without definitive answers, evidence, or warrants. Honestly acknowledging that reality is an unending festival of interpretation weakens and "lightens" our understanding of being, of objectivity, and of truth.

Given this philosophical approach, how does Vattimo regard the Christian faith? Rather than taking an imperious and dismissive attitude toward religious belief, à la Enlightenment modernity, Vattimo thinks that religion must again be permitted a public, societal role; it cannot be excluded from the life of the *agora*. But if religion is to be once again allowed into the societal drawing room, what price must be paid? Just there's the rub. For the religion welcomed into public discourse must be a faith that has passed through the ringers of Heidegger and Nietzsche, both of whom have shown that "truth" is deeply historicized and epiphanic rather than solid and unchanging. As such, there can be no dogmatic or disciplinary Christianity which insists on the objectivity and certainty of its doctrinal and moral claims. To assert otherwise would be to sanction a recrudescence of philosophical and theological fundamentalism—of an approach that has been unmasked as intellectually illegitimate. Rather, the true meaning of Christianity—the meaning that has been "received" in contemporary, educated, Europe—is the notion of *caritas* or charity, now understood as tolerance toward all nonviolent positions.

In other words, the philosophies of Nietzsche and Heidegger, with their strong accent on the historicity and contingency of all assertions, help us to see the true meaning of the Christian faith—tolerance towards all—and this inexorably implies the embrace of unlimited interpretative plurality. It is precisely the humane tolerance of every point of view—the accent on *caritas* rather than *veritas*—that has replaced a notion of religion which insists on doctrinal, creedal, and moral truths. Properly understood, philosophy and Christian belief have now happily converged, with both recognizing the infinite interpretability of the world, thereby overcoming and abjuring "strong" truth-claims in the process.

Vattimo argues, consequently, that the contemporary secularized world represents not an antagonistic opponent of Christian faith, but Christianity's ultimate triumph. Why? Because secularized Europe attests to the gradual realization of the central Christian idea—charity-as-tolerance—now working its way through history. Rightly understood, "charity" means that everyone, no matter his or her belief, is equally welcomed in public life. The aggressive and assertive demands of doctrinal, "fundamentalist" Christianity have receded from view, allowing a secularized world to come into being. Indeed, it is the Christian faith, with its insistence on charity, which is the *fons et origo* of secularization.

Can any dialogue whatsoever be established between Catholic Christianity and Vattimo's "religion 'after religion'"? Are there any "spoils from Egypt" that can be retrieved for orthodox Christian theology from his understanding of postmodern philosophy? Or has the Nietzschean, Heideggerian Vattimo simply offered us one more *Aufhebung* of Christianity which, in the final analysis, is not so different from the Enlightenment modernity he intends to heal and overcome?

The Return of Religion in Europe? The Postmodern Christianity of Gianni Vattimo

With the onslaught of recent books extolling atheism, speaking of the contemporary "return to religion" sounds a bit naïve, akin to nervous whistling in the dark rather than to the rigors of critical analysis. Yet there is such a movement afoot, often linked to the rise of postmodernism. Vattimo is one of its most acute practitioners.

In this essay, I would like to introduce the reader to the fundamental themes that characterize Vattimo's philosophical work—particularly his reading of Christianity's contributions to contemporary culture—and then offer an evaluation of his thought. Despite its patent opposition to anything resembling historic Christian orthodoxy, Vattimo's interpretation of Christianity constitutes an influential achievement that has proven, either explicitly or implicitly, to be attractive to large segments of contemporary society.

Gianni Vattimo was born in Turin, Italy in 1936. After graduating from the university there, he went on to Heidelberg, studying with K. Löwith and H.-G. Gadamer. From the early 1960s onwards, he was a professor at the University of Turin (retiring in 2008)—with specialties in hermeneutics, Nietzsche, and Heidegger—as well as a visiting professor at several American universities, including Stanford and Yale. Vattimo has amassed an impressive array of publications, with scores of volumes and hundreds of articles both in professional journals as well as in general-interest newspapers and magazines. He has continued to engage the thought of Heidegger and Nietzsche (with his work on the latter sustained and even groundbreaking) and is the Italian translator of Hans-Georg Gadamer's magnum opus on hermeneutics, *Truth and Method*. Recently, the Torinese philosopher's work has centered on the role of religion in contemporary life and thought as well as the possible convergences of postmodernity with the Christian faith. He was a

* Originally published as "The Return of Religion in Europe? The Postmodern Christianity of Gianni Vattimo," *Logos: A Journal of Catholic Thought and Culture* 14, no. 2 (2011): 15–36. Republished with permission.

member of the European parliament for several terms and has continued to be involved with reform political movements in Italy.

Given Vattimo's contemporary influence, it is worth examining the fundamental linchpins of his philosophy and his recent reinterpretation of Christianity.

POSTMODERNISM

A term frequently heard in recent days is the "postmodern return of religion 'after religion.'" This enigmatic phrase wishes to say that postmodernity has shattered and transgressed the constricting canons of modern rationalism, allowing religion to reappear in the process, albeit in a changed form, differing from prior understandings of its societal role. Of course, contemporary definitions of postmodernism are legion and even conflicting, so one is wary of invoking the term. Nonetheless, one may outline some broad contours of this movement.

In general, the term "postmodernism" refers to the continually growing critique of Enlightenment construals of rationality. *Modern* rationality is understood as attempting to pin down reason to the limited canons of empiricism, positivism, or some equally narrow form of thinking and knowing. Modernity is equated with a reductive attempt to reduce truth to methodology, particularly those methods and canons associated with scientific inquiry, leading inexorably to the detriment of philosophical wonder, to the rise of rationalism, and to the equation of thinking with mere *techné*. *Post*modernity's contemporary ascent, then, is fueled by its opposition to modernity's simplistic trust in scientism, its devaluation of the truth mediated by the arts and by tradition, and its marginalization of religion under the banner of the Enlightenment claim that science has unmasked faith as little more than superstitious mythology. Postmodernity argues, in fact, that *modern* forms of rationality are now in deep retreat. The rationalization thesis itself, that God would eventually disappear in the face of continuing education, has been entirely discredited. And rationalist approaches have hardly solved the intractable problems of human suffering or global warfare. In general, then, modernity's colonization of the world by a luminous, scientific reason now seems a misguided and constricting utopian dream.

Deeply entwined with postmodernity's reproach of modernity is its critique of the banishment of religion from the public square. It is precisely here that one sees the meaning of the contemporary phase, "the postmodern return of religion." The Enlightenment dispelled religion from the *agora* on the grounds that it fomented the passions of men and women, was not grounded by empirical science, and inexorably led to obscurantist dogmatism, loathsome intolerance, and anarchic violence. Modernity argued that religion's explosive potency could only be domesticated and neutered by reducing it to an entirely private affair, shorn of any public role in everyday societal intercourse. Vattimo and postmodernism argue, however, that this imperious attitude of modern rationalism has itself been exposed as defective. Modernity's colonization of the world by scientism, its exclusion of "hot religion" in the name of "cool reason," now seems a cramped and insular project. And so with the revealing of modernity's unfounded pretensions, religion must once again be accorded a central role in society. Religion has now returned, and robustly so, to the public square.

But this implies a critical question: For if religion has, indeed, returned to a public role and been allowed back into the societal drawing room, by what manners must it now abide? It is precisely here that we shall see how Vattimo conceives "postmodern religion" and so the kind of Christianity that is welcome in the contemporary world. But to bring Vattimo's religious understanding into clearer focus, we need first to explain his signature philosophical idea, the triumph of "weak thought" (*il pensiero debole*).

WEAK THOUGHT

It is perhaps best to understand Vattimo's "weak thought" as an attempt to reconstruct rationality in a postmodern way.[2] By this I mean that the Torinese philosopher intends to move contemporary construals of rationality away from modern notions of reason, with their aggressive assertions about the "certainly true," the "really real," and "absolute objectivity," and with their insinuations that evidence and warrants are unproblematic concepts, readily available to settle questions of interpretative adequacy. Weak thought, on the contrary, holds that the world is not simply "given" to us as pure, uninterpreted, unmediated reality.

If contemporary philosophy has taught us anything, it is that the world is known by men and women who are already deeply enmeshed in history and tradition, who are themselves entirely theory laden. Vattimo is convinced, then, that the world is "given" to us as an *always-already interpreted reality.* And precisely because of this, we must avoid "strong thought" with

---

2 In the sections that follow, I rely on material found in Thomas G. Guarino, *Vattimo and Theology* (New York: T & T Clark, 2009).

its blinkered claims to truth, finality, and objectivity and with its concomitant avoidance of historical contingency. There exist no ultimate, normative
foundations that are available to us "outside" of interpretation. There exists
no "evidence" that is not already deeply implicated in determinate socio-
cultural forms of life and in already elaborated interpretive structures.
Consequently, we have no clearly available *archai* or *Gründe*, undisputed
first principles or warrants, that could settle matters finally, that could offer
definitive notions of truth which would escape perpetual provisionality.[3]

The internet serves as a good example of what Vattimo is driving at. As
any casual user of the web can attest, the internet displays to us a profligate
interpretive bazaar, since it provides access to a vast collection of machine-
readable texts indexed by powerful search engines. We might pose to this
bazaar a range of questions about virtually any topic:

> What is the nature of humanity?
> What is the good we should pursue?
> Which values are ultimate?
> Is there a God?
> Do we know anything about him?

In the answers proffered to these questions, we have the multivalent, infinitely interpretable world on full view. The internet, with its inexhaustible
explanations of reality, makes patently clear that we reside in a world of competing and proliferating interpretations without a defined center. And precisely
this is Vattimo's point. Our world is without Archimedean levers that offer us
evidence to decide these fundamental questions. In fact, it is just on the fundamentals that we see an array of highly variable answers. Strong thought
insists on its objectivity and final truth; it contends that it has irrefutable proof
to buttress its case, to make final decisions, to offer clear answers. As such it
tends toward positivism, aggression, and intolerance. Weak thought, on the
contrary, recognizes that all claims to adduce definitive evidence and indis-
putable warrants are themselves riddled with theoretical commitments and
prior suppositions. No final or uncomplicated "givenness" is to be found in
evidence itself. Weak thought, in a word, recognizes the deeply interpretive
nature of human life and discourse. And such recognition ineluctably weakens
and "lightens" our sense of the finality of being and truth.

---

3 *Il pensiero debole,* ed. Pier Aldo Rovatti and Gianni Vattimo (Milano: Feltrinelli, 1983), 18; "Dialectic, Difference, Weak Thought," *Graduate Faculty Philosophy Journal* 10, no. 1 (1984): 155.

Vattimo, of course, is hardly the only thinker to insist on the primacy of interpretation or on the hermeneutical nature of human experience. One hears with growing frequency these days the pithy claim that "it's interpretation all the way down." This maxim, cited by several recent authors, finds its *fons et origo* in Nietzsche's assertion: there are no facts, only interpretations. And this, too, is an interpretation![4] This passage, cited frequently by Vattimo,[5] is meant to remind us that we are embedded and conditioned observers, that we "perform" within different language games, that there exist no universal or unambiguous warrants for knowledge. All warrants for truth, rather, are deeply embedded in specific forms of life, in contingent cultural circumstances. This claim—that all knowledge is, necessarily and without exception, rooted in interpretation—helps us to see more clearly what "weak thought" actually means. It signifies that there exists a multiplicity of interpretations, none of which is self-justifying by virtue of appeals to universally available first principles or evidence. We should understand, rather, that evidence and criteria are not unproblematic concepts. Evidence varies from community to community, from person to person. For example, while the believer may see the world as attesting to God's goodness and wisdom, a nonbeliever may see only a variety of biological, chemical, and material causes. This is something of what Nietzsche meant by the phrase "God is dead." God can no longer serve as an unproblematic first principle for objectivity and meaningfulness because "God" is also an interpreted reality. Nietzsche's point about the inextricable interweaving of facts and interpretations constitutes one reason why Vattimo resists lumping him together with Marx and Freud. It is true that they were all "masters of suspicion." But Nietzsche was no subscriber to the claim that the idea of God will inevitably decline as education advances. Unlike Marx and Freud, Nietzsche mocked scientific positivism as a hopelessly utopian imposter; science gives us no more access to "truth" and "objectivity" than does religion.

4 Friedrich Nietzsche, *The Will to Power*, trans. Walter Kaufmann and R. J. Hollingdale (New York: Random House, 1967), no. 481. Several commentators echo Nietzsche's point. For example, Brice Wachterhauser avers, "[. . .] We seem to be in the uneasy position of having to admit that interpretation goes, as it were, 'all the way down.'" See "Getting it Right: Relativism, Realism and Truth," in *The Cambridge Companion to Gadamer*, ed. Robert J. Dostal, 52–78 (Cambridge: Cambridge University Press, 2002), 53.

5 *Nihilism and Emancipation: Ethics, Politics, and Law*, ed. Santiago Zabala and trans. William McCuaig (New York: Columbia University Press, 2004), 155; *Dialogue with Nietzsche*, trans. William McCuaig (New York: Columbia University Press, 2006), 74.

A good example of Nietzsche's philosophy is his parable "How the World Became a Fable" from *The Twilight of the Idols*, a story often repeated by Vattimo. In this parable, the "true world," the truth, was first available to the wise and virtuous man, the follower of Plato. But, gradually, the "true world" or the "really real" became successively more unattainable. It was *promised* to the Christian who committed himself to living an ascetical and virtuous life; later, the true world became entirely unknowable and unattainable in Kantian philosophy, wherein the noumenal world (reality itself) escaped humanity's cognitive grasp. Finally, the idea of the "true world" no longer even served a purpose. It became a superfluous notion, best abolished. The "true world" in fact, no longer even exists![6] Vattimo is deeply attracted to this passage. Nietzsche's point (reaffirmed by Vattimo) is not only that we have no universal, self-justifying warrants which give us access to "reality" but that, in fact, reality itself *is constituted* by the interpretations we offer. The world is, in fact, simply a play of interpretations.[7] Weak thought, with its profound doubts about "objective reality" and "absolute certainty" serves, for Vattimo, as a way of liberating human *freedom* from those who would stifle emancipation and creativity with bellicose claims to certitude and finality. Weak thought allows the human being to seize fully his or her own life, to mold and shape it in new ways, apart from predetermined structures and assertive claims about truth or "unchanging human nature."

For Vattimo, this difficulty of knowing "the truth" or "reality itself" necessarily grants some opening to religion. There is little room for religion in the man of the Enlightenment, the *Aufklärer*. In modernity, *if* religion is admitted into the societal drawing room, it is consigned to an obscure corner, considered as belonging to the realm of the affective but cognitively empty, and, often enough, regarded as suffocatingly repressive and authoritarian. As Vattimo says, the modern West was increasingly founded "on the self-assurance of scientistic and historicist reason that saw no limit to increasingly total domination [. . .]."[8] And, of course, a spate of popular books claiming to defend atheism on the grounds of scientific discoveries

---

6 Friedrich Nietzsche, *Twilight of the Idols*, trans. R. J. Hollingdale (London: Penguin, 1990), 50–51.

7 *Beyond Interpretation: The Meaning of Hermeneutics for Philosophy*, trans. David Webb (Stanford: Stanford University Press, 1997), 7; "Conclusion: Metaphysics and Violence," in *Weakening Philosophy: Essays in Honour of Gianni Vattimo*, ed. Santiago Zabala (Montreal and Kingston: McGill-Queens University Press, 2007), 402.

8 *Belief*, trans. Luca D'Isanto and David Webb (Stanford: Stanford University Press, 1999), 56.

shows that this trend is not altogether moribund. Some still long for the recrudescence of a modern spirit which occludes religion.[9] Vattimo, however, regards this kind of militant atheism to be as much a phenomenon of strong thought as is religious fundamentalism, noting that the end of modernity is also the end of positivist science and Marxist historicism with their aggressive claims to have mastered the deep, underlying structure of the universe and to have destroyed religion in the process. Vattimo is convinced that faith in the progress of reason (and even faith in objective truth) has now broken down. Atheist manifestos, then, even with all their *Sturm und Drang*, their anti-religious huffing and puffing, are arriving at the scene in need of an oxygen tank, badly out of theoretical breath.

VATTIMO AND RELIGION

But what kind of religion does Vattimo now allow? Of course, Vattimo is writing in Europe where Christian practice is on the wane but where European intellectuals are besieged by an assertive Islam, with large mosques sprouting in every major city. What happens to secularized, "laicist" Europe in the face of this confident expression of religion? Just here Vattimo gives an indication of the *kind* of religion that is acceptable to contemporary Western society. If scientific and rationalist modernity can no longer be presumptuous and self-assured about its strong claims to truth, then neither can religion. Consequently, while Vattimo thinks postmodernity and weak thought make room for religion, it is always religion of a certain type and shape. We cannot simply "return" to religion, as if our eyes have not been opened by further reflection, particularly the contributions of Nietzsche and Heidegger. Both of these philosophers have shown us that truth is deeply historicized and evanescent rather than solid and unchanging. Any contemporary rediscovery of religion (and of Christianity in particular), then, necessarily entails the theoretical overcoming of "objectivistic-dogmatic philosophies." As such, Vattimo insists that "dogmatic and disciplinary Christianity [. . .] has nothing to do with what I and my contemporaries 'rediscover'" when speaking of faith.[10]

Indicating his chosen path between the *Aufklärer* and the "fundamentalist," Vattimo argues that neither modern scientism (with its positivistic

---

9 See, for example, Christopher Hitchens, *God is Not Great* (New York: Twelve, 2007); and Richard Dawkins, *The God Delusion* (New York: Houghton Mifflin, 2006).

10 *Belief*, 61.

methods) nor premodern dogmatism (with its precipitous enclosing of truth's boundaries) duplicates contemporary retrievals of faith. The "return of religion" demands the concomitant acknowledgment that religion can rely on no strong body of doctrine, or on claims to absolute and definitive knowledge. Dogmatic assertions, with their claim to know reality, the *ontos on*, with certainty and finality, represent precisely the kind of objectifying, metaphysical thought that has been discredited by the historical and hermeneutical character of existence. Christian faith must now be understood in light of the profound provisionality and contingency that inexorably distinguishes contemporary thought and life. And this leads Vattimo to his own interpretation of the essence of Christianity.

Absent any strong claims, any belief or doctrine that can adequately mediate the world, any revelation that can tell us "final" and "objective" truth, then what is the cognitive yield of the Christian faith? For Vattimo, the theoretical resolution of Christianity is found not in doctrine, but only in the notion of *caritas*, charity (understood now as tolerance of plurality). As he says, "The Christian inheritance that 'returns' in weak thought is primarily the Christian precept of charity and its rejection of violence."[11] Precisely here we see, Vattimo insists, the happy convergence between the weak thought of contemporary philosophy and the fundamental teaching (*caritas*) of Christian faith. Both faith (theology) and reason (philosophy) now renounce and repudiate all strong, dogmatic assertions which allegedly offer access to the *logos* structure of reality, the *ontos on*. Both faith and reason willingly embrace the "twilight of Being," that "lightening" of the solidity of reality that is the necessary residue of the dilution of objectivity.

This helps to explain why Vattimo is fond of citing the well-known dictum rooted in Aristotle's *Ethics*: *Amicus Plato sed magis amica veritas*,[12] a noble sentiment indicating that truth must take priority over friendship, even an intimate one. But he uses this phrase with a purpose, showing how, in our day, it has been contravened. He observes, for example, that when one sees large crowds coming out to cheer the pope, this is not an instance of "*amicus Plato*," that is, of love for some assertive dogmatic or moral truth represented by the pope. No one is claiming that the huge throngs of well-wishers who usually greet the pope's arrival agree with him on many dis-

---

11 *Belief*, 44.

12 "A 'Dictatorship of Relativism'?" trans. Robert Valgenti, *Common Knowledge* 13 (2007): 218; *Beyond Interpretation*, 40.

puted matters; no one is affirming that this man speaks the truth on controversial issues. Rather, one is applauding his universal call to charity, to friendship, to common understanding among all peoples. What is at stake here is *caritas*, charity, tolerance toward others, not some determinate principle of moral or dogmatic truth.

KENOSIS

Given his claim that the retrievable part of Christianity is its accent on *caritas*, it is no surprise that Vattimo is deeply taken with the biblical notion of kenosis (the self-emptying that occurs in the Incarnation), an image that figures prominently in his thought. For the kenosis of God, the Incarnation, helps us to see why charity (tolerance toward interpretative plurality) is the living fruit of Christian faith. A central passage of the New Testament attesting to the self-emptying of the Son is Philippians 2: 6–8: "Though he was in the form of God, Christ did not consider equality with God something to be grasped at; rather, he took the form of a slave, being made in the likeness of men. He humbled himself becoming obedient unto death, even death on a cross." This passage, one of the few biblical citations adduced by Vattimo, indicates a "weakening" of God, a renunciation of power and authority, a self-abasement which is the "dissolution of divine transcendence."[13] In the story of the Son of God become man, Vattimo sees a self-emptying of divine sovereignty, a vulnerability now unexpectedly convergent with the "weak thought" of Heidegger who teaches the end of objectifying metaphysics and of Nietzsche who argues for the death of the moral-metaphysical God.

In the kenosis of the Son, God renounces power and authority—just as contemporary philosophy has renounced its claims to finality and truth. Both theology and philosophy, then, harbor deep currents tending in the same direction: both are concerned with overcoming strong claims, whether philosophical (I now have certitude about the stable structure, the final system, the *ontos on*.) or theological (determinate biblical, doctrinal and moral teachings are absolutely and universally true.) This is why Vattimo says, in a truly revelatory statement, that "Christianity is a stimulus, a message that sets in motion a tradition of thought that will eventually realize its freedom from metaphysics"[14] In other words, the kenotic action of God

---

13 *After Christianity*, trans. Luca D'Isanto (New York: Columbia University Press, 2002), 27.

14 John Caputo and Gianni Vattimo, *After the Death of God*, ed. Jeffrey W. Robbins (New York: Columbia University Press, 2007), 35.

preached by the Christian faith has come to fruition in philosophy's renunciation of strong, objective claims to truth; contemporary thought thereby confirms the fundamental message of the Gospel: what is enduringly important is charity, *caritas*, rather than any determinate claims to truth. The "end of metaphysics" as proclaimed by Nietzsche and Heidegger is simply a philosophical transcription of the New Testament's message of charity and love. Rather than being sworn enemies, the beating heart of Christian faith and "weak thought" are deeply and inextricably related. The divine kenosis revealed in Jesus of Nazareth teaches us that God manifests himself as the vulnerable one who willingly renounces authority, as the one who undermines assertive declarations of truth. It is precisely in the weakness of kenotic Christianity that Vattimo discerns the root and paradigm of secularization.

SECULARIZATION

Secularization is a word that, in a religious context, usually carries pejorative overtones. But Vattimo's contention is just the opposite: Christianity should see secularization not as a development to be decried and reversed, but as a triumph of Christian belief, as a beneficent and propitious impulse given life by Christianity itself. In fact, when we come to understand that the real fruit of religion is charity-as-tolerance and that charity is rooted in God's kenosis (which is itself a parable about the renunciation of power and ascendency), we gradually come to see that secularization is not the opponent of religion, but one of its most vibrant fruits. Secularization is, in fact, the gradual realization in history of the kenotic self-abasement of God; it is the result of *caritas* working its way through history. Rather than an adversary of the Christian message, secularization is, on the contrary, an *essential component* of it. According to Vattimo, "Christianity's vocation consists in deepening its own physiognomy as source and condition for the possibility of secularity."[15]

But why, we may ask, is continuing secularization the happy issue and not the deadly foe of fervent Christian belief and practice? One reason is because secularization, properly understood, means that there is "room" for everyone, no matter his or her belief (or lack of belief), in the public square; no one is excluded from equal participation in the realm of public life and discourse. Secularization is, in fact, the dynamic consequence of Christian *caritas* because it opens society to every point of view, thereby rejecting an aggressive religiosity that degenerates into fundamentalist ideology, seeking

15 *After Christianity*, 98.

to exclude those viewpoints not conforming to the prevailing wisdom. On the Vattimian reading, secularization is the recognition that the world is a festival of interpretative plurality with no one claiming privileged access to the *ontos on*. After all, Vattimo asks, in this era of global cultural and religious conflict, does it make sense for Christianity to insist on "strong" doctrinal claims, on the truth of its own positions?

And this view, with its marked epistemological and ontological humility, is entirely convergent, Vattimo insists, with the Christian understanding of kenosis, the self-renunciation of power and authority by God. This is why Christianity's actual achievement does not consist in its strong claims, in its creeds or its system of dogma or doctrine; its stunning achievement, in fact, is the secularized truth of *caritas*–as-tolerance) which has led to the modern understanding of rights, to the humanization of social relations, to the dissolution of class structures. These achievements exemplify Christianity's historical and societal triumph. It is precisely these "secularized" accomplishments that represent the positive way in which modern civilization has responded to the announcement of the Christian tradition.[16] Indeed, the West acknowledges its proper self-identity when recognizing that it is nothing other than secularized Christianity (kenotic *caritas*-as-tolerance unfurled in history). Vattimo concludes, therefore, that secularization must always be viewed positively by the Christian faith, must be considered as one of its greatest successes. Indeed, the contemporary missionary task of Christianity is not to strengthen its own doctrinal, moral, and disciplinary specificity and concreteness (for this would be a return to a discredited "objectivism" and would make little sense in a world deeply riven with religious strife), but to accent its unique contribution to world culture which consists in the opening of the secular sphere to wide interpretative plurality, an opening rarely found in other cultures or religions. In Vattimo's interpretation, Christianity's new and apposite mission to the world is the spreading of the gospel of charity-as-tolerance, thereby introducing other cultures to the wisdom of secularization.

The parable of the Incarnation, then, the divine self-emptying, leads straight to a welcoming of secularization. As Vattimo revealingly states: "[. . .] if I have a vocation to recover Christianity, it will consist in the task of rethinking revelation in secularized terms in order to 'live in accord with one's age,' therefore in ways that do not offend my culture [. . .] as a man who

---

16 *After Christianity*, 26.

belongs to his age."[17] A helpful clue to Vattimo's notion of secularization may be seen in his comments on the symbols of the crucifix and the chador (the full-length garment worn by many Muslim women). The Torinese philosopher's observations on religious imagery are revelatory insofar as they illustrate just how devitalized and denuded of strong and specific religious assertions the public square must be. He does not object, for example, to the large crucifixes that are often displayed in the classrooms, courtrooms, and public buildings of countries with a Catholic heritage. He does, however, object to the wearing of the chador by Muslim women. Is this a patent case of anti-Muslim prejudice? Not at all. Vattimo makes clear that the crucifix is acceptable precisely because it has *lost its assertive power*. It now serves simply as a cultural accoutrement, hardly noticeable anymore to the passerby, blending meekly into the background. The crucifix, in other words, the central image of Christianity, has grown "weak" and attenuated by its acculturation to secular, Western society. The chador, however, is a powerfully aggressive symbol of strong thought, of an exclusionary and dogmatic truth-claim. As such, Vattimo holds it should be banned from the secular sphere in order to allow and encourage tolerance and interpretative plurality.[18]

THE "NATURAL SACRED"

Vattimo tells us that one reason that Christians should beneficently welcome secularization is because the drifting away from an apparently "sacral core" is the way in which God's kenosis continues to realize itself in history, overcoming, in the process, the originary violence associated with the "natural sacred."[19] What precisely does this statement mean? Why is a central part of Vattimo's eulogistic analysis of secularization rooted in a polemic against the natural sacred?

The Torinese philosopher relies heavily here on the thought of René Girard who, in a plethora of studies, has argued that Christ's death and resurrection fully unveils the "scapegoat mechanism" that is part and parcel of the naturally sacred. A cultural anthropologist as well as a philosopher, Girard observes that, throughout the whole of human history, societies have retained their unity and social cohesion by identifying various persons, groups, or classes as "evil ones," that is, as causes of social and cultural dis-

---

17 *Belief*, 75.
18 *After Christianity*, 95–97; 101–2.
19 *Belief*, 48.

sension. Only when violent action is taken against the malefactors, when they are wounded or killed, is society cleansed and healed, with cohesive social unity now fully restored. It is Girard's brief that the violence against Christ, leading to his ultimate death, finally unmasked this scapegoat mechanism as belonging to the naturally sacred. But this ritual cycle of violence and cleansing has now been exposed by the New Testament (and, indeed, by aspects of the Old Testament as well) as illegitimate and antihuman.[20]

Vattimo is deeply taken with Girard's point that the death of Christ discloses and lays bare the violence of natural, sacrificial religion. He says, in fact, that his reading of Girard led him to thinking about secularization (the drifting away from natural religion) as a positive development. For secularization necessarily entails the corrosion of the naturally sacred core of societies, particularly those repugnant exclusionary actions committed in the name of religion. Secularization is a Christian triumph precisely because it moves societies away from the crippling discriminatory tendencies of natural religion toward the essence and core of true biblical religion which is charity and fraternity. For if, in the Christian parable, God did not hesitate to humble himself, if God willingly took the form of a slave, then how much more should men and women be willing to renounce not only strong thought (with its assertive insistence on certitude) but also natural religion, with its skewed understanding of God's identity and action in history?

The self-emptying of God, then, bespeaks a divine weakening and charity that enfeebles and destabilizes primitive conceptions of religion. Here, Vattimo goes beyond Girard (as he admits) offering a list of exclusionary (and therefore violent) characteristics which are manifestations of the primitive, natural religion that needs to be exposed. He says, for example, that the great scandal of Christian revelation, the kenosis, occasions "the removal of all the transcendent, incomprehensible, mysterious and even bizarre features" traditionally assigned to God.[21] Other elements of the natural sacred not yet purified by Christian *caritas* include: the refusal to ordain women to the priesthood in Catholicism;[22] the Church's opposition to the distribution of condoms during the AIDS crisis in order to avoid "the impression

---

20 Vattimo cites Girard's *Violence and the Sacred* as important to his thought. See *After Christianity*, 38. For a crisp account of Girard's fundamental insights, see Michael Kirwan, *Discovering Girard* (Cambridge, MA: Cowley Publications, 2005).

21 *Belief*, 55.

22 *After Christianity*, 47; *A Farewell to Truth*, trans. William McCuaig. (New York: Columbia University Press, 2011), 15.

that Christian morality and doctrine may be weakening";[23] and, the condemnation of homosexual activity, on the grounds that this is sick or disordered behavior.[24]

All of these instances, Vattimo insists, smack of a primitive notion of God, rooted in precepts of exclusionary violence, far from the kenotic charity in which God has manifested himself as weak, as friend, and as love. Such positions try to pass off historically contingent judgments (such as the nature of human sexuality or various gender roles) as inescapably identical with a universal human nature or a generalized metaphysical anthropology. But these judgments, Vattimo is convinced, have not been properly "cleansed" by the Gospel's central message of *caritas* and so remain deeply corroded by the violent, constricted sense of primitive religion.[25] Such elements, Vattimo contends, represent the sacred as read through the lens of nature, rather than accenting the God revealed in the kenotic message of the Gospels, the God who appears "after metaphysics." Thus, the Torinese philosopher can assert that he has rediscovered "salvation as the dissolution of the sacred as natural-violent."[26] Vattimo's attack on the natural sacred here echoes (and supersedes) Heidegger's well-known comment about overcoming the God of metaphysics, the *causa sui* before whom one can neither dance nor pray, the god of natural religion who does not reflect the biblical God of the Old and New Covenants.[27]

CONCLUSIONS

This chapter offers just a glimpse at Vattimo's provocative thought, briefly outlining a few pillars of his philosophy, particularly his understanding of the postmodern return to religion "after religion." How may Christian theology evaluate his rethinking of religious belief?

While Vattimo's "weak thought" appears to be at antipodes to anything resembling historic Christian orthodoxy, we do well to remember the classic

---

23 *Belief*, 57; *A Farewell to Truth*, 79.

24 *Belief*, 73.

25 As Vattimo says to René Girard in one of their dialogues: "If the orthodox Catholic declares that one is unable to abort, or to divorce or to experiment with embryos and so on, does there not persist here a certain violence of natural religion [. . .] ?" Gianni Vattimo and René Girard, *Verità o fede debole?: Dialogo su cristianesimo e relativismo* (Massa: Transeuropa, 2006), 9.

26 *Belief*, 61.

27 Martin Heidegger, *Identity and Difference*, trans. Joan Stambaugh (New York: Harper and Row, 1969), 72.

principle, with deep roots in the third century theologian Origen, of taking "spoils from Egypt," that is, of utilizing truth wherever it is found, even in those who ardently oppose the Christian faith.[28] In the 1998 encyclical *Fides et ratio*, John Paul II gave contemporary force to this position by citing Aquinas's axiom: "Truth, whatever its source, is from the Holy Spirit."[29]

And, indeed, there are several elements in Vattimo's philosophy that have something important to contribute. Is it not the case that, at least in his general diagnosis, Vattimo has his finger on the pulse of contemporary society? Is not everyone exasperated by aggressive claims to truth no matter the quarter from which they emerge? Are not people tired to the point of exhaustion by the brutal paroxysms of violence born of clashing ethnic and religious identities? Does not Vattimo's thought legitimately seek to respond to the rise in extremism, in fundamentalism, in global animosity? Is this not the basis for the Torinese philosopher's attraction: the contemporary desire to avoid hectoring fundamentalisms of every stripe, to elude the kind of passion that fosters an intolerant crusade for truth apart from human dignity and freedom? Is this not the reason that men and women find a certain resonance with the call for weak thought?

And does not Vattimo's philosophy have the ring of authenticity when it contends that in a world of competing interpretations, we should allow one fundamental contribution of religion to shine forth: a strong sense of fraternity and solidarity among all peoples, thereby fostering tolerance toward a wide variety of beliefs?[30] After all, is not one goal of ecumenical and interreligious dialogue to promote bonds of fellowship and common humanity despite differences in terms of "strong" doctrinal assertions? It is true, of course, that Vattimo's understanding of charity is not at all equivalent to that of Christianity's, which understands *caritas* as supernatural love poured into human hearts through the agency of the Holy Spirit. Nonetheless, the Torinese thinker's accent on fraternity and nonviolence surely allows glimpses of a bolder, transcendent charity that supersedes mere tolerance and insists that fraternal love is a living proof that God abides in

---

28 So, Origen could say regarding Celsus's unrelenting attack on Christianity, "We are careful not to raise objections to any good teachings, even if their authors are outside the faith [. . .] nor to find a way of overthrowing statements which are sound" (*Contra Celsum*, VII, 46).

29 "*Omne verum a quocumque dicatur a Spiritu Sancto est.*" See *Summa theologiae* I-II, q. 109, a. 1, ad 1.

30 On just this point, for example, we may see a convergence between Vattimo's thought and the encyclical letter of Pope Francis, *Fratelli tutti* (October 3, 2020).

us.[31] Moreover, in Vattimo's attraction to the kenosis one finds a clear affinity for the vulnerable and loving God revealed in Jesus Christ, even if he does not allow himself, because of his philosophical allegiances, to make any ontological commitment to the full reality of the Incarnation or even to the existence of God.

Lastly, even if one cannot sanction Vattimo's rereading of Christianity, who cannot concur with his evenhanded critique of the naively rationalist modernity of the Enlightenment which, in the name of reason, shunted religion from the public square, desperately trying to reduce the most comprehensive and foundational of realities to a private, cognitively empty affair? Here, too, Vattimo's thought is to be welcomed for unmasking the colonization of life sought by imperious and suffocating secular reason trading under the banner of enlightened rationality.[32]

Of course, even an appreciative reading of Vattimo's thought cannot disguise those elements of his work worthy of criticism. Vattimo has often described his philosophy as "optimistic nihilism"—and nihilism is, indeed, the key word.[33] For Vattimo, nihilism (the end of belief in fixed, stable structures or truths) *is* emancipation. This is the case precisely because nihilism recognizes the world for what it is: a multicultural Babel, an irreducible web of vast interpretative plurality. As Nietzsche observes in the *Will to Power*, humanity is entirely deracinated, "rolling from the center toward 'X'"[34] Like Nietzsche, Vattimo also has a strong sense of the triumph of the sovereign, autonomous will. This means, in essence, that the world possesses no *logos*-structure, no fundamental architecture which itself bestows meaning and wisdom. "Nature," taken in the sense of the comprehensible and preexisting contours of reality, necessarily becomes here the irremediable and menacing enemy of human liberty. Only if *kosmos* and *physis* are stripped of their pre-

---

31 1 John 4:12.

32 I note, however, that Vattimo's evaluation of the Enlightenment is mixed. An alteration/healing (*Verwindung*) of modernity is certainly required, but it cannot simply be "overcome" (*Überwindung*). See *Vattimo and Theology*, 8–10. Benedict XVI provides his own careful evaluation of Enlightenment modernity, including Vatican II's guarded appropriation of it, in his Christmas address to the Roman Curia of December 22, 2005.

33 Anthony Sciglitano (when speaking of Kant) uses the apt term "urbane Prometheanism," a phrase which may be properly applied to Vattimo as well, although the Torinese philosopher, while surely an urbane nihilist, can also be quite aggressive about religion's societal role. See Sciglitano, "Prometheus and Kant: Neutralizing Theological Discourse and Doxology," *Modern Theology* 25, no. 3 (2009): 387–414.

34 Nietzsche, *The Will to Power*, no. 1 of "European Nihilism."

tensions to provide a rule and measure for human being and acting is existence entirely pliant and malleable—and, therefore, free. Any attempt to
establish an ontological norm or canon, to assert a constraining *ontos on*, is
to illegitimately insist on strong thought, on fixed, stable, metaphysical structures, thereby limiting personal independence. This complete plasticity of
nature is essential if Promethean human freedom is to be fully unfurled. And
this accounts for Vattimo's profound voluntarism and his insistence on tolerance (named *caritas*) toward virtually any (non-violent) point of view.[35]

The historical roots of Vattimo's thought are not difficult to identify. As
Louis Dupré has argued, the ancients were constructivists only to the extent
that culture represented a further molding of a given nature.[36] With Descartes
and Kant, the form-giving principle of the subject is intensified. There is a
gradual loss of cosmic intelligibility, of the truth mediated by nature, of the
link between God and creatures. By the time one reaches Nietzsche, as the
aforementioned parable from *The Twilight of the Idols* makes clear, meaning
is entirely bestowed by human subjectivity. This is why Vattimo insists that
Nietzsche and Heidegger complete the turn toward subjectivity and interiority
that began with Christianity. It is the Nietzsche of the "death of God" and the
Heidegger of the epiphanic and evanescent notion of being that brings to
fruition the allegedly anti-metaphysical philosophy initiated by Christianity's
interest in the soul rather than in the cosmos. This is why Vattimo insists that
"postmodern nihilism constitutes the actual truth of Christianity."[37]

Needless to say, this kind of Promethean nihilism regards traditional
Christian teachings and beliefs as entirely outdated. The uniqueness of the
Jewish law and prophets, of Christ's historical Incarnation and Resurrection,
are swallowed by Vattimo's weak thought, by the claim that there are no
finalities, no enduring, objective truths. The Torinese's philosophy sublates
the concrete and determinately historical dimensions of Christianity into
the philosophical idea of an overarching weak thought, with religion now
emptied of its authentic specificity for the sake of the secularized philosophy
of nihilism. Christianity here is a parable which only reaches its zenith (now
stripped of mythology) in the insights of Heidegger and Nietzsche. But this

---

35 One may contrast Vattimo's position with Pope Benedict XVI's encyclical (June 29, 2009) on
caritas wherein the proper exercise of charity is necessarily linked with enduring truth: Only the
truth sets us free (Jn 8:22) while charity itself "rejoices in the truth" (1 Cor 13:6). See *Caritas in
veritate*, no.1.

36 Louis Dupré, *Passage to Modernity* (New Haven: Yale University Press, 1993).

37 *A Farewell to Truth*, 47.

dissolution of historical Christianity into a philosophical universality is, ironically, the quintessential strategy of modernity, leading one to wonder to what extent the overcoming of the modern attitude toward religion (even in the highly nuanced Vattimian understanding of "overcoming") has been accomplished. The fundamental narrative of modernity remains the same; only the philosophers invoked (Nietzsche and Heidegger rather than Kant and Hegel) have exchanged places. Christian faith is *aufgehoben* by a nihilism which alone allows true freedom. No less than modernity, Vattimo wants to defang religion by dissolving it into an inoffensive charity-as-tolerance without any truth-claims, thereby (once again) allowing the public square to be entirely secular, absent any strong religious claims.

As is clear, then, Vattimo refuses to commit himself to the kind of definitive and specific claims that Christ and the Christian message inexorably make. These assertions seem to him to replicate a Platonic escape to a reified, ahistorical fable—far from the incessant and enveloping tides of contingency and provisionality, of the dialectic of *lēthē* and *alētheia*, of hiddenness and truth. His religious identity, therefore, despite his continuing fascination with Christianity, is entirely reconceived according to his own philosophical faith, a faith that cannot see the unconditioned revealed in the historically concrete. The *scandalum particularitatis*, the shorthand term referring to the scandal of the Incarnation, is indeed, an obstacle for Vattimo's deeply historicized notion of truth. The Torinese philosopher certainly wishes to give Christianity a hearing, even to reintroduce its lexicon into the public square, but it must now be deeply reconceived and reinterpreted, indeed, betrayed in its fundamental instincts.[38]

At the same time, one must nonetheless call attention to the desire for God that animates much of Vattimo's recent writing. Like a moth drawn to a flame, he returns again and again to the God-question and to the person of Jesus of Nazareth. To be sure, Vattimo is no paradigm of Christian orthodoxy—as he willingly admits—offering interpretations deeply incongruous

---

38 Yet Vattimo would do well to see that there are convergences between his understanding of secularity and the historical emphasis on the Incarnation. Catholicism has always recognized a "healthy secularity"—i.e., a natural sphere that has an excellence in and of itself. But the intelligibility and autonomy of the natural estate is rooted in the *logos*-structure of reality. And *logos*, or reason, is at the heart of who God is and how God acts, as Benedict XVI pointed out insistently in his Regensburg address (September 12, 2006). So there is a decided accent on fraternity and tolerance in Christianity—and a consequent lessening of violence. But this fraternity and healthy secularity is not based on "weak thought." It is based, rather, on the belief in the *logos* become flesh in Jesus Christ. See chapters six and seven for further development of these points.

with the God of Abraham, Isaac, Jacob, and Jesus Christ preached by historical Christianity. But his work represents a desire for God, a desire making it difficult for him simply to walk away from religion entirely. In the last analysis, we may see in Vattimo's provocative work something of St. Augustine's uneasy heart: "You have made us for yourself, O Lord, and our hearts are restless until they rest in you."[39]

39 *Confessions* 1.1.1.

Chapter Six

Introduction:
The God of Philosophy and of the Bible: Theological Reflections on Regensburg

enedict XVI's September 12th, 2006, lecture to scholars of the University of Regensburg became an international *cause célèbre* when the pope's comments (recounting a dialogue between a Byzantine Emperor and an educated Persian) were interpreted as profoundly insulting to Islam. Unfortunately, the subsequent furor and indignation overshadowed the central theme of the lecture which was to reflect, once again, on the proper relationship between faith and reason. As we have seen, in his 1998 encyclical *Fides et ratio*, Pope John Paul II summed up much of the Catholic tradition by insisting on the conjunctive confluence of human rationality and Christian faith.

John Paul's unambiguous endorsement of philosophy was repeated by Benedict XVI in the Regensburg Lecture. Indeed, Benedict argues that the encounter between the biblical message and Greek philosophy was providential, as attested by the vision of St. Paul in Acts 16 wherein his path to Asia was blocked while, at the same time, a Macedonian pleaded for his aid. Benedict invokes this biblical passage in order to overturn and confound what has become a central trope in certain theological precincts: the Hellenization thesis, tendered most forcefully by Adolf von Harnack who argued that the simple message of the Bible had been deformed and defaced by Greek philosophy. The straightforward instruction of Jesus—God is our father and all men are brothers—had been badly contorted by later "metaphysical" talk about eternal persons, processions, and relations.

Benedict, echoing themes he had first developed as a young theologian, ardently opposed Harnack and his thesis, arguing that the intimate rapprochement between biblical faith and Greek inquiry was born of an "intrinsic necessity." The name of God revealed in Exodus 3:14—which clearly resonates with the "I am" of John's Gospel (8:24 and 8:58)—suggested to several Fathers of the Church the unity of philosophy and faith. The biblical name "I am" was now united with the notions of existence and being; the primacy and plenitude of the existing real was conjoined with the identity of the Lord of history. In the Christian tradition, Benedict insists, the choice was made to utilize, even while purifying and surpassing, the truth discovered by the philosophers.

Benedict accents the importance of Greek philosophy for several reasons. But central to his lecture—indeed, the very crux of his argument—is this: "not to act in accordance with reason is contrary to God's nature." With this insight, "the heart of Greek thought" is now conjoined with Christian faith. God's sovereign will cannot be understood as so transcendent to human categories that rationality itself is inapplicable to the Creator. Benedict goes on to firmly reprove the medieval Islamic writer, Ibn Hazm, for holding that if God so willed it, men would have to practice idolatry. This misplaced emphasis on the unknowability and even irrationality of God, Benedict continues, was not limited to Islamic thinkers. Even some Christian theologians, abandoning the intellectualism of Augustine and Aquinas, became captive to a voluntarism which defends limitless divine freedom, not bound even by truth and goodness. Against this position, Benedict cites the famous statement of Lateran IV (1215)—that although the dissimilarity between God and humanity is always greater, there nonetheless remains a true similarity between Creator and creatures. God is not sheer caprice; *he acts with reason*—a reason that is analogically related to our own.

Finally, Benedict argues that Western technocratic rationality, with its emphasis on positivist reason and empirical verification, has illegitimately circumscribed speculative intelligence. The pope makes clear that his comments are not intended as an overarching critique of modernity—for modernity has yielded many benefits—but represent a plea for a more capacious and encompassing vision of human rationality, a breadth of perception allowing reason to achieve a deeper, more far-reaching understanding of humanity, the cosmos, and of God himself.

In the Regensburg Lecture, Pope Benedict deftly scores the irrationality of certain religious movements, even while taking to task the limited philosophical vision of much contemporary Western scientism. The profound insights embedded in this short lecture—with its insistence that religious faith needs reason just as reason cannot do without faith—will remain consequential far into the future.

The God of Philosophy and of the Bible: Theological Reflections on Regensburg

There has been ample commentary on Pope Benedict XVI's remarks about Islam in his Regensburg Lecture of Sept. 12, 2006. But there has been very little sustained comment on the other major story that emerged from that lecture: the relationship between Christian faith and human rationality. For the pope not only derided the kind of reason that proceeds without faith, he also took to task those who failed to grasp that faith is inextricably bound up with reason, even with a certain kind of philosophical thinking. This was the major story that went largely unreported, and yet is of enduring importance for understanding Christian life and thought.

The conjunctive coherence of faith and reason is a position that has a long and venerable heritage extending through many of the earliest fathers of the Church. They recognized that reason, *logos*, already said something important about God, even if this needed to be amplified, corrected, and transformed by revelation. Second and third-century Christians such as Justin Martyr, Clement of Alexandria, and Origen all had something to contribute on this question. On the other hand, the third-century theologian Tertullian famously asked, "What does Athens have to do with Jerusalem, the Academy with the Church?" Precious little, Tertullian thundered: "Away with all attempts to produce a mottled Christianity of Stoic, Platonic and dialectic composition! We want no curious disputation after possessing Christ Jesus, no inquisition after enjoying the Gospel!"[1] For the North African thinker, philosophy represented, at least often enough, an attempt to deform and mutilate transparent biblical truth.

---

* Originally published as "The God of Philosophy and of the Bible: Theological Reflections on Regensburg," *Logos: A Journal of Catholic Thought and Culture* 10, no. 4 (2007): 120–30. Republished with permission.

1 Tertullian, *The Prescription against Heretics*, vol. 3 of *The Ante-Nicene Fathers*, ed. Alexander Roberts and James Donaldson (Grand Rapids: Eerdmans Publishing, 1957), chapter 7, 246.

While many remember Tertullian's pointed remarks, fewer are likely to be familiar with a Tertullian *redivivus*, the medieval friar Jacopone da Todi, long considered the author of the beautiful Latin hymn about Mary, the *Stabat Mater*. In the middle of the thirteenth century, Jacopone was irritated with the growing number of Franciscan friars leaving Assisi for the allurements of learning available at the University of Paris, inspiring his mocking couplet, "The *frati* flock to Paris schools/And all Assisi's ardor cools." Philosophical reasoning, for Jacopone, deadens and defaces the fiery spirit of Christian piety. The poet could not resist expanding on his sentiments:

> Plato and Socrates may contend
> And all the breath in their bodies spend
> Arguing without an end
> What's it all to me?
> Only a pure and simple mind
> Straight to heaven its way does find
> Greets the King [. . .] while far behind
> Lags the world's philosophy [. . .].[2]

The Church warmly embraced Jacopone's graceful Marian hymn, but stayed at arm's length from his dyslogistic view of philosophy and reason. In fact, just as the Franciscan poet was railing against philosophical exposition, St. Thomas Aquinas was further developing the consensual tradition of the early Church: there exists a deep convergence between the best of philosophy and the Christian faith; grace perfects nature and reason, it does not destroy them.[3] Ever aware of St. Paul's assertion, "I will destroy the wisdom of the wise," Aquinas says that the Apostle is not rejecting philosophy per se, but warning against trusting in one's personal erudition.[4]

In his Regensburg Lecture, Benedict's concern for a proper balancing of faith and reason reprised several of these significant issues.[5] The encounter

---

2 Jacopone da Todi's poems can be found in a translation rendered by Anne MacDonell, *Sons of Francis* (London: J. M. Dent and Co., 1902), 369.

3 *Summa theologiae* I, 1, 8.

4 For Aquinas' comments on this point, see his *Expositio super librum Boethii De Trinitate*, q. 2, a. 3, ad 2.

5 Pope Benedict XVI's interest in the faith/reason question has repeatedly come to the fore over the years as evidenced, for example, by his 2004 dialogue with Jürgen Habermas on the role of reason and religion in contemporary societies. See Joseph Ratzinger and Jürgen Habermas, *The Dialectics of Secularization: On Reason and Religion* (San Francisco: Ignatius Press, 2007).

between the biblical message and Greek thought was providential, he argues, as witnessed by the vision of St. Paul in Acts 16 wherein his path to Asia is blocked while a Macedonian pleads for his aid. Paul's vision, in fact, may be interpreted as indicating a necessary and fruitful rapprochement between biblical faith and Greek inquiry. The pope recounts that the name of God revealed in Exodus 3:14 suggested to the fathers of the Church a unity of belief and thought, of philosophy and faith. The biblical name for God, "I am," is here unified with a philosophical idea, the notion of existence and being. As the younger Ratzinger says in his *Introduction to Christianity* (explicitly invoked in a footnote to the Regensburg lecture), in this union, one finds that "belief is wedded to ontology."[6] One should look very carefully, however, at this marriage between *ontos* (being) and *theos* (God). It is decidedly not the subordination of God to an *a priori* philosophical idea. Nor does it counsel a Christian accommodation to a foreign worldview. Such a position is rightly derided as "ontotheology" in the worst possible sense.[7]

What the pope *is* suggesting, rather, is that in this marriage of faith and philosophy, one sees the commingling of the philosophical insight into the primacy of *the existing real, of being itself*, with the revelation of the Lord of the universe manifested in the history of Israel and in Jesus of Nazareth. The "I am" of Exodus and again, for example, of Isaiah 48:12, "I am He, the first and the last," and finally, the "I am" of John's Gospel (John 8:24; 8:58) all converge. The fullness of existence prized by ancient philosophy and the revelation of God's name in Exodus, Ratzinger argues, comes to fruition and fulfillment in the identity of Christ. Precisely here one detects the proper conjunction and transformation of philosophy by faith and revelation.

Again in the early Church, the pope insists, a choice was boldly made for utilizing and purifying the God of the philosophers, even while rejecting the gods of various mythic religions. Our God, the early Christian writers say, is the highest being of whom your philosophers speak. Our faith is, in fact, the "true philosophy" as so many Christian thinkers called it, a faith that embodies the fullness of the *logos*.[8] What occurs here is the triumph of

---

6 Joseph Ratzinger, *Introduction to Christianity*, trans. J. R. Foster (London: Search Press, 1969), 79.

7 "Ontotheology," in this definition, means an understanding of God overshadowed by the philosophical notion of being. For the meaning of ontotheology in several contemporary thinkers, see Thomas G. Guarino, *Foundations of Systematic Theology* (New York: T & T Clark, 2005), 9–20.

8 See Pierre Hadot, *Philosophy as a Way of Life*, trans. Michael Chase (Oxford: Blackwell, 1995), 141n15, citing Clement of Alexandria's *Stromateis* I, 13, 57.

logos over *mythos*, of existing actuality over fiction and fable. It is no surprise, then, that the pope, near the close of his Regensburg lecture, invokes Plato's *Phaedo*. There, Socrates observes:

> [It is possible that] a man should have lighted upon some argument or other which at first seemed true and then turned out to be false, and instead of blaming himself and his own want of wit, because he is annoyed, should at last be too glad to transfer the blame from himself to arguments in general; and forever afterwards should hate and revile them, and lose the truth and knowledge of realities.[9]

Socrates, it is clear, is interested in actuality, in the existing real, over and against the world of appearance and falsehood. One discerns, Benedict argues, that both the Bible and the best of philosophical thought strive for reality, for truth, rather than for mythology. This is why the pope insists that the encounter of biblical faith with Greek thought resulted in a "mutual enrichment." Christians rejected the folk customs of ancient *religio* in favor of the truth of being, but this truth now expanded and transformed by the incomparably new wine of Revelation. Something like this is in evidence in Pascal's distinction between *le Dieu des philosophes* and *le Dieu d'Abraham, d'Isaac, et de Jacob*. Pascal recognized that the God of love and fire, the God of the patriarchs, outstripped anything that the philosophers could imagine. But, Ratzinger insists, the God of Abraham does not cease to be what the philosophers had discovered: the truth and ground of being. Christianity's task is to comprehend, surpass, and correct the God of the philosophers.

It is unsurprising, then, that Ratzinger, in his earlier work, warmly embraces the incisive comment of Tertullian, "Our Lord Christ called himself truth, not custom," labeling this insight one of the "great assertions" of the early Church.[10] For in rejecting myth and custom for the truth of being, the Church undertook the abiding task of insisting on the uniqueness of her own claims. Of course, one may legitimately object that this emphasis on the knowledge of the existing real was also appropriated by modernity. But the difference is that modernity, in a logic unthinkable for the ancients and their medieval successors, severed the real from the One who is the source, the *fons et origo* of all existence, the One who is himself the most

---

9 90c-d; See *The Dialogues of Plato*, trans. B. Jowett, vol. 1 (New York: Random House, 1920), 475.

10 Ratzinger, *Introduction to Christianity*, 97, citing Tertullian, *De virginibus velandis*, I, 1.

intelligible, even if the human intellect, finite and sinful, can only glimpse him obliquely and obscurely. It is just here, in the quest for the full intelligibility of the universe, that philosophy and faith closely merge. For there exists an ascent of our spirits, by way of the theatre of the world, to the intelligibility and luminosity of the cosmos and to the infinite source of existence and truth. Here the complex but unified real opens our vision to the fountainhead of all reality. Under the influence of Kant and a later positivism, modernity tended toward a sensibility and empiricism cut off from the natural goal of both speculative intelligence and mysticism. This *gran rifiuto* is finely summarized by the Jesuit patrologist Henri de Lubac who once remarked: modernity will always *know* more, it will always *explain* more, but it will never *understand* more, because it has refused mystery.[11] What is at stake here is mystery both in the specifically religious sense, and in the sense of the fullness of being that yields itself to the penetrating intellect.

At Regensburg, Benedict is concerned not only with an untenable Western rationalism that refuses mystery, but also with a dichotomous understanding of faith and reason haunting religion itself. One may not entertain the deformed image of a voluntarist God any more than one may sanction the unbridled use of a truncated reason. The pope takes specific note of Ibn Hazm's claim that God's transcendence is such that he is not bound even by his own word. But the eleventh century Muslim thinker is not the only one guilty of this charge. Benedict recognizes that in late medieval Christianity the scent of voluntarism also entered the Church, whereby God's ordained will was considered distinct from his absolute will, so that God's absolute freedom could contradict, at least theoretically, what he himself had instituted. In the classic example, God could have, in his transcendent power, condemned the just to eternal damnation, thereby introducing into the Godhead an element of caprice and whimsy severed from right reason. Rather than human reason being an icon and image of God, God becomes a totally distant figure, whose life and mind remain entirely unfathomable by humanity. Precisely here the pope invokes the important teaching of Lateran IV in 1215: there exists an analogical similitude between creatures and God, even if always within a greater dissimilitude. God, Benedict insists, has revealed himself as truth, as one who acts with reason, not as sheer *arbitrium* with a profligate freedom of will that contravenes every law.

11 Henri de Lubac, *A Theologian Speaks* (Los Angeles: Twin Circle, 1985), 25. This pamphlet is an English translation of an interview of de Lubac by Angelo Scola that first appeared in the Italian journal *30 Giorni* (July 1985).

This is also why Benedict so strongly and insistently opposes a severe disjunction between the God of the philosophers and the God of the Bible, thereby explaining his direct and sustained attack at Regensburg on the idea of "dehellenization," on any attempt to sever the Christian faith from the heritage of Hellenistic inquiry. Of course, the pope is very careful here. With the entire prior tradition, he insists that Greek inquiry must be "critically purified." By this he means that all philosophy, of Greek provenance or otherwise, must be transformed and recreated by theology. This position was championed by virtually every father of the Church as well as every later thinker committed to historic Christian orthodoxy. As Aquinas says, to take one example, when one uses philosophy in service to the faith, one does not mix water with wine; one *changes* water into wine.[12] The history of theology is replete with such instances: witness Augustine's use of Plotinus, Aquinas's adoption of Aristotle, Newman's employment of Locke and Hume, and the contemporary theological use and modification of Kant, Heidegger, and Husserl. It is precisely by an assimilation and creative transformation of philosophy (along with other disciplines) that proper theological development occurs.[13] Of course, Christian faith is not to be accommodated to an alien ideology or tied to the bed of some latter-day Procrustes. Benedict himself, in his book on eschatology, offers an example of a critically purified philosophy, observing that Aquinas defined the human soul as *forma corporis*, the form of the body. But this seemingly Aristotelian definition manifested in reality "a complete transformation of Aristotelianism" since in Aristotle, the soul is entirely bonded to matter, while Aquinas is concerned to protect the biblical affirmation that union with Christ overcomes death. In this instance, philosophical concepts are used to champion what amounts to an impossibility in Aristotle's own thought.[14]

But having registered a necessary and cautionary accent on "critical purification," Benedict is nonetheless averse to the program of dehellenization because of its tendency to separate faith and reason. The Reformation was right to fear a Gospel dominated by an alien philosophical system. The pope suggests, however, that the Church's interest in meta-

---

12 *De Trinitate*, q. 2, a. 3, ad 5.

13 I have treated the issue of how theology properly uses philosophy and other disciplines, in "'Spoils from Egypt': Yesterday and Today," *Pro Ecclesia* 15, no. 4 (2006): 403–17.

14 Joseph Ratzinger, *Eschatology*, trans. Michael Waldstein (Washington, DC: The Catholic University of America Press, 1988), 146–47.

physics should not be regarded as an attempt to achieve a conceptual integration of Christianity on something other than biblical grounds, but as an employment of philosophical reasoning in service to the Gospel's own purposes, in particular its insistent claims to transcultural and transgenerational truth and universality. So when Luther says, for example, "No one can become a theologian unless he becomes one without Aristotle," he is entirely right, but only in the sense that neither Aristotle nor any other philosopher may be uncritically adopted without modification by Christian faith and doctrine.[15] Although the pope mentions Kant as radicalizing the dehellenization program, a more recent paradigm is Martin Heidegger who, like Kant, tries to limit theology's speculative reach. Heidegger claims, for example, that "faith does not need the thought of Being. When faith has recourse to this thought, it is no longer faith."[16] Heidegger here not only misunderstands how "being" is used within the tradition, he also drives a stake between faith and reason in service to his own project of making theology merely a regional discipline (as he says, like chemistry or mathematics) reflecting simply on faith-filled life.[17] But this illegitimately attempts to overturn the traditional notion that theology is the highest discipline precisely because it offers knowledge of the *Creator* of being while all other disciplines, including philosophy, study one or another aspect of created *esse*.

The pope also criticizes the historian Adolf von Harnack, who was influential in both Catholic and Protestant theology. Harnack's famous manifesto, *Das Wesen des Christentums*, is based on the claim that the simple Hebraic message of Jesus of Nazareth, "God is our father and all men are brothers," was badly distorted by Hellenistic philosophy, forcing useless speculation about the Eternal Logos generated from the Father and about three hypostases sharing one divine nature. Historical fact, Harnack says, is here drawn into the realm of philosophy and metaphysics, making the Christian teaching on the Trinity reek of philosophical obscurantism and overweening

---

15 *Luther's Works*, ed. Jaroslav Pelikan and Helmut T. Lehmann, vol. 31 (St. Louis: Concordia, 1955–1986), 12.

16 "Der Glaube hat das Denken des Seins nicht nötig. Wenn er das braucht, ist er schon nicht mehr Glaube." Martin Heidegger, "Séminaire de Zurich," trans. F. Fédier, *Po&sie* 13 (1980): 52–63, at 60. The passage may also be found in *Heidegger et la question de Dieu*, ed. Richard Kearney and Joseph S. O'Leary (Paris: Bernard Grasset, 1980), 334.

17 Martin Heidegger, *The Piety of Thinking*, trans. J. Hart and J. Maraldo (Bloomington: Indiana University Press, 1976), 6. These comments are also found in Martin Heidegger, *Pathmarks*, ed. William McNeill (Cambridge: Cambridge University Press, 1998), 41.

supernaturalism.[18] Having denied the possibility that Christian faith assimilated and transformed certain Greek ideas in *service* to the faith, Harnack
can only conclude that the council of Nicea was the triumph of the priests
over the people, that is, of a Hellenistically educated clergy over an allegedly
simple and uncomplicated faith.[19] Benedict strongly rebukes Harnack's
methodological reductionism, his trimming the Gospel's claim that Jesus of
Nazareth is the Eternal Word made flesh to the pre-existing parameters of a
human reason that limits itself to the empirically verifiable.

Benedict's final point about dehellenization concerns the contemporary
claim that the Church's early synthesis of faith and Hellenistic thought is
not binding on others. Different cultures, it is sometimes argued, can go
"behind" the convergence of Greek thought and biblical inspiration in order
to inculturate the Gospel "in their own particular milieux." The pope
sharply concludes, "This thesis is not simply false, but it is coarse and lacking
in precision." Why this stinging rebuke? Because, he says, the fundamental
decisions made about the relationship between faith and reason are themselves part of the faith; they are developments consonant with the nature of
the faith itself.

The pope surely cannot intend to contravene here what Vatican II
taught so forcefully as a general hermeneutical principle: the deposit of faith
is one matter, the way in which it is expressed, without violence to its meaning, is another.[20] With this formulation the council wished to open the way
to an authentic theological pluralism that nonetheless maintains a fundamental unity of faith and doctrine. It is a principle that, over the course of
decades, has yielded significant ecumenical and theological fruit. Not bound
simply to the linguistic conventions of one particular epoch, theology—
African and Asian certainly, but also Western—could express the faith using
other forms of thought. Further, Christian communities could come to
agreements about substantial matters while using different vocabularies and
semantic lexicons. An example would be the issue of justification. At the

---

18 Adolf Harnack, *What is Christianity?* trans. Thomas Bailey Saunders (Gloucester, MA: Peter
Smith, 1978), 204–5; 236–37.

19 Harnack, vol. 4 of *History of Dogma*, trans. Neil Buchanan (Boston: Little, Brown, and Company, 1898), 106.

20 Vatican Council II, *Gaudium et spes* (December 7, 1965), no. 62. In fact, Benedict XVI benignly
cited this distinction (in its original context which was John XXIII's opening speech to the council
on October 11, 1962) when indicating the legitimate "hermeneutic of reform" inaugurated by
Vatican II. See Benedict's important *Christmas Address to the Roman Curia* of December 22,
2005.

council of Trent, Catholicism used the language of causality, characteristic of Aristotelian thought, to express its understanding of how men and women are justified by faith and grace, while in the *Joint Declaration on Justification*, signed with the Lutheran World Federation in 1999, the Catholic Church intends the same understanding promulgated by Trent, but without using the earlier conceptual forms.

But if such reconceptualization is not the target, what exactly is? The pope refers, I suspect, to the aforementioned Trinitarian and Christological formulations of the early Church, with three Persons sharing one divine essence and, in the case of Jesus of Nazareth, two natures subsisting in the one Person of the Eternal Logos. These conciliar formulations, achieved from within the biblical, liturgical, and performative life of Christian faith, cannot be understood simply as early, premodern, Hellenistically-tinged attempts to objectify the Gospel. They must be understood as a use of Greek concepts disciplined and purified by a living, scriptural faith. To affirm this is not to forestall continuing theological investigation. It is to say that such investigation must always take place within the boundaries achieved by the early Christian Church in obedience to the truth of scripture.

Ultimately, Benedict's lecture at Regensburg was a forceful affirmation of several traditional themes concerning reason as a gift from God with its own *relative* autonomy. Most assuredly it does not echo some of the baneful comments about philosophy issued by Tertullian and Jacopone (even while recognizing their legitimate concerns). Positively, it expands upon what John Paul II had written in 1998 in the encyclical *Fides et ratio*, which itself sums up the earlier tradition: "Faith asks that its object be understood with the help of reason; and at the summit of its searching, reason acknowledges that it cannot do without what faith presents."[21]

Pope Benedict again makes clear at Regensburg a position to which virtually the entire Christian tradition bears witness: properly understood, the God of the philosophers and the God of Abraham, Isaac, and Jacob cannot be placed at antipodes.

---

21 John Paul II, *Fides et ratio* (September 14, 1998), no. 42.

Chapter Seven

Introduction: Nature and Grace: Seeking the Delicate Balance

I t is not unusual for theologians to ignore papal remarks made to civil authorities. Such comments, usually tendered at the beginning of apostolic journeys, are often little more than scripted greetings to duly assembled dignitaries. Pope Benedict XVI, however, frequently used these occasions to offer insightful primers on the relationship between civil society and the Church, between nature and grace, between reason and faith.

One example of this is Benedict's 2008 visit to France, wherein he endorsed President Nicholas Sarkozy's call for a *laïcité positive*—or a healthy secularism. A couple of years later, the pope repeated this idea when speaking to the diplomats accredited to the Holy See. He argued for the "urgent need to delineate a positive and open secularity [. . .] grounded in the just autonomy of the temporal order and the spiritual order."[1]

Pope Benedict's accent on a healthy secularism has its proximate roots in Vatican II's Pastoral Constitution, *Gaudium et spes*, which speaks of the relative autonomy of the natural order: "By the very fact of their creation, all things are endowed with their own stability, truth, goodness, their own laws and their proper order."[2] This statement reflects the traditional Catholic theme that the natural sphere possesses an integral excellence and stability even "apart" from the order of revelation and grace.

And within this natural sphere, moral truth and meaning are visible. For example, Pope John Paul II insisted in his 1995 encyclical *Evangelium vitae*—when discussing abortion and euthanasia—that despite the negative consequences of sin, "*it* [the moral law] *can also be known in its essential traits by human reason.*"[3] Pope Benedict frequently affirmed the same point,

---

1 Benedict XVI, *Address of His Holiness Pope Benedict XVI to the Members of the Diplomatic Corps for the Traditional Exchange of New Year Greetings* (January 11, 2010).

2 Vatican Council II, *Gaudium et spes* (December 7, 1965), no. 36.

3 John Paul II, Encyclical Letter *Evangelium vitae* (March 25, 1995), no. 29.

perhaps most clearly in his 2010 address at Westminster Hall in London, before the most distinguished academic and political classes of British society. He noted that if fundamental moral issues are decided by nothing more solid than societal consensus "then the fragility of the [democratic] process becomes all too evident."

This fragility, however, can be surmounted. Benedict notes that one of the great achievements of the British Parliament, the abolition of the slave trade, was built upon "firm ethical principles rooted in the natural law." He adds that the "Catholic tradition maintains that the objective norms governing right reason are accessible to reason, [even] prescinding from the content of revelation."[4] Both John Paul II and Benedict XVI are arguing that there is a *natural visibility* to truth. *Kosmos* and *physis* teach us something about the human person and his proper flourishing. Nature, while wounded by sin, has an authentic independence, even if it is never entirely self-sufficient.

Of course, care must be taken with this issue precisely because there exists no natural realm completely apart from the order of grace. As Hans Urs von Balthasar argued in the 1940s, the entire Catholic tradition, including the High Middle Ages, invoked the order of nature only within the *unicus ordo realis supernaturalis*. In other words, the natural order is already deeply participative in the life of grace. To speak of nature—whether human nature, natural law, natural virtue, or a natural pathway to God—is always to invoke the overarching estate of grace which inexorably commands, irradiates, and transforms every natural reality. To express this carefully calibrated relationship, Balthasar invoked the Latin phrase *aliter, non alter* which is to say: nature is always itself (and so not other) even though it has become something "different" through divine grace.

Consequently, when Benedict XVI speaks of a "healthy secularism," or when John Paul II defends philosophy's "legitimate autonomy," neither pope is extolling an entirely autonomous natural sphere. Each, rather, is seeking to uphold the delicate theological balance between the orders of nature and grace. The Church has a profound respect for the natural, created estate, a domain with its own integrity and stability. At the same time, even with all its integral excellence, the natural realm has palpable limits; the truth it yields needs to be purified and strengthened by divine revelation. As Vatican

---

4 Benedict XVI, *Address of His Holiness Benedict XVI, Westminster Hall—City of Westminster,* September 17, 2010. The text may be found in *Origins* 39 (January 21, 2010): 518–21.

II taught, any good that exists in the minds and hearts of men needs to be healed and perfected by Christ unto the glory of God.[5] The natural order, in all its various dimensions—philosophy, the civil state, anthropology, natural virtue—must ultimately come face-to-face with Jesus Christ.

---

5 Vatican Council II, *Lumen gentium* (November 21, 1964), no. 17; Vatican Council II, *Ad gentes* (December 7, 1965), no. 9.

Nature and Grace:
Seeking the Delicate Balance

When Pope Benedict XVI visited France in September of 2008 and endorsed French President Nicolas Sarkozy's call for a *laïcité positive*, some Christians may have thought that the pope was slightly addled—given to fuzzy thinking, perhaps, after an extended bout of travel.[6] More benignly, it was supposed that Benedict was simply engaging in a *captatio benevolentiae*, wisely ingratiating himself with his rabidly secular hosts. In fact, Benedict's remark was carefully calculated, perfectly echoing the comments offered after his remarkable pastoral visit to the United States earlier in 2008. Impressed by his pilgrimage to America, Benedict gratefully acknowledged the country's "healthy secularism"—the anglicized version of "*laïcité positive*."[7] But why, one asks, is the pope endorsing a secular view of society, even a healthy one? Is it not his mission to foster and maintain a thick Christian and religious culture, a vision of public life which is a robust competitor to secularism of any kind, especially to the poisonous *laïcisme* with its deeply truncated anthropology and its militant privatization of religious belief and activity?

In fact, Benedict's comments about the need for an authentic and healthy secularity underscore the Catholic understanding of the autonomy belonging to the natural, created order. Invoking the word "autonomy" in its simple and freestanding sense is not entirely helpful here, conjuring up, as it inexorably does, images of enraged *illuminati* railing against an oppressive God and a benighted Church with its allegedly unending campaigns to deprive humanity of unfettered freedom. The term "*relative*

---

* Originally published as "Nature and Grace: Seeking the Delicate Balance," *Josephinum Journal of Theology* 18, no. 1 (2011): 151–62. Republished with permission.

6 See Benedict XVI, *Meeting with Authorities of the State* (September 12, 2008). Text may be found in *Origins* 38 (September 25, 2008): 245–47, at 247.

7 See Benedict XVI, *General Audience* (April 30, 2008). Subsequently, Benedict spoke of the "urgent need to delineate a *positive and open secularity* which, grounded in the just autonomy of the temporal order and the spiritual order, can foster healthy cooperation." See Benedict XVI, *Address to the Members of the Diplomatic Corps* (January 11, 2010), 520 (emphasis added).

autonomy" more precisely names the reality at stake, insisting that nature, in its own sphere, possesses an intrinsic stability and integral excellence. Such constancy and excellence is neither overthrown nor disrupted by the uniqueness or stark singularity of—dare it be said without irony—"transgressive" Judeo-Christian revelation. As Aquinas put it in the thirteenth century, in a lapidary formulation of extraordinary influence but intended simply to recapitulate the prior Christian tradition: *Gratia perficit, non destruit naturam.*[8] Grace does not destroy nature but perfects it, bringing it to fruition. This statement should not be understood as mitigating the stark "alterity" of revelation, the fact that it speaks uniquely of the "Other," that it necessarily shatters totality systems—as the postmoderns love to say—particularly those boundaries artificially imposed by rationalist modernity. Univocal reductionism and unimaginative predetermination are precisely what is *not* asserted by positing the "relative autonomy" of the natural order. It is simply to insist that the created estate possesses an inner identity, an inherent essence with its own capacities and power, even "apart" from the further molding that is bestowed by revelation and grace.[9] Vatican II gives us some sense of this when it says, "By the autonomy of earthly affairs, we mean that created things and societies themselves enjoy their own laws and values." And again, "By the very fact of their creation, all things are endowed with their own stability, truth, goodness, their own laws and their proper order."[10]

The council is hardly denying the preeminence of the Christian narrative—or the absolute *novum* that revelation assuredly introduces—any more than Benedict himself is doing. In fact, Vatican II firmly insists that any understanding of the created order's autonomy must be intrinsically linked with humanity's profound dependence on God. Nonetheless, it is a matter

---

8 Thomas Aquinas, *Summa theologiae* I, q. 1, a. 8, ad 2.

9 This traditional theme in Catholic thought, the "relative autonomy" of the natural, created order, is developed by Hans Urs von Balthasar in his 1951 volume, an extended dialogue with Karl Barth. See Hans Urs von Balthasar, *The Theology of Karl Barth*, trans. Edward T. Oakes (San Francisco: Ignatius Press, 1992), 120, 242.

10 *Gaudium et spes*, no. 36. Benedict XVI also makes this point in his first encyclical, *Deus caritas est* (December 25, 2005) at no. 28: "Fundamental to Christianity is the distinction between what belongs to Caesar and what belongs to God (cf. *Mt* 22:21), in other words, the distinction between Church and State, or, as the Second Vatican Council puts it, the autonomy of the temporal sphere." In *Acta apostolicae sedis* 98 (2006), 217–52, at 238. For a detailed analysis of Benedict's attempt to balance the realms of nature and grace, see Serge-Thomas Bonino, "Nature et grâce dans l'encyclique *Deus caritas est*," *Revue Thomiste* 105 (2005): 531–49.

of recognizing the role of nature in its own sphere, with its own excellence and goodness, its own essence and constancy.[11]

Deeply related to this accent on the quasi-autonomy of nature is the traditional Catholic accent on natural law, natural virtue, a natural path to God's existence, and a stable human nature. With regard to natural law, for example, John Paul II insisted, in the course of discussing evils such as abortion and euthanasia, "... *despite the negative consequence of sin, it* [the moral law] *can also be known in its essential traits by human reason.*"[12] The Vatican's own website (in its English version) fails to indicate that the official text of the document italicizes these words for a precise reason: to display boldly and without hesitation the stability and knowability of the natural order. One need not be a Christian, or, indeed, an explicitly religious person of any kind, to maintain the principal truths concerning the defense and promotion of human life. Of course, a fuller discussion of natural law would require reflection on a complex of elements inescapably entering the cognitive equation: the role of antecedent subjective interests, for example, or the cultural background of the inquirer, or a life of sinfulness or holiness. Nevertheless, the fundamental point is clear: nature has its own stability, its own integral autonomy, whose demands may be known by the discerning, reasonable individual. It must be immediately added that nature has only a "*relative* autonomy" precisely because it is always deeply embedded in the one and only supernatural order of God's action in history. But what is affirmed here is that, because nature does, indeed, have a certain autonomy, arguments may be made regarding the moral order which have a rational validity even apart from full-blooded, "intrasystemic" religious belief. Nature and natural reason, although wounded by sin, have a genuine, if not total, independence.[13]

---

11 As Benedict said to the American bishops in April 2008: "Of course, what is essential is a correct understanding of the just autonomy of the secular order, an autonomy which cannot be divorced from God the Creator and his saving plan." *Responses of His Holiness Benedict XVI to the Questions Posed by the US Bishops* (April 16, 2008). In *Acta apostolicae sedis* 100 (2008), 314–19, at 314.

12 John Paul II, *Evangelium vitae*, no. 29. In *Acta apostolicae sedis* 87 (1995), 401–522, at 434. An English translation may be found in *Origins* 24 (April 6, 1995): 689–727, at 700. The *Origins* translation, however, does not italicize the remarks found in the authentic Latin text.

13 While debates continue about the precise contours of natural law reasoning, most parties agree with the claim that reason, although weakened by sin, is nonetheless able to discern certain normative precepts of the moral law. One may take as an example Benedict XVI's address to the International Theological Commission of October 5, 2007, in which he states that the natural law is "in itself accessible to any rational creature" and that with the aid of natural law

Benedict's endorsement, then, of a "healthy secularism" is one way of speaking about the quasi-autonomy of the created, natural order, just as natural law reasoning offers another venue, allowing one to declare that particular practices—on the basis of their *natural visibility*—either contribute to humanity's nobility and dignity or debase and deform the human estate. Such intrinsic honorability or unworthiness is, of course, confirmed, strengthened, and purified by revelation. But the intrinsic visibility of the true and good remains, at least potentially, even for those who are not religious "insiders."[14]

A further example will indicate how deeply this delicate relationship between nature and grace, between the relative autonomy of the natural order and the more comprehensive domain of revelation and faith, is enshrined within the Christian tradition. In his 1998 encyclical, *Fides et ratio*, John Paul II ardently defends the capacities of human reason in an age when rationality is derided for its impotence, fragmentation, and easy subjugation to power.[15] The pope also upholds philosophy's legitimate and essential independence by reminding his readers that the ancient discipline is "rightly jealous" of its autonomy. Even when philosophy is used by theology, he insists, its freedom remains unimpaired; for the "content of revelation can never debase the legitimate autonomy of reason."[16] Indeed, the pope goes so far as to insist that the venerable designation of philosophy as

---

reasoning "the foundations are laid to enter into dialogue with all people of good will and, more generally, with civil and secular society." An English translation may be found in *Origins* 37 (November 8, 2007): 352–54, at 353. At the same time, in his well-known 2004 dialogue with Jürgen Habermas, Ratzinger stated that, although the natural law had remained the "key issue" in the Church's dialogue with secular society, "this instrument has become blunt" given the challenges of evolutionary biology. See Ratzinger and Habermas, *The Dialectics of Secularization*, trans. Brian McNeil (San Francisco: Ignatius Press, 2006), 69–70. For a discussion of varying contemporary positions on natural law reasoning, see Matthew Levering, *Biblical Natural Law* (Oxford: Oxford University Press, 2008), 1–21; Martin Rhonheimer, "The Moral Significance of Pre-Rational Nature in Aquinas," in *The Perspective of the Acting Person*, ed. William F. Murphy, 129–57 (Washington, DC: The Catholic University of America Press, 2008); Patrick Riordan, "Natural Law Revivals: A Review of the Recent Literature," *Heythrop Journal* 51, no. 2 (2010): 314–23 and the various essays in *Intractable Disputes about the Natural Law*, ed. Lawrence Cunningham (Notre Dame: University of Notre Dame Press, 2009).

14 The term "natural visibility" may be found in an article by Robert Sokolowski, "What is Natural Law? Human Purposes and Natural Ends," *The Thomist* 68, no. 4 (2004): 507–29, at 524.

15 See John Paul II, Encyclical Letter *Fides et ratio* (September 14, 1998). In *Acta apostolicae sedis* 91 (1999), 5–88. An English translation may be found in *Origins* 28 (October 22, 1998): 317–47.

16 *Fides et ratio*, no. 79.

ancilla theologiae, the term describing the discipline's traditional role as the handmaiden of theological reflection, "can scarcely be used today" given philosophy's rightful independence.[17] With such a marked accent on philosophy's autonomy, some may have wondered if the pope was unwittingly encouraging rationalist tendencies.

A careful reading of the encyclical, however, reveals that John Paul II was actually defending reason's *relative* autonomy. For the pope insists that, in the light of divine revelation, philosophy itself must undergo "profound transformations." And the document makes a clear distinction between philosophy's valid autonomy and its entirely *illegitimate* "self-sufficiency," a self-determination that is wholly invalid precisely because of a refusal to be enlightened by divine truth. The pope's letter, then, calls to mind the fuller maxim concerning philosophy's traditional servant role: *ancilla theologiae sed non ancilla nisi libera*. Philosophy can only be a proper handmaiden to theology if she herself is not an abject slave but a free woman, exercising her own comparative independence, at liberty to wander into new realms of thought and covetous of her freedom.[18] The sciences, for example, are entirely free with regard to their own authentic discoveries. Their autonomy is uninhibited and unrestrained, even if necessarily inscribed within the larger narrative of Christian faith. Such is the basis for John Paul's contention that faith and reason offer each other a mutually "purifying critique" as well as for Benedict's assertion at Regensburg of the "mutual enrichment" between biblical faith and (Hellenistic) philosophy.[19]

But it is precisely these confident assertions concerning the autonomy of nature, of philosophy and of the secular estate, that some Christians find disconcerting. Such language appears to mark out an area of reality that is resistant to conversion, or, perhaps to formulate it better, not in need of conversion at all and, therefore, in some way "independent" of the Gospel of grace. The "autonomous order" appears, at least on the surface, to be a competitor to the estate of revelation and faith, a realm that finds the Christian story alien and constraining. Indeed, invoking nature's "autonomy"

---

17 *Fides et ratio*, no. 77.

18 John Paul II draws a further analogy in the same encyclical: "And just as in giving her assent to Gabriel's word, Mary lost nothing of her true humanity and freedom, so too when philosophy heeds the summons of the Gospel's truth its autonomy is in no way impaired. Indeed, it is then that philosophy sees all its enquiries rise to their highest expression." See *Fides et ratio*, no. 108.

19 *Fides et ratio*, no. 100. Benedict XVI, *Regensburg Lecture* (September 12, 2006). An English translation may be found in *Origins* 36 (September 28, 2006): 248–52.

seems to chain rationality to Enlightenment mythology, with reason regarded as a critical and supervisory faculty to which every reality—revelation included—must be subjected.

Equally damaging to the notion of "autonomy" is the widespread philosophical suspicion that any reference to nature and the natural order implies a universal reality that is not only autarchic and neutral, but that is easily accessible by all inquirers. But to speak of a humanity capable of reasoning to the existence of God, to the dictates of the moral law and to the just ordering of secular society bears the unmistakable patina of epistemological naiveté. For human reason is profoundly circumscribed—deeply embedded within determinate cultures, languages, and traditions. The recognition of just such immersion has utterly dethroned the claim that rationality is exercised apart from a world of enveloping historical contingencies. For precisely this reason, one significant chant of the contemporary academy is that "it's interpretation all the way down."[20] This is simply to acknowledge that there exists no unconditioned exercise of reason; "knowing reality" is always a matter of knowing an *already interpreted* reality. As Thomas Kuhn insisted, the idea that one can know "facts" apart from "theories," apart from the prejudices of the theory-laden observer, is simply the tattered, chimerical remnant of a positivist fantasy, a layer-cake approach to reality (hard facts alone, then larger theories) that has no traction in the actual world of deeply conditioned observers.[21]

The danger of speaking of an autonomous natural order, then, is that it seems to buttress the possibility of theory-free ways of knowing. And this, in turn, provides unwitting aid and comfort to the Enlightenment claim that some aspects of reality are clearly known by all, while other assertions (religious ones, in particular) are simply and unabashedly sectarian, faith-based, dogmatic, and ideological. Christians should recognize, therefore, that it is in their interest to redeem reason from the mythology of Enlightenment rationality, to *undermine* the claim that there exists a neutral and

---

20 The *fons et origo* of this oft-repeated claim is Nietzsche's statement: there are no facts, only interpretations—and this, too, is an interpretation. See *The Will to Power*, trans. Walter Kaufmann and R. J. Hollingdale (New York: Random House, 1967), no. 481. Of course, the maxim, "it's interpretation all the way down," can also simply mean that all knowing occurs within determinate socio-cultural circumstances, without necessarily entailing Nietzsche's relativistic conclusions.

21 Kuhn argues this point in his ground-breaking manifesto, *The Structure of Scientific Revolutions* (Chicago: University of Chicago Press, 1970), with later developments outlined in *The Road since Structure*, ed. James Conant and John Haugeland (Chicago: University of Chicago Press, 2000).

autonomous natural order (at least one that is easily discernable). Participatory commitment is intrinsic to understanding; every construal of reality is socially and culturally determined. Acknowledging such embeddedness supports the religion-friendly idea that *all* claims to "rigorous" objectivity are just as contingent and contextualized as the assertions posited by Christian faith. And this, in turn, subverts the primary shibboleth of modernity: Christian and religious beliefs are insular and obscurantist while secular claims are entirely verifiable by unbiased observers. While primarily concerned with epistemological issues, these insights nonetheless call into question the easy invocation of an autonomous natural, created, order since such language seems to perpetuate the dogmas of modernity—naively ignoring the profoundly immersed character of human life and thought.

From an explicitly theological point of view, Karl Barth, the influential Reformed theologian, argued that the Catholic accent on nature—particularly as offering a pathway to God—was, to speak demurely, overblown. Barth's legitimate concern was that assertive and aggressive human nature—indeed, a human nature that insisted precisely on its own autonomy—sought constantly to justify Christianity on its own terms, according to its own standards. But God is known through God alone, through his own Word, his own self-manifestation, not through the fictions and fantasies concocted by an allegedly autonomous humanity. Christian warrants are not answerable to a depraved "nature" but only to the clear command of the Gospel. Indeed, when one looks to nature for knowledge of God, one moves inexorably toward idolatry, toward the antichrist. This, of course, was the root of Barth's polemic, at least in his early days, against the "analogy of being," the claim that there exists an intrinsic relationship between humanity and God on the very basis of creation—of nature—itself. Barth found this concept idolatrous insofar as it jeopardized both the abject fallenness of humanity and the unique biblical locus of revelation. Catholicism's concern with nature appeared to establish an ontological *a priori*, that is, a philosophical starting point outside of faith that, in turn, became determinative of the content of faith.[22]

---

22 I have recounted Barth's arguments against the revelatory character of a comparatively autonomous natural order in *Foundations of Systematic Theology* (New York: T & T Clark, 2005), 218–23. Indications that a more positive account of the natural order is emerging in Protestant thought (despite Barth's claims) may be found, for example, in Stephen J. Grabill, *Rediscovering the Natural Law in Reformed Theological Ethics* (Grand Rapids: Eerdmans Publishing, 2006) and J. Daryl Charles, *Retrieving the Natural Law: A Return to Moral First Things* (Grand Rapids: Eerdmans Publishing, 2008).

Among Barth's Catholic interlocutors was Hans Urs von Balthasar whose deep agreement with—yet concomitant challenge to—Barth's theology was developed in the midst of theological battles waged during the 1940s and 1950s, when the issue of an autonomous human nature and its relationship to the graced estate dominated Catholic theological discussion. Several thinkers, the Jesuit patrologist Henri de Lubac preeminent among them, argued that there slowly developed in Catholic thought, in response to certain sixteenth and seventeenth century controversies, a notion of "human nature" as increasingly independent, to the point that "nature" seemed to be an entirely self-sufficient, self-determined entity. Grace, in this reading, appeared to be only a subsequent "elevation" of a fully formed, preexistent natural reality. Although the issue is not reducible to easy stereotypes, the perilous implication was that nature existed as an autonomous entity distinct unto itself while grace was conceived, so to speak, as a "second-story" on a previously elaborated notion of humanity. At work here was the additive trope which, while legitimately seeking to protect both God's freedom and revelation's gratuity, imagined grace as a final capstone on an *a priori* natural edifice.[23]

It is precisely this image of a bifurcated nature and grace—of a fully autonomous philosophical realm apart from the supernatural order—that certain theologians forcefully challenged. Balthasar, for example, insisted that Catholic theology needed to recover the teaching of the early Church: "The whole patristic tradition, right up to the High Middle Ages—even Thomas himself, for the most part—conceives the issue [the invocation of categories such as "nature" and the *analogia entis*] within the *unicus ordo realis supernaturalis,* and thus within the analogy of faith."[24] In other words, there exists only one order of divine revelation in which all human beings are unalterably embedded; the so-called "natural order" is always deeply participative in the life of grace. To speak of "nature," then, in any context—whether natural law, human nature, a natural pathway to God, or the natural order of secular, public life—is always to invoke the wider and overarching

---

23 See Henri de Lubac, *Surnaturel: Études historiques* (Paris: Aubier, 1946). A salutary warning against simplifying this difficult issue may be found in Ralph McInerny, *Praeambula Fidei* (Washington, DC: The Catholic University of America Press, 2006), especially 69–90.

24 *The Theology of Karl Barth,* 261. As Balthasar says in a slightly earlier (1947) work: "The world, considered as an object of knowledge, is always already embedded in this supernatural sphere, and in the same way man's cognitive powers operate either under the positive sign of faith or under the negative sign of unbelief." See vol. 1 of *Theo-Logic,* trans. Adrian J. Walker (San Francisco: Ignatius Press, 2000), 11, 30.

supernatural sphere. There exists no entity such as pure nature that can be surgically abstracted from the domain of grace. The concrete supernatural estate *commands and transforms* every natural reality, just as the concrete goal or *telos* for actual human nature is always and only the beatific vision of God.[25]

Equally important was the argument marshaled by de Lubac and Balthasar that the theological accent on an autonomous human nature had an unforeseen but deeply pernicious *cultural* effect. After all, if one could posit a fully formed philosophical order entirely at home within its own sphere, then why was it necessary to bother with God at all? Neo-scholasticism, at times, appeared to conceive of nature much as modernity itself, as an entity that was largely self-enclosed and self-sufficient, possessed of an habitual and fully formed autonomy. Was it not the case that neo-scholasticism had imbibed the very presuppositions of modernity, transforming itself into a rationalist *Doppelgänger* in the process? The abstract construct of an independent natural order unwittingly played into secularism's wily hands: revelation could now be construed simply as an unwarranted intrusion on promethean human liberty, illicitly jeopardizing personal freedom by usurping the autonomy of the unrestricted self. The Enlightenment had simply to lop off the additive dimension of revelation and grace in order to defend, cogently and decisively, a completely autonomous, secular person who is able to live without God—*etsi Deus non daretur*—for a divine Being was now understood as a purely private option, an entirely superfluous accoutrement (for those who needed this sort of prosthesis).

In response to this *aporia*, de Lubac and Balthasar drew inspiration not only from early Christian writers (particularly the Greek Fathers) but also from the French *fin de siècle* philosopher, Maurice Blondel, who argued in his great work, *L'Action* (1893), that the human will is always restless and uneasy, never satisfied with limited, finite goals, always actively

---

25 Because of his insistent accent on the one and only supernatural order, Balthasar's response to Barth on the issue of the *analogia entis* remains one of the most theologically incisive dimensions of his work. Balthasar argues convincingly that the metaphysics of causality and participation, on which the analogy of being (and so analogical language) is founded, indefeasibly exists within the estate of grace since creation itself is an entirely gratuitous gift of God. At the same time, Balthasar contends, one need not denigrate the order of creation in order to exalt the order of salvation. There exists a legitimate "philosophical moment," indeed, a certain "autonomy" of the natural sphere, even if this is always inscribed within the one and only domain of grace. As Balthasar says, presumably with Barth in mind, "the intrinsic fullness of philosophical truth—even apart from the theological light that may fall upon it—is much richer than many accounts of it would lead us to suspect." See vol. 1 of *Theo-Logic*, 14.

(if unconsciously) seeking a reality beyond its grasp.[26] In many ways, Blondel's work was a philosophical reprise of St. Augustine's well-known maxim, "You have made us for yourself, O Lord, and our hearts are restless until they rest in you." For Blondel, as for Augustine, to speak of man is to imply God; anthropology arrives at the very threshold of theology. Naively invoking an autonomous human nature is to try to separate realities that are inseparable—as the early Christian tradition bore witness. The Enlightenment notion of men and women as wholly sovereign agents was a failed idea, a truncated and exhausted view of humanity which could not account for the endlessly restless human heart; its anthropology paled in comparison to the robust and powerful Christian notion of the intrinsic and indelible link between God and humanity. Speaking of an autonomous natural order served only to buttress an unsustainable Enlightenment perspective which fatefully traduced the extraordinary depths and singular drama of human existence.

At the same time, Balthasar and de Lubac argued the traditional Catholic point that while always existing within the one estate of God's graciousness, nature is and always must be *relatively* autonomous because it possesses a certain freedom and essence in itself and distinct from God. It would be a serious mistake to impoverish or denigrate the actual autonomy of nature, its stability and internal excellence, precisely because God has graciously established creatures and creation in truth and goodness. One may acknowledge the tangible goodness of creation (which is, ultimately, the recognition of God's own gift) even while asserting that nature itself has no final or absolute claims. For this reason, Balthasar insists, when theology uses a deeply Aristotelian concept such as "nature," it should always be understood as *analogically* valid rather than as univocally so. For any invocation of the natural order ineluctably involves a profound relationship with God, even while maintaining its own created constancy and internal coherence. This intrinsic excellence is never abandoned although nature is, in the final analysis, always a theological concept. Nature exists, then, in the one order of grace—which irradiates and transforms the natural realm—but without annulling its own properties or collapsing it into the supernatural estate.[27] To express this del-

---

26 Maurice Blondel, *Action (1893)*, trans. Oliva Blanchette (Notre Dame: University of Notre Dame Press, 1984).

27 Balthasar expresses this delicate balance well when he says that "philosophy can indeed highlight certain fundamental natural structures of the world and knowledge, because this embedding [in the domain of revelation and grace] does not do away with, or even alter the

icately balanced idea, Balthasar invokes the paradoxical Latin phrase "*aliter,
non alter,*" which is to say that nature is always itself (and so "not other")
even when it has, through the divine gift of grace, become "different" than it
would have been.[28]

In light of these reflections, it is perhaps clearer that when Benedict
XVI speaks of a "healthy secularism" or of a "*laïcité positive,*" he is assuredly
not capitulating to the Enlightenment fantasy of a nakedly secular state
where religion is marginalized from public life, prohibited from making
theologically informed arguments in the *agora.* Nor is he launching a weak
and ineffective counteroffensive waged on enemy terrain—anymore than
John Paul II, when boldly defending philosophy's "legitimate autonomy" is
extolling reason's complete self-sufficiency. Both popes, rather, with the
prior Christian tradition, are seeking to uphold the subtle balance between
the two orders of nature and grace. Nature does indeed have its own essence
and integral identity, at least analogically so. Human reasoning, even apart
from the infused light of Judeo-Christian revelation, can achieve palpable
insight into the true and the good, into the dignity and nobility of human
beings, into the establishment of a just public realm. Because of the relative
autonomy of the created order, the secular state (like other institutions, such
as universities) has its proper and legitimate sphere of competence. All
socio-political-educational institutions need not be explicitly religious in
nature to fulfill their just mission.[29]

Another example in which this comparative autonomy is sanctioned
may be found in Benedict's letter to Chinese Catholics, wherein he invokes

essential core of, such structures." But he immediately adds, "After all, the supernatural takes
root in the deepest structures of being, leavens them [. . .] and permeates them like a breath or
omnipresent fragrance." See vol. 1 of *Theo-Logic,* 11–12. This desire to balance deftly nature and
grace is also displayed in Balthasar's exegesis of Anselm's work, particularly the argument for
God's existence found in the *Proslogion.* Balthasar contends that Anselm's argument has a certain philosophical independence, even while concomitantly insisting that other passages in the
Benedictine's writings make clear that "the full realization of the true philosophical act" is found
only in the theological sphere, the order of revelation and grace. For a discussion of the attempt
by Balthasar (and, with similar intent, Henri Bouillard) to offer an Anselmian via media between
Barthian fideism and neo-scholastic rationalism (and, therefore, between excessive views of
the grace/nature relationship), see Thomas G. Guarino, "Contemporary Lessons from the *Proslogion,*" chapter three of this volume.

28 *The Theology of Karl Barth,* 281.

29 Robert A. Markus has mounted a convincing argument that St. Augustine held for the autonomy of the secular order (as distinct from both the sacred and the profane) not insisting, therefore, that all cultural or political institutions be subject to explicitly religious views. See
Christianity and the Secular (Notre Dame: University of Notre Dame Press, 2006).

Gaudium et spes, "The political community and the Church are autonomous and independent of each other in their own fields. They are both at the service of the personal and social vocation of the same individuals, though under different titles."[30] In the same letter, Benedict makes clear that when the Church teaches, she does not intend to trespass upon the independence that legitimately belongs to the State, the secular space, so to speak, that is essential for the contemporary *polis*: "It [the Church's activity in China] is not, therefore, a question of a political authority, unduly asserting itself in the internal affairs of a State and offending against its sovereignty."[31]

This emphasis on the relative independence of the natural order is also inscribed in Benedict's (abortive) 2008 talk to the faculty and students at La Sapienza, the University of Rome. The pope speaks of the "autonomy which [. . .] has always been part of the nature of universities, which must be tied exclusively to the authority of the truth." Here, the pope invokes Aquinas who "highlighted the autonomy of philosophy, and with it, the laws and the responsibility proper to reason which enquires on the basis of its own dynamic." Benedict then offers an intriguing theological analogy to express the relative independence of the natural (philosophical) order: "I would say that St. Thomas's idea concerning the relationship between philosophy and theology could be expressed in the formula that the Council of Chalcedon adopted for Christology: philosophy and theology must be interrelated 'without confusion and without separation.' [. . .] Philosophy must truly remain a quest conducted by reason with freedom and responsibility; it must recognize its limits, and likewise its grandeur and vastness."[32]

---

30 *Letter to Catholics in the People's Republic of China* (May 27, 2007). An English translation may be found in *Origins* 37 (August 2, 2007): 145–58.

31 *Letter to Catholics*, 153. In an address to the ambassador of the Philippines, Benedict makes a similar point (as he often does with civil authorities) regarding the spheres of nature and grace: "She [the Church] carries out this mission fully aware of the respective autonomy and competence of Church and State. Indeed, we may say that the distinction between religion and politics is a specific achievement of Christianity and one of its fundamental historical and cultural contributions." See *Address to the Ambassador of the Philippines to the Holy See* (October 27, 2008). One suspects that Benedict made this remark with an eye on Islam, which, of course, by conjoining the political, legal, and theological orders, leaves little or no space for a comparatively autonomous secular sphere. As Martin Rhonheimer says, "[. . .] the Islamic tradition has no notion of a purely secular legitimacy and justification of the state, a notion that was never missing in the Christian tradition." See Martin Rhonheimer, "Christian Secularity, Political Ethics, and the Culture of Human Rights," *Josephinum Journal of Theology* 16, no. 2 (2009): 320–38, at 327.

32 Extending Benedict's Chalcedonian analogy, one may add that a significant danger is always to be found in two types of "monophysitism." On the one hand, there is a deeply deformed

Both Benedict's letter to Chinese Catholics and his address to the students and faculty of the University of Rome are recent instances, chosen from among many possible examples, displaying the Church's deep respect for the comparative independence of the created, secular order, an order with its own integrity, stability, and goodness. It is precisely because of this respect that Catholicism staunchly defends natural law, natural virtue, an authentic secularity, and the integrity and liberty of the philosophical and scientific disciplines. This esteem for the natural sphere is also manifest in Benedict's comments about the unique contributions to Catholic theology of Albertus Magnus and Thomas Aquinas. The pope argues that both thinkers defend the actual autonomy of—but also the necessary cooperation between—the estates of faith and reason. Faith protects reason from misunderstanding its own capacities, while simultaneously exposing it to grander, more capacious horizons; reason, for its part, establishes the *praeambula fidei*, offers analogies to clarify truths of faith and helps to defend faith itself against those who register objections to its intelligibility.[33]

---

understanding of nature—with the created, philosophical, secular order regarding itself as wholly complete and entirely sovereign, closing itself, therefore, to the wisdom of religious insights (*laïcité negative*); on the other hand, there is the danger of an overweening theological imperialism which leaves little or no room for the created order's *relative* autonomy, thereby devaluing reason and philosophy. Neither view allows the proper independence, yet essential interrelationship, of the respective spheres. See *Lecture of Benedict XVI at the University of Rome 'La Sapienza'* (January 17, 2008). The text may be found in *Acta apostolicae sedis* 100 (2008), 107–14, at 113. Various protests by students and faculty led to the cancellation of Benedict's visit to the university. The prepared address was subsequently released by the Vatican.

33 Of Albert, Benedict writes that he "contributed to the formation of an autonomous philosophy, distinct from theology and united with it only by the unity of truth." See *General Audience* (March 24, 2010). The pope makes use of Thomas's *De Trinitate* q. 2, a. 3, to explain how reason renders important services to faith. To buttress his argument for reason's significance (including its ability to discern the natural moral law), Benedict also cites the bold statement of Aquinas: "Even if grace is more efficacious than nature, nonetheless, nature itself is more essential for man." (*Summa theologiae*, I-II, q. 94, a. 6 ad 2), (*Gratia etsi sit efficacior quam natura, tamen natura essentialior est homini, et ideo magis permanens*). See *General Audience* (June 16, 2010). In his dialogue with Habermas, Ratzinger strongly accented the interrelationship (but distinction) between the orders of faith and reason. He concludes that reason helps to purify and structure "the *pathologies in religion* that are extremely dangerous." But he insists that there exist "*pathologies of reason*" as well. If these are to be healed, reason needs to stay within its proper limits, "and it must learn a willingness to listen to the great religious traditions of mankind." Failing to do so results in a reason (and a created order generally) that is reckless and destructive. See *Dialectics of Secularization*, 77–78.

A final illustration of the Church's interest in the relative independence of natural order may be found in Benedict's comments inaugurating the "Pauline year" in the Catholic Church (2008–2009). In his first catechesis, the pope reflected on the Apostle's letter to the Philippians:

> When Paul wrote, "Whatever is true, whatever is honorable, whatever is just, whatever is pure, whatever is lovely, whatever is gracious, if there is any excellence, if there is anything worthy of praise, think about these things," he was only taking up a purely humanist concept proper [. . .] to philosophical wisdom."[34]

Benedict adds that in Stoic philosophers such as Seneca and Epictetus "the loftiest values of humanity and wisdom are found which were naturally to be absorbed by Christianity."[35] This is simply to say that natural human wisdom—in its relative autonomy—is good and proper, even if it must ultimately be brought to fruition and completion by the Gospel of grace. This is why the "spoils from Egypt" trope (implicitly invoked by Benedict with his citation of the ancient Stoic thinkers) has been so theologically powerful throughout the entire history of the Catholic Church. There exists a "natural visibility" of the true and the good, even if this must always be ultimately disciplined by the light of revelation.[36]

By endorsing a healthy secularism, then, Benedict is hardly abandoning a full-blooded, thickly Christian approach to human life and thought, retreating into an unseemly pusillanimity in the face of secular modernity's boldness. Nor is he insisting that Christianity must justify its claims before an allegedly neutral and critical rationality. The pope, rather, is defending reason's and nature's inherent capacities, while simultaneously insisting on the essential and necessary openness of this sphere to the purifying and transforming light of revelation.[37]

---

34 Phil. 4:8.

35 *General Audience* (July 2, 2008).

36 I have treated "spoils from Egypt" and related tropes (such as the "comely captive") at length in *Foundations of Systematic Theology*, 269–310.

37 So, in his "La Sapienza Address" of 2008, Benedict extols the Christian faith as a "purifying force for reason." Indeed, if "reason, out of concern for its alleged purity, becomes deaf to the great message of Christian faith and wisdom, then it withers like a tree whose roots can no longer reach the waters that give it life." In *Acta apostolicae sedis* 100 (2008), 114. The inexorable result of such deafness is a positivist, truncated notion of rationality and an unhealthy secularism, a *laïcité négative*. What is at stake here, once again, is the claim that reason's autonomy is

Benedict has been at pains to establish a precise calibration between the realms of nature and grace, between the created order of reason and the gratuitous gift of revelation. *Laïcité* in its negative sense—entailing a societal structure and a positivistic reason that is anti-religious at its core—represents the collapse of grace into (deformed) nature, with the created sphere now closed in upon itself, unhealthily spurning the light and living water of revealed truth. Conversely, those religious societies which have no room for a comparatively autonomous secular space (a *laïcité positive*), devalue the gift of created reason and inexorably proscribe religious freedom, thereby infringing on the domain of nature by ignoring rights to which every human being is entitled. This is why Benedict has assiduously defended the relative autonomy of the secular sphere at every opportunity, simultaneously insisting that this estate is only properly understood when secularity itself is receptive to the wisdom and truth of divine revelation.[38]

Of course, in the last analysis, even with all of its integral excellence, nature, too, must finally come face-to-face with Christ crucified. But Benedict resolutely maintains that belief in the Christian narrative, in the salt and light and power of Jesus Christ, can never be at antipodes with the essential integrity that rightly pertains to the created order. A proper and apposite secularism, indeed, an appropriate understanding of the natural order in all its various dimensions, only becomes fetid and degrading when rationality is reduced to positivism, when anthropology is truncated by scientism, when the secular is rendered opaque to God's action in history. This is, indeed, to become something less than fully human, leading inexorably to a deeply impoverished and wholly erroneous view of both human-

---

only *relative* in kind. It must itself be deeply nourished by faith, allowing its deliberations to open out to the beauty of the world, to the fullness of being, and, ultimately, to the Creator of all that is true and good. As Benedict says elsewhere: "Accordingly, I would speak of a necessary relatedness between reason and faith and between reason and religion, which are called to purify and help one another. They need each other, and they must acknowledge this mutual need." See *Dialectics of Secularization*, 78.

38 In this delicate balance of nature and grace, traditional philosophical analogues may be found in the representative figures of Hegel and Kierkegaard/Barth, with the former representing rationalist and positivist reason deprived of that revealed truth which serves to purify the philosophical order and with the latter deprived of a strong sense of the relative autonomy of the created estate and tending, therefore, towards fideism. It was, of course, one intention of the Regensburg Lecture to warn Islam—while conceding that Christianity, too, has not been entirely untouched by this phenomenon—against a fideism that, precisely because of its radical devaluation of the created order of reason and philosophical insight, courts the danger of irrationality.

ity and society. Properly understood, the created order possesses an authentic beauty, truth, and goodness which must, finally, be perfected, strengthened, and purified by the light of grace and faith.[39]

---

39 As Newman says in his *"Biglietto"* speech: "There is much in the liberalistic theory which is good and true; for example, not to say more, the precepts of justice, truthfulness, sobriety, self-command, benevolence, which, as I have already noted, are among its avowed principles, and the natural laws of society. It is not till we find that this array of principles is intended to supersede, to block out, religion, that we pronounce it to be evil. There never was a device of the Enemy so cleverly framed and with such promise of success." Newman's point, of course, is that, while the natural order has much to commend it, when a despotic *laïcité* becomes closed against transcendence and religious belief, then the natural order becomes unworthy of the autonomy which is properly its own. See *Addresses to Cardinal Newman with his Replies* (1879–1881), ed. W. P. Neville (London: Longmans, Green, and Co., 1905), 61–70, at 68–69.

Bibliography

Adorno, Theodor. *Negative Dialectics*. Translated by E. B. Ashton. New York: Seabury Press, 1973.

Alberigo, Giuseppe. "Formazione, contenuto e fortuna dell'allocuzione *Gaudet Mater Ecclesia*." In *Fede tradizione profezia*, edited by G. Alberigo, et al., 187–222. Brescia: Paideia, 1984.

_____. "Facteurs de 'Laïcité' au Concile Vatican II." *Revue des sciences religieuses* 74, no. 2 (2000): 211–25.

_____. "Fedeltà e creatività nella ricezione del concilio Vaticano II. Criteri ermeneutici." *Cristianesimo nella storia* 21 (2000): 383–402.

Anselm of Canterbury. "*Proslogion.*" In *S. Anselmi Opera Omnia*. Edited by Franciscus Salesius Schmitt. Edinburgh: Thomas Nelson and Sons, 1946.

Aquinas, Thomas. *Summa Theologiae*. Blackfriars edition. Edited by Thomas Gilby, O.P. London: Eyre and Spottiswoode, 1964.

_____. *On the Unity of the Intellect Against the Averroists*. Translated by Beatrice H. Zedler. Milwaukee: Marquette University Press, 1968.

_____. *Summa Contra Gentiles*: Book One, God. Translated by Anton C. Pegis. Notre Dame: University of Notre Dame Press, 1975.

_____. *Faith, Reason and Theology: Questions I–IV of the* De Trinitate *of Boethius*. Translated by Armand Maurer. Toronto: Pontifical Institute of Medieval Studies, 1987.

_____. *De Trinitate in Thomae Aquinatis. Opera omnia*. Vol. 50. Rome-Paris: Commissio Leonina, 1992.

Arthos, John. "Gadamer at the Cumaean Gates." *American Catholic Philosophical Quarterly* 74, no. 2 (2000): 223–48.

Aristotle. *The Basic Works of Aristotle*. Translated by Richard McKeon. New York: Random House, 1941.

Augustine. *The City of God*. Translated by Henry Bettenson. London: Penguin Classics, 1972.

_____. *De doctrina christiana*. Translated by Edmund Hill. Hyde Park: New City Press, 1996.

_____. *Confessions*. Translated by Maria Boulding. Hyde Park: New City Press, 1997.

_____. *Soliloquies*. Translated by Kim Paffenroth. Hyde Park: New City Press, 2000.

Azkoul, Michael. *The Influence of Augustine of Hippo on the Orthodox Church*. Lewiston, ME: The Edwin Mellen Press, 1990.

Balthasar, Hans Urs von. *The Theology of Karl Barth*. Translated by Edward T. Oakes. San Francisco: Ignatius Press, 1992.

_____. "On the Tasks of Catholic Philosophy in Our Time." Translated by Brian McNeil. *Communio: International Catholic Review* 20, no. 1 (1993): 147–87.

_____. *Love Alone Is Credible.* Translated by A. Dru. New York: Herder and Herder, 1969.

_____. *The Glory of the Lord.* Vol. 1, Translated by Erasmo Leiva-Merikakis. San Francisco: Ignatius Press, 1982.

_____. *The Glory of the Lord.* Vol. 2, Translated by Andrew Louth, et al. San Francisco: Ignatius Press, 1984.

_____. *The Glory of the Lord.* Vol. 4, Translated by Brian McNeil, et al. San Francisco: Ignatius Press, 1989.

_____. *Theo-Logic.* Vol. 1. Translated by Adrian J. Walker. San Francisco: Ignatius Press, 2000.

Barth, Karl. *Church Dogmatics* I/1. Translated by G. T. Thomson. Edinburgh: T & T Clark, 1949.

_____. *Church Dogmatics* II/I. Edited by G. W. Bromiley and T. F. Torrance. Edinburgh: T & T Clark, 1957.

_____. *Anselm: Fides Quaerens Intellectum.* Richmond: John Knox Press, 1960.

Basil. "Address to Young People on Reading Greek Literature." In Vol. 4 of *The Letters.* Translated by R. Deferrari and M. McGuire, 379–435. Cambridge, MA: Harvard University Press, 1934.

Bayer, Oswald. "Philipp Melanchthon." *Pro Ecclesia* 18, no. 2 (2009): 134–61.

Benedict XVI. *Christmas Address to the Roman Curia.* December 22, 2005.

_____. *Deus caritas est.* Encyclical Letter. December 25, 2005. *Acta apostolicae sedis* 98 (2006), 217–52. English translation: *Origins* 35 (Feb. 2, 2006), 541–57.

_____. *Regensburg Lecture.* September 12, 2006. English translation *Origins* 36 (September 28, 2006): 248–52.

_____. *Christmas Address to the Roman Curia.* December 22, 2006.

_____. *Letter to Catholics in the People's Republic of China.* May 27, 2007. English translation: *Origins* 37 (August 2, 2007): 145–58.

_____. *Address of His Holiness Benedict XVI to Members of the International Theological Commission.* English translation: *Origins* 37 (November 8, 2007): 352–54.

_____. *Lecture of Benedict XVI at the University of Rome 'La Sapienza.'* January 17, 2008. *Acta apostolicae sedis* 100 (2008), 107–14.

_____. *General Audience.* April 30, 2008.

_____. *General Audience.* July 2, 2008.

_____. *Responses of His Holiness Benedict XVI to the Questions Posed by the US Bishops.* April 16, 2008. *Acta apostolicae sedis* 100 (2008), 314–19.

_____. *Meeting with Authorities of the State.* September 12, 2008. *Origins* 38 (September 25, 2008): 245–47.

_____. *Address to the Ambassador of the Philippines to the Holy See*. October 27, 2008.

_____. *Address of His Holiness Pope Benedict XVI to the Members of the Diplomatic Corps for the Traditional Exchange of New Year Greetings*. January 11, 2010.

_____. *General Audience*. March 24, 2010.

_____. *Address of His Holiness Benedict XVI, Westminster Hall—City of Westminster*. September 17, 2010.

Bernstein, Richard J. *Beyond Objectivism and Relativism: Science, Hermeneutics, and Praxis*. Philadelphia: University of Pennsylvania Press, 1983.

Blondel, Maurice. *Action (1893)*. Translated by Oliva Blanchette. Notre Dame: University of Notre Dame Press, 1984.

Boersma, Hans. *Nouvelle Théologie and Sacramental Ontology: A Return to Mystery*. Oxford: Oxford University Press, 2009.

_____. "Nature and the Supernatural in *la nouvelle théologie*: The Recovery of a Sacramental Mindset." *New Blackfriars* 93, no. 1043 (2012): 34–46.

Boethius. "Letter to John the Deacon." In *The Theological Tractates*. The Loeb Classical Library, translated by H. F. Stewart and E. K. Rand, 2–129. Cambridge, MA: Harvard University Press, 1962.

_____. *The Consolation of Philosophy*. Translated by Richard Green. Indianapolis: Bobbs-Merrill, 1962.

Bonino, Serge-Thomas. "'Nature et grâce' dans l'encyclique *Deus caritas est*." *Revue Thomiste* 105, no. 4 (2005): 531–49.

Bonsor, Jack. "History, Dogma, and Nature: Further Reflections on Postmodernism and Theology." *Theological Studies* 55, no. 2 (1994): 295–313.

_____. *Athens and Jerusalem*. New York: Paulist Press, 1993.

Bouillard, Henri. *Conversion et Grâce chez S. Thomas d'Aquin: Étude Historique*. Paris: Aubier, 1944.

_____. *Karl Barth: Parole de Dieu et Existence Humaine*. 2 vols. Paris: Aubier, 1957.

_____. *Blondel and Christianity*. Translated by James M. Somerville. Washington: Corpus Books, 1969.

Brill, Susan. *Wittgenstein and Critical Theory*. Athens, OH: Ohio University Press, 1995.

Browning, Don S. and Francis Schüssler Fiorenza, eds. *Habermas, Modernity and Public Theology*. Chestnut Ridge, NY: The Crossroad Publishing Company, 1992.

Bryant, David. "Christian Identity and Historical Change: Postliberals and Historicity." *Journal of Religion* 73, no. 1 (1993): 31–41.

Bulgakov, Sergius. *The Holy Grail and the Eucharist*. Translated by Boris Jakim. Hudson, NY: Lindisfarne Books, 1997.

Burr, David. "Petrus Ioannis Olivi and the Philosophers." *Franciscan Studies* 31 (1971): 41–71.

Burrell, David. "Reflections on 'Negative Theology' in the Light of a Recent Venture to Speak of '*God Without Being*.'" In *Postmodernism and Christian Philosophy*, edited by Roman T. Ciapalo, 58–67. Mishawaka, IN: American Maritain Association, 1997.

Campbell, Richard. *Truth and Historicity.* Oxford: Clarendon Press, 1992.

Caputo, John D. *Heidegger and Aquinas: An Essay on Overcoming Metaphysics.* New York: Fordham University Press, 1982.

_____. *Radical Hermeneutics.* Bloomington: Indiana University Press, 1987.

_____. "Gadamer's Closet Essentialism." In *Dialogue and Deconstruction: The Gadamer-Derrida Encounter*, edited by Diane P. Michelfelder and Richard E. Palmer, 258–64. Albany: SUNY Press, 1989.

_____. *Demythologizing Heidegger.* Bloomington: Indiana University Press, 1993.

_____. "Heidegger and Theology." In *The Cambridge Companion to Heidegger*, edited by Charles Guignon, 270–88. Cambridge: Cambridge University Press, 1993.

_____. "The Good News about Alterity: Derrida and Theology." *Faith and Philosophy* 10, no. 4 (1993): 453–70.

_____. "Philosophy and Prophetic Postmodernism: Toward a Catholic Postmodernity." *American Catholic Philosophical Quarterly* 74, no. 4 (2000): 549–67.

_____. *On Religion.* New York: Routledge, 2001.

_____. *Philosophy and Theology.* Nashville: Abingdon, 2006.

Caputo, John D. and Gianni Vattimo. *Radical Hermeneutics.* Bloomington: Indiana University Press, 1987.

_____. *After the Death of God.* Edited by Jeffrey W. Robbins. New York: Columbia University Press, 2007.

Caputo, John D. and Michael Scanlon, eds. *God, the Gift and Postmodernism.* Bloomington: Indiana University Press, 1999.

Carabine, Deirdre. "*Apophasis* East and West." *Recherches de théologie ancienne et médiévale.* 55 (1988): 5–29.

Charles, J. Daryl. *Retrieving the Natural Law: A Return to Moral First Things.* Grand Rapids: Eerdmans Publishing, 2008.

Chenu, Marie-Dominique. *Le Saulchoir: Une école de théologie.* Kain-Lez-Tournai: Le Saulchoir, 1937. Reprint Paris: Cerf, 1985.

Clement. *Stromateis.* In *The Ante-Nicene Fathers.* Vol. 2, edited by Alexander Roberts and James Donaldson. Grand Rapids: Eerdmans Publishing, 1956.

Congar, Yves. *Divided Christendom.* London: Centenary, 1939.

_____. *Tradition and Traditions.* Translated by Michael Naseby and Thomas Rainborough. New York: MacMillan Publishers, 1967.

_____. *Situation et tâches présentes de la théologie.* Paris: Cerf, 1967.

_____. *A History of Theology.* Translated by Hunter Guthrie. Garden City, NY: Doubleday, 1968.

_____. *After Nine Hundred Years*. Westport, CT: Greenwood Press, 1978.

_____. *Diversity and Communion*. Translated by John Bowden. Mystic, CT: Twenty-Third Publications, 1985.

Congregation for the Doctrine of the Faith. *Mysterium ecclesiae*. Declaration. June 24, 1973.

Conway, Gertrude. *Wittgenstein on Foundations*. Atlantic Highlands, NJ: Humanities Press, 1989.

Corbin, Michel. *Prière et raison de la foi: Introduction à l'oeuvre de saint Anselme de Cantorbéry*. Paris: Cerf, 1992.

Cunningham, Lawrence, ed. *Intractable Disputes about the Natural Law*. Notre Dame: University of Notre Dame Press, 2009.

Daley, Brian. "The *Nouvelle Théologie* and the Patristic Revival: Sources, Symbols and the Science of Theology." *International Journal of Systematic Theology* 7, no. 4 (2005): 362–82.

Dallmyer, Fred. *Between Freiburg and Frankfurt: Toward a Critical Ontology*. Amherst: University of Massachusetts Press, 1991.

Daniélou, Jean. "Les orientations preésentes de la pensée religieuse." *Études* 79 (1946): 5–21. Translated into English as "The Present Orientations of Religious Thought." *Josephinum Journal of Theology* 18, no. 1 (2011): 51–62.

Dartigues, André. "À propos de la vérité philosophique. En echo à encyclique *Fides et Ratio*." *Bulletin de littérature ecclésiastique* 101, no. 1 (2000): 15–36.

Da Todi, Jacopone. *Sons of Francis*. Translated by Anne MacDonell. London: J.M. Dent and Co., 1902.

Davies, Brian and Brian Leftow, eds. *The Cambridge Companion to Anselm*. Cambridge: Cambridge University Press, 2004.

Dawkins, Richard. *The God Delusion*. New York: Houghton Mifflin, 2006.

de Lubac, Henri. *Surnaturel: Études historiques*. Paris: Aubier, 1946.

_____. *The Drama of Atheist Humanism*. Translated by E. Riley. London: Sheed and Ward, 1949.

_____. *Catholicism*. Translated by L. Sheppard. New York: Longmans, Green, and Co., 1950.

_____. "A propos de la formule: *Diversi, sed non adversi*." *Recherches de science religieuse* 40 (1952): 27–40.

_____. *The Motherhood of the Church*. Translated by Sr. Sergia Englund. San Francisco: Ignatius Press, 1982.

_____. *A Brief Catechesis on Nature and Grace*. Translated by R. Arnandez. San Francisco: Ignatius Press, 1984.

_____. *A Theologian Speaks*. Los Angeles: Twin Circle Publishing, 1985.

Denifle, H., ed. *Chartularium Universitatis Parisiensis*. Vol. 1, Paris: Delalain, 1899.

Denzinger, Heinrich. *Enchiridion symbolorum*. 37th ed. Edited by Heinrich Denzinger and Peter Hünermann. Freiburg im Breisgau: Herder, 1991.

Derrida, Jacques. *Of Grammatology*. Translated by G. Chakravorty. Baltimore: Johns Hopkins University Press, 1976.

———. *Writing and Difference*. Translated by Alan Bass. Chicago: University of Chicago Press, 1978.

———. *Positions*. Translated by Alan Bass. Chicago: University of Chicago Press, 1981.

———. *The Post Card: From Socrates to Freud and Beyond*. Translated by Alan Bass. Chicago: University of Chicago Press, 1987.

———. "How to Avoid Speaking: Denials." In *Languages of the Unsayable: The Play of Negativity in Literature and Literary Theory*, edited by S. Budick and W. Iser, 3–70. New York: Columbia University Press, 1989.

Diggins, John Patrick. *The Promise of Pragmatism*. Chicago: University of Chicago Press, 1994.

Dilthey, Wilhelm. *Introduction to the Human Sciences*. Translated by Ramon J. Betanzos. Detroit: Wayne State University Press, 1988.

Dragseth, Jennifer Hockenbery, ed. *The Devil's Whore: Reason and Philosophy in the Lutheran Tradition*. Minneapolis: Fortress, 2011.

Dulles, Avery. *The Craft of Theology*. Chestnut Ridge, NY: The Crossroad Publishing Company, 1992.

———. *The Assurance of Things Hoped For*. Oxford: Oxford University Press, 1994.

———. "Can Philosophy Be Christian?" *First Things* 102 (April 2000): 24–29.

———. *Newman*. London: Continuum, 2002.

———. *Church and Society*. New York: Fordham University Press, 2008.

Dunne, Joseph. *Back to the Rough Ground: "Phronesis" and "Techne" in Modern Philosophy and in Aristotle*. Notre Dame: University of Notre Dame Press, 1993.

Dupré, Louis. *Passage to Modernity: An Essay in the Hermeneutics of Nature and Culture*. New Haven: Yale University Press, 1993.

———. "Postmodernity or Late Modernity?" *Review of Metaphysics* 47, no. 2 (1993): 277–95.

———. *Religious Mystery and Rational Reflection*. Grand Rapids: Eerdmans Publishing, 1998.

Eagleton, Terry. *The Ideology of the Aesthetic*. Cambridge, MA: Blackwell, 1990.

Elshtain, Jean Bethke. "Augustine and Diversity." In *A Catholic Modernity? Charles Taylor's Marianist Award Lecture and Four Responses*, edited by James Heft, 95–104. Oxford: Oxford University Press, 1999.

Florovsky, Georges. *The Collected Works of Georges Florovsky*. Vol. 1, Belmont, MA: Nordland, 1972.

Flogaus, Reinhard. "Inspiration-Exploitation-Distortion: The Use of St. Augustine in the Hesychast Controversy." In *Orthodox Readings of Augustine*, edited by George E. Demacopoulos and Aristotle Papanikolaou, 63–80. Crestwood, NY: St. Vladimir's Seminary Press, 2008.

Floucat, Yves. "L'être de Dieu et l'onto-théo-logie." *Revue thomiste* 95, no. 3 (1995): 437–84.

Fiorenza, Francis Schüssler. "Systematic Theology: Task and Methods." In Vol. 1 of *Systematic Theology: Roman Catholic Perspectives*, edited by F. S. Fiorenza and John P. Galvin, 1–88. Minneapolis: Fortress, 1991.

_____. "Introduction: A Critical Reception for Practical Public Theology." In *Habermas, Modernity and Public Theology*, edited by Browning and Fiorenza, 1–17. Chestnut Ridge, NY: The Crossroad Publishing Company, 1992.

_____. "The Church as a Community of Interpretation." In *Habermas, Modernity and Public Theology*, edited by Browning and Fiorenza, 19–42. Chestnut Ridge, NY: The Crossroad Publishing Company, 1992.

Francis. *Fratelli tutti.* Encyclical Letter. October 3, 2020.

Frank, G. L. C. "The Incomprehensibility of God in the Theological Orations of St. Gregory the Theologian." *Greek Orthodox Theological Review* 39 (1994): 95–107.

Gadamer, Hans-Georg. *Truth and Method.* Translated and edited by Garrett Barden and John Cumming. New York: Seabury Press, 1975.

_____. "Correspondence concerning *Wahrheit und Methode.*" *Independent Journal of Philosophy* 2 (1978): 5–12.

_____. *Truth and Method*, 2nd rev. ed. Translated by Joel Weinsheimer and Donald G. Marshall. New York: Continuum, 1993.

_____. *Heidegger's Ways.* Translated by John Stanley. Albany: State University of New York Press, 1994.

Galvin, John. "Fides et Ratio." *The Downside Review* 118, no. 410 (2000): 1–16.

Gavrilyuk, Paul L. *The Suffering of the Impassible God.* Oxford: Oxford University Press, 2004.

_____. "The Reception of Dionysius in Twentieth Century Eastern Orthodoxy." *Modern Theology* 24, no. 4 (2008): 707–23.

Geiselmann, Josef R. *Die lebendige Überlieferung als Norm des christlichen Glaubens.* Freiburg: Herder, 1959.

Gill, James. *The Council of Florence.* Cambridge: Cambridge University Press, 1959.

Gilson, Etienne. *Reason and Revelation in the Middle Ages.* New York: Charles Scribner's Sons, 1938.

Goetz, Ronald. "The Suffering God: The Rise of a New Orthodoxy." *Christian Century* 103, no. 13 (1986): 385–89.

Grabill, Stephen J. *Rediscovering the Natural Law in Reformed Theological Ethics.* Grand Rapids: Eerdmans Publishing, 2006.

Greco, Joseph. "Foundationalism and Philosophy of Religion." In *Philosophy of Religion*, edited by Brian Davies, 34–41. Washington, DC: Georgetown University Press, 1998.

Guarino, Thomas G. "Between Foundationalism and Nihilism: Is *Phronēsis* the *Via Media* for Theology?" *Theological Studies* 54, no. 1 (1993): 37–54.

_____. *Revelation and Truth: Unity and Plurality in Contemporary Theology*. Scranton: University of Scranton Press, 1993.

_____. "Vincent of Lérins and the Hermeneutical Question." *Gregorianum* 75, no. 3 (1994): 491–523.

_____. "Spoils from Egypt: Contemporary Theology and Nonfoundationalist Thought." *Laval théologique et philosophique* 51, no. 3 (1995): 573–87.

_____. "Vatican I and Dogmatic *Apophasis*." *Irish Theological Quarterly* 61, no. 1 (1995): 70–82.

_____. "*Fides et Ratio*: Theology and Contemporary Pluralism." *Theological Studies* 62, no. 4 (2001): 675–700.

_____. "Postmodernity and Five Fundamental Theological Issues." *Theological Studies* 57, no. 4 (2001): 654–89.

_____. "Rosmini, Ratzinger, and Kuhn: Observations on a Note by the Doctrinal Congregation." *Theological Studies* 64, no. 1 (2003): 43–68.

_____. *Foundations of Systematic Theology*. New York: T & T Clark, 2005.

_____. "'Spoils from Egypt:' Yesterday and Today." *Pro Ecclesia* 15, no. 4 (2006): 403–17.

_____. "The God of Philosophy and of the Bible: Theological Reflections on Regensburg." *Logos: A Journal of Catholic Thought and Culture* 10, no. 4 (2007): 120–30.

_____. "Contemporary Lessons from the *Proslogion*," *Nova et Vetera* English edition 7, no. 1 (2009): 125–52

_____. *Vattimo and Theology*. New York: T & T Clark, 2009.

_____. "Nature and Grace: Seeking the Delicate Balance." *Josephinum Journal of Theology* 18, no. 1 (2011): 151–62.

_____. "The Return of Religion in Europe? The Postmodern Christianity of Gianni Vattimo," *Logos: A Journal of Catholic Thought and Culture* 14, no. 2 (2011): 15–36.

_____. "*Philosophia Obscurans*? Six Theses on the Proper Relationship between Theology and Philosophy," *Nova et Vetera* English edition 12, no. 2 (2014): 349–94.

_____. "Vattimo, Diversity and Catholicism." In *Justice Through Diversity?*, edited by Michael J. Sweeney, 533–50. Lanham, MD: Rowman and Littlefield, 2016.

_____. *The Disputed Teachings of Vatican II: Continuity and Reversal in Catholic Doctrine*. Eerdmans Publishing, 2018.

Gunton, Colin. *Act and Being*. London: SCM Press, 2002.

Habermas, Jürgen. *Postmetaphysical Thinking*. Translated by William Mark Hohengarten. Cambridge, MA: The MIT Press, 1992.

_____. "Transcendence from Within, Transcendence in this World." In *Habermas, Modernity, and Public Theology*, edited by Browning and Fiorenza, 226–50. Chestnut Ridge, NY: The Crossroad Publishing Company, 1992.

Hadot, Pierre. *Philosophy as a Way of Life*. Translated by Michael Chase. Oxford: Blackwell, 1995.

Harnack, Adolf von. *History of Dogma*. Vols. 1–4. Translated by Neil Buchanan. Boston: Little, Brown and Company, 1898. Reprint. New York: Russell and Russell, 1958.

_____. *What is Christianity?* Translated by Thomas Bailey Saunders. Gloucester, MA: Peter Smith Publisher, 1978.

_____. "Erik Peterson's Correspondence with Adolf von Harnack." Translated by Michael J. Hollerich. *Pro Ecclesia* 2, no. 3 (1993): 333–44.

Haslanger, Sally. "Feminism in Metaphysics: Negotiating the Natural." In *The Cambridge Companion to Feminism in Philosophy*, edited by Miranda Fricker and Jennifer Hornsby, 107–26. Cambridge: Cambridge University Press, 2000.

Hauerwas, Stanley. *With the Grain of the Universe*. Grand Rapids: Brazos, 2001.

_____. "Connections Created and Contingent." In *Grammar and Grace: Reformulations of Aquinas and Wittgenstein*, edited by Jeffrey Stout and Robert MacSwain, 75–102. London: SCM Press, 2004.

_____. *Performing the Faith*. Grand Rapids: Brazos, 2004.

Hebblethwaithe, Brian. "God and Truth." *Kerygma und Dogma* 40, no. 1 (1994): 2–19.

Heidegger, Martin. *Being and Time*. Translated by John Macquarrie and Edward Robinson. New York: Harper and Row, 1962.

_____. *Identity and Difference*. Translated by Joan Stambaugh. New York: Harper and Row, 1969.

_____. *The Piety of Thinking*. Translated by J. Hart and J. Maraldo. Bloomington: Indiana University Press, 1976.

_____. *Heidegger et la question de Dieu*. Edited by Richard Kearney and Joseph S. O'Leary. Paris: Bernard Grasset, 1980.

_____. *Basic Writings*. Edited by David Farrell Krell. San Francisco: HarperCollins, 1993.

_____. "Overcoming Metaphysics." In *The Heidegger Controversy: A Critical Reader*, edited by Richard Wolin, 67–90. Cambridge, MA: The MIT Press, 1993.

_____. *Pathmarks*. Edited by William McNeill. Cambridge: Cambridge University Press, 1998.

_____. *The Phenomenology of Religious Life*. Translated by Matthias Fritsch and Jennifer Anna Gosetti-Ferencei. Bloomington: Indiana University Press, 2004.

Hennessy, Kristin. "An Answer to de Régnon's Accusers: Why We Should Not Speak of 'His' Paradigm." *Harvard Theological Review* 100, no. 2 (2007): 179–97.

Henrici, Peter. "The One Who Went Unnamed: Maurice Blondel in the Encyclical *Fides et Ratio*." *Communio: International Catholic Review* 26, no. 3 (1999): 609–21.

Hill, William. *Knowing the Unknown God*. New York: Philosophical Library, 1971.

_____. *The Three-Personed God.* Washington, DC: The Catholic University of America Press, 1982.

Hitchens, Christopher. *God is Not Great.* New York: Twelve, 2007.

Hodgson, Peter E. "Galileo the Theologian." *Logos: A Journal of Catholic Thought and Culture* 8, no. 1 (2005): 28–51.

International Theological Commission. *In Search of a Universal Ethic: A New Look at the Natural Law.* 2009.

_____. *On the Interpretation of Dogmas.* October 1989. English translation: *Origins* 20 (May 17, 1990): 1–14.

Jenson, Robert. *Unbaptized God.* Minneapolis: Fortress, 1992.

John of Damascus. *On the Divine Images.* Translated by David Anderson. Crestwood, NY: St. Vladimir's Seminary Press, 1980.

John Paul II. "Letter to George V. Coyne, S.J., Director of the Vatican Observatory." *Acta Apostoliciae Sedis* 81 (1989): 274–83.

_____. *Address to the Participants in the Plenary Session of the Pontifical Academy of Sciences.* October 31, 1992. English translation: "Lessons of the Galileo Case." *Origins* 22 (November 12, 1992): 371–73.

_____. *Veritatis splendor.* Encyclical Letter. August 6, 1993. *Acta apostolicae sedis* 85 (1993), 1133–1228. English translation: *Origins* 23 (Oct. 14, 1993), 297–334.

_____. *Evangelium vitae.* Encyclical Letter. March 25, 1995. *Acta apostolicae sedis* 87 (1995), 401–522. English translation: *Origins* 24 (April 6, 1995): 689–727.

_____. *Ut unum sint.* Encyclical Letter. May 25, 1995. *Acta Apostolicae Sedis* 87 (1995), 921–982. English translation: Origins 25, no. 4 (June 8, 1995): 49–72.

_____. *Fides et ratio.* Encyclical Letter. September 14, 1998. *Acta apostolicae sedis* 91 (1999), 5–88. English translation: *Origins* 28 (October 22, 1998): 317–47.

Johnson, Elizabeth A. *She Who Is: The Mystery of God in Feminist Theological Discourse.* Chestnut Ridge, NY: The Crossroad Publishing Company, 1992.

Jüngel, Eberhard. *God as Mystery of the World.* Translated by Darrell L. Guder. Grand Rapids: Eerdmans Publishing, 1983.

Junker-Kenny, Maureen. *Habermas and Theology.* New York: T & T Clark, 2011.

Juntunen, Sammeli, "Christ." In *Engaging Luther,* edited by Olli-Pekka Vainio, 59–79. Eugene, OR: Wipf and Stock Publishers, 2010.

Kallenberg, Brad J. "Praying for Understanding: Reading Anselm through Wittgenstein." *Modern Theology* 20, no. 4 (2004): 527–46.

Kaufman, Gordon. *In the Face of Mystery.* Cambridge, MA: Harvard University Press, 1993.

Kasper, Walter. *Theology and Church.* Translated by Margaret Kohl. Chestnut Ridge, NY: The Crossroad Publishing Company, 1989.

_____. "Unité ecclesiale et communion ecclésiale dans une perspective catholique." *Revue des sciences religieuses* 75, no. 1 (2001): 6–22.

Kerr, Fergus. "Thomas Aquinas: Conflicting Interpretations in Recent Anglophone Literature." In *Aquinas as Authority,* edited by Paul van Geest, et al., 165–86. Leuven: Peeters, 2002.

Kirwan, Michael. *Discovering Girard.* Cambridge, MA: Cowley Publications, 2005.

Klenicki, Leon. "Se il rabbino commenta l'enciclica." *Studi Cattolici* 44 (October 2000): 660–72.

Kuhn, J. E. *Einleitung in die katholische Dogmatik.* 2 vols. Tubingen: 1846–1847.

Kuhn, Thomas. "The Function of Dogma in Scientific Research." In *Scientific Change,* edited by A.C. Crombie, 347–69. New York: Basic Books, 1963.

_____. *The Structure of Scientific Revolutions.* 2nd ed. Chicago: University of Chicago Press, 1970.

_____. *The Road since Structure.* Edited by James Conant and John Haugeland. Chicago: University of Chicago Press, 2000.

Lakeland, Paul. *Theology and Critical Theory: The Discourse of the Church.* Nashville: Abingdon, 1990.

Langford, Jerome. *Galileo, Science and the Church.* 3rd ed. Ann Arbor: University of Michigan Press, 1992.

Lafont, Ghislain. *Histoire théologique de l'Église catholique.* Paris: Les Éditions du Cerf, 1994.

Lamb, Matthew. "Praxis communicationnelle et théologie par-delà le nihilisme et le dogmatisme." In *Habermas et la théologie,* edited by Edmund Arens, translated by D. Trierweiler, 123–56. Paris: Les Éditions du Cerf, 1993.

Levering, Matthew. *Biblical Natural Law.* Oxford: Oxford University Press, 2008.

Lindbeck, George A. *The Nature of Doctrine.* Philadelphia: The Westminster Press, 1984.

Lints, Richard. "The Postpositivist Choice: Tracy or Lindbeck?" *Journal of the American Academy of Religion* 61, no. 4 (1993): 655–77.

Lonergan, Bernard. *Method in Theology.* London: Darton, Longman and Todd, 1971.

_____. *Doctrinal Pluralism.* Milwaukee: Marquette University Press, 1971.

_____. "The Dehellenization of Dogma." In *A Second Collection.* Edited by William Ryan and Bernard Tyrrell, 11–32. Philadelphia: The Westminster Press, 1974.

_____. *Insight: A Study of Human Understanding.* Edited by Frederick E. Crowe and Robert M. Doran, 117–34. Collected Works of Bernard Lonergan 3. Toronto: University of Toronto Press, 1992.

_____. "Natural Knowledge of God." In *A Second Collection,* edited by William F. J. Ryan and Bernard J. Tyrrell, 117–34. Toronto: University of Toronto Press, 1996.

Long, D. Stephen. *Speaking of God: Theology, Language, and Truth.* Grand Rapids: Eerdmans Publishing, 2009.

Lowe, Walter. *Theology and Difference: The Wound of Reason.* Bloomington: Indiana University Press, 1993.

Luther, Martin. *Luther's Works.* Edited by Jaroslav Pelikan and Helmut T. Lehmann. St. Louis: Concordia Publishing House, 1955–1986.

Lutheran World Federation and the Catholic Church. *Joint Declaration on the Doctrine of Justification.* 1997. English translation: *Origins* 28, no. 8 (July 16, 1998): 120–27.

Lyon, David. *Postmodernity.* Minneapolis: University of Minnesota Press, 1994.

MacIntyre, Alasdair. *God, Philosophy, Universities: A Selective History of the Catholic Philosophical Tradition.* New York: Sheed and Ward: 2009.

Marion, Jean-Luc. *God Without Being.* Translated by Thomas Carlson. Chicago: University of Chicago Press, 1991.

_____. "Saint Thomas d'Aquin et l'onto-théologie." *Revue Thomiste* 95, no. 1 (1995): 31–66.

_____. "Metaphysics and Phenomenology: A Summary for Theologians." In *The Postmodern God,* edited by Graham Ward, 279–96. Oxford: Blackwell Publishers, 1997.

_____. *Prolegomena to Charity.* Translated by Stephen E. Lewis. New York: Fordham University Press, 2002.

Maritain, Jacques. *An Essay on Christian Philosophy.* Translated by Edward H. Flannery. New York: Philosophical Library, 1955.

Markus, Robert A. *Christianity and the Secular.* Notre Dame: University of Notre Dame Press, 2006.

Marsh, James, John Caputo, and Merold Westphal, eds. *Modernity and Its Discontents.* New York: Fordham University Press, 1992.

Marshall, Bruce D. *Trinity and Truth.* Cambridge: Cambridge University Press, 2000.

_____. "In Search of an Analytic Aquinas." *Grammar and Grace,* edited by Stout and MacSwain, 55–74. 2004.

McCool, Gerald. *Catholic Theology in the Nineteenth Century.* New York: Seabury Press, 1977.

_____. *From Unity to Pluralism: The Internal Evolution of Thomism.* New York: Fordham University Press, 1989.

McGrath, Alister. *The Genesis of Doctrine.* Oxford: Blackwell Publishers, 1990.

McInerny, Ralph. *Aquinas on Human Action.* Washington, DC: The Catholic University of America Press, 1992.

_____. *Praeambula Fidei.* Washington, DC: The Catholic University of America Press, 2006.

Meijering, E. P. *Melanchthon and Patristic Thought.* Leiden: Brill, 1983.

Melanchthon, Philip. *Loci Communes Theologici. 1521.* In *Melanchthon and Bucer,* edited by Wilhelm Pauck, 18–119. Philadelphia: The Westminster Press, 1969.

Merrill, Clark A. "Leo Strauss's Indictment of Christian Philosophy." *The Review of Politics* 62, no. 1 (2000): 77–105.

Meyer, William. "Private Faith or Public Religion? An Assessment of Habermas's Changing View of Religion." *Journal of Religion* 75, no. 3 (1995): 371–91.

Milbank, John. *Theology and Social Theory*. Oxford: Blackwell, 1990.

_____. "The Theological Critique of Philosophy in Hamann and Jacobi." In *Radical Orthodoxy*, edited by John Milbank, Catherine Pickstock, and Graham Ward, 21–37. London: Routledge, 1999.

Newman, John Henry. *An Essay on the Development of Christian Doctrine*. London: Longmans, Green, and Co., 1894.

_____. *Apologia Pro Vita Sua*. London: Longmans, Green, and Co., 1895.

_____. *The Via Media of the Anglican Church*. Vol. 1, 3rd ed. London: Longmans, Green, and Co., 1901.

_____. *Addresses to Cardinal Newman with his Replies* (1879–1881). Edited by W. P. Neville. London: Longmans, Green, and Co., 1905.

Nichols, Aidan. "Thomism and the *Nouvelle Théologie*." *The Thomist* 64, no. 1 (2000): 1–19.

Nicolas, J. H. "La suprême logique de l'amour et la théologie." *Revue thomiste* 83 (1983): 639–59.

Nietzsche, Friedrich. *The Will to Power*. Translated by Walter Kaufmann and R. J. Hollingdale. New York: Random House, 1967.

_____. *Human, All Too Human*. Translated by R. J. Hollingdale. Cambridge: Cambridge University Press, 1986.

_____. *Twilight of the Idols*. Translated by R. J. Hollingdale. London: Penguin, 1990.

Origen. "Letter to Gregory." In *The Ante-Nicene Fathers*. Vol. 4, edited by Alexander Roberts and James Donaldson. Grand Rapids: Eerdmans Publishing, 1956.

O'Rourke, Fran. *Pseudo-Dionysius and the Metaphysics of Aquinas*. Leiden: Brill, 1992.

Pannenberg, Wolfhart. *Systematic Theology*. Vol. 1, translated by Geoffrey W. Bromiley. Grand Rapids: Eerdmans Publishing, 1988.

_____. "Christianity and the West: Ambiguous Past, Uncertain Future." *First Things* 48 (December 1994): 18–23.

Pascal, Blaise. *Pensées*. Paris: Charpentier, 1861.

_____. *Pensées*. Translated by W. F. Trotter. Mineola, NY: Dover Publications, 2003.

PCCU. "The Greek and Latin Traditions regarding the Procession of the Holy Spirit." *Information Service* 89 (1995): 88–92.

Peddicord, Richard. *The Sacred Monster of Thomism*. South Bend, IN: St. Augustine's Press, 2005.

Pelikan, Jaroslav. *Christianity and Classical Culture*. New Haven: Yale University Press, 1993.

Peukert, Helmut. "Enlightenment and Theology as Unfinished Projects." In *Habermas, Modernity and Public Theology*, edited by Browning and Fiorenza, 43–65. Chestnut Ridge, NY: The Crossroad Publishing Company, 1992.

Phan, Peter. "*Fides et Ratio* and Asian Philosophies." *Science et esprit* 51, no. 3 (1999): 333–49.

Piché, David and Claude LaFleur. *La condemnation parisienne de 1277.* Paris: Vrin, 1999.

Pius X. *Pascendi dominici gregis.* Encyclical Letter. September 8, 1907.

Pius XII. *Humani generis.* Encyclical Letter. August 12, 1950.

Placher, William. *Unapologetic Theology.* Louisville: Westminster/John Knox Press, 1989.

Plantinga, Alvin. *The Analytic Theist: An Alvin Plantinga Reader.* Edited by James F. Sennett. Grand Rapids: Eerdmans Publishing, 1998.

_____. "Faith and Reason." *Books and Culture* 5 (July/August 1999): 32–35.

_____. *Where the Conflict Really Lies.* Oxford: Oxford University Press, 2011.

Plato. *The Dialogues of Plato,* trans. B. Jowett, vol. 1. New York: Random House, 1920.

Pottmeyer, Hermann. *Der Glaube vor dem Anspruch der Wissenschaft.* Freiburg: Herder, 1968.

Powell, Samuel M. *The Trinity in German Thought.* Cambridge: Cambridge University Press, 2001.

Preller, Victor. "Water into Wine." In *Grammar and Grace,* edited by Jeffrey Stout and Robert MacSwain, 253–69. London: SCM Press, 2004.

Rahner, Karl. "*Mysterium Ecclesiae.*" In *Theological Investigations.* Vol. 17. Translated by Margaret Kohl, 139–55. Chestnut Ridge, NY: The Crossroad Publishing Company, 1981.

_____. "Yesterday's History of Dogma and Theology for Tomorrow." In *Theological Investigations.* Vol. 18. Translated by Edward Quinn, 3–34. Chestnut Ridge, NY: The Crossroad Publishing Company, 1983.

_____. *I Remember.* Translated by Harvey D. Egan. Chestnut Ridge, NY: The Crossroad Publishing Company, 1985.

_____. *Karl Rahner in Dialogue.* Edited and translated by Harvey D. Egan. Chestnut Ridge, NY: The Crossroad Publishing Company, 1986.

_____. "Theology and the Roman Magisterium." In *Theological Investigations.* Vol 22. Translated by J. Donceel. Chestnut Ridge, NY: The Crossroad Publishing Company, 1991.

_____. "Experiences of a Catholic Theologian." Translated by Gesa Elsbeth Thiessen. *Theological Studies* 61, no. 1 (2000): 3–15.

Ramshaw, Gail. *God Beyond Gender: Feminist Christian God-Language.* Minneapolis: Fortress, 1995.

Ranieri, John. *Disturbing Revelation: Leo Strauss, Eric Voegelin, and the Bible.* Columbia: University of Missouri Press, 2009.

Ratzinger, Joseph. *Introduction to Christianity.* Translated by J. R. Foster. London: Search Press, 1969.

_____. *Principles of Catholic Theology.* Translated by Mary Frances McCarthy. San Francisco: Ignatius Press, 1987.

_____. *Eschatology*. Translated by Michael Waldstein. Washington, DC: The Catholic University of America Press, 1988.

_____. *Theological Highlights of Vatican II*. Translated by Henry Traub, Gerard C. Thormann, and Werner Barzel. Mahwah, NJ: Paulist Press, 2009.

Ratzinger, Joseph and Jürgen Habermas. *The Dialectics of Secularization: On Reason and Religion*. Translated by Brian McNeil. San Francisco: Ignatius Press, 2006.

Reeve, C. D. C. *Practices of Reason: Aristotle's Nicomachean Ethics*. Oxford: Clarendon, 1992.

Régnon, Théodore de. *Etudes de théologie positive sur la Sainte Trinité*. Paris: Victor Retaux, 1892–1896.

Rhonheimer, Martin. "The Moral Significance of Pre-Rational Nature in Aquinas." In *The Perspective of the Acting Person*, edited by William F. Murphy, 129–57. Washington, DC: The Catholic University of America Press, 2008.

_____. "Christian Secularity, Political Ethics, and the Culture of Human Rights." *Josephinum Journal of Theology* 16, no. 2 (2009): 320–38.

Riordan, Patrick. "Natural Law Revivals: A Review of the Recent Literature." *Heythrop Journal* 51, no. 2 (2010): 314–23.

Rist, John. *Augustine: Ancient Thought Baptized*. Cambridge: Cambridge University Press, 1994.

Rocca, Gregory P. "The Distinction between the *Res Significata* and *Modus Significandi* in Aquinas's Theological Epistemology." *The Thomist* 55, no. 2 (1991): 173–97.

_____. "Aquinas on God-Talk: Hovering over the Abyss." *Theological Studies* 54, no. 4 (1993): 641–61.

Rockmore, Tom and Beth J. Singer, eds. *Antifoundationalism Old and New*. Philadelphia: Temple University Press, 1992.

Rorem, Paul. "Martin Luther's Christocentric Critique of Pseudo-Dionysian Spirituality." *Lutheran Quarterly* 11, no. 3 (1997): 291–307.

_____. "Negative Theologies and the Cross." *Harvard Theological Review* 101, no. 3 (2008): 451–64.

Rorty, Richard. *Philosophy and the Mirror of Nature*. Princeton: Princeton University Press, 1979.

_____. "Heideggerianism and Leftist Politics." In *Weakening Philosophy: Essays in Honour of Gianni Vattimo*, edited by Santiago Zabala, 149–58. Montreal: McGill-Queens University Press, 2007.

Rorty, Richard and Gianni Vattimo. *The Future of Religion*. Edited by Santiago Zabala. New York: Columbia University Press, 2005.

Rosen, Stanley. *Hermeneutics as Politics*. Oxford: Oxford University Press, 1987.

Sauter, Gerhard. *What Dare We Hope? Reconsidering Eschatology*. Harrisburg: Trinity Press, 1999.

Sciglitano, Anthony. "Prometheus and Kant: Neutralizing Theological Discourse and Doxology." *Modern Theology* 25, no. 3 (2009): 387–414.

Silvestre, Hubert. *"Diversi sed non adversi."* *Recherches de théologie ancienne et médiévale* 31 (1964): 124–32.

Simon, Yves. *The Tradition of Natural Law.* New York: Fordham University Press, 1965.

_____. *Practical Knowledge.* New York: Fordham University Press, 1991.

Sokolowski, Robert. "Knowing Essentials." *The Review of Metaphysics* 47, no. 4 (1994): 691–709.

_____. *Introduction to Phenomenology.* Cambridge: Cambridge University Press, 2000.

_____. "What is Natural Law? Human Purposes and Natural Ends." *The Thomist* 68, no.4 (2004): 507–29.

Spiegelberg, Herbert. *The Phenomenological Movement.* Vol. 1. The Hague: Martinus Nijhoff, 1969.

Strauss, Leo and Hans-Georg Gadamer. "Correspondence concerning *Wahrheit und Methode.*" *Independent Journal of Philosophy* 2 (1978): 5–12.

Stump, Eleonore. "Aquinas on the Foundations of Knowledge." *Canadian Journal of Philosophy* 17, Supplement (1992): 125–58.

Taminiaux, Jacques. *Heidegger and the Project of Fundamental Ontology.* Translated and edited by M. Gendre. Albany: SUNY Press, 1991.

Tatian. *Oratio ad Graecos.* Edited and translated by Molly Whittaker. Oxford: Clarendon, 1982.

Taylor, Charles. "Engaged Agency and Background in Heidegger." In *The Cambridge Companion to Heidegger,* edited by Charles B. Guignon, 317–36. Cambridge: Cambridge University Press, 1993.

Tertullian. *The Prescription against Heretics.* In *The Ante-Nicene Fathers.* Vol. 3, edited by Alexander Roberts and James Donaldson. Grand Rapids: Eerdmans Publishing, 1957.

Thiel, John. *Nonfoundationalism.* Minneapolis: Fortress, 1994.

_____. "Perspectives on Tradition." *Proceedings of the Catholic Theological Society of America* 54 (1999): 1–18.

Thiemann, Ronald. *Revelation and Theology.* Notre Dame: University of Notre Dame Press, 1985.

Thundy, Z. P. "Sources of *Spoliatio Aegyptiorum.*" *Annuale mediaevale* 21 (1981): 77–90.

Tillich, Paul. *Christianity and the Encounter of the World Religions.* New York: Columbia University Press, 1963.

Tracy, David. *The Analogical Imagination.* Chestnut Ridge, NY: The Crossroad Publishing Company, 1981.

_____. *Plurality and Ambiguity: Hermeneutics, Religion, Hope.* San Francisco: Harper and Row, 1987.

_____. *Dialogue with the Other.* Grand Rapids: Eerdmans Publishing, 1990.

_____. *On Naming the Present*. Maryknoll, NY: Orbis Books, 1994.

_____. "Evil, Suffering, Hope: The Search for New Forms of Contemporary Theodicy." *Proceedings of the Catholic Theological Society of America* 50 (1995): 15–36.

Triplett, Timm. "Recent Work on Foundationalism." *American Philosophical Quarterly* 27, no. 2 (1990): 93–116.

Tocqueville, Alexis de. *Journeys to England and Ireland*. Translated by G. Lawrence and K. P. Mayer. London: Faber and Faber, 1957.

Turner, Denys. *Faith, Reason, and the Existence of God*. Cambridge: Cambridge University Press, 2004.

US Lutheran-Roman Catholic Dialogue. *The Hope of Eternal Life*. Minneapolis: Lutheran University Press, 2011.

Vatican Council I. *Dei filius*. Dogmatic Constitution. April 24, 1870.

Vatican Council II. *Lumen gentium*. November 21, 1964.

_____. *Unitatis redintegratio*. November 21, 1964.

_____. *Dei verbum*. November 18, 1965.

_____. *Ad gentes*. December 7, 1965.

_____. *Dignitatis humanae*. December 7, 1965.

_____. *Gaudium et spes*. December 7, 1965.

Vattimo, Gianni. *Il pensiero debole*. Edited by Pier Aldo Rovatti and Gianni Vattimo. Milano: Feltrinelli, 1983.

_____. "Dialectics, Difference, and Weak Thought." *Graduate Faculty Philosophy Journal* 10, no. 1 (1984): 151–64.

_____. *Beyond Interpretation: The Meaning of Hermeneutics for Philosophy*. Translated by David Webb. Stanford: Stanford University Press, 1997.

_____. *Belief*. Translated by Luca D'Isanto and David Webb. Stanford: Stanford University Press, 1999.

_____. *After Christianity*. Translated by Luca D'Isanto. New York: Columbia University Press, 2002.

_____. *Nihilism and Emancipation: Ethics, Politics, and Law*. Edited by Santiago Zabala. Translated by William McCuaig. New York: Columbia University Press, 2004.

_____. *Dialogue with Nietzsche*. Translated by William McCuaig. New York: Columbia University Press, 2006.

_____. "A 'Dictatorship of Relativism'?" Translated by Robert Valgenti. *Common Knowledge* 13, no. 2 (2007): 214–18.

_____. "Toward a Nonreligious Christianity." In *After the Death of God*, by John Caputo and Gianni Vattimo, edited by Jeffrey W. Robbins, 27–46. New York: Columbia University Press, 2007.

_____. *Weakening Philosophy: Essays in Honour of Gianni Vattimo*. Edited by Santiago Zabala. Montreal: McGill-Queens University Press, 2007.

_____. *A Farewell to Truth*. Translated by William McCuaig. New York: Columbia University Press, 2011.

Vattimo, Gianni and René Girard. *Verità o fede debole?: Dialogo su cristianesimo e relativismo*. Massa: Transeuropa, 2006.

Virgoulay, R. "Dieu ou l'Être." *Recherches de science religieuse* 72, no. 2 (1984): 163–98.

Wachterhauser, Brice, ed. *Hermeneutics and Truth*. Evanston, IL: Northwestern University Press, 1994.

_____. "Getting It Right: Relativism, Realism, and Truth." In *The Cambridge Companion to Gadamer*, edited by Robert J. Dostal, 52–78. Cambridge: Cambridge University Press, 2002.

Wainwright, Geoffrey. *Is the Reformation Over?* Milwaukee: Marquette University Press, 2000.

Webster, John. "*Fides et Ratio*: Articles 64–79." *New Blackfriars* 81, no. 948 (2000): 68–76.

Weinandy, Thomas. *Does God Suffer?* Notre Dame: University of Notre Dame Press, 2000.

_____. "*Fides et Ratio*: A Response to John Webster." *New Blackfriars* 81, no. 951 (2000): 225–35.

Wellmer, Albrecht. *The Persistence of Modernity*. Translated by David Midgley. Cambridge, MA: The MIT Press, 1991.

Westphal, Merold. "Overcoming Onto-theology." In *God, the Gift, and Postmodernism*, edited by John Caputo and Michael Scanlon, 146–69. Bloomington: Indiana University Press, 1999.

_____. "Postmodernism and the Gospel: Onto-theology, Metanarratives, and Perspectivism." *Perspectives: A Journal of Reformed Thought* 15, no. 4 (2000): 6–10.

Wicks, Jared. *Investigating Vatican II*. Washington, DC: The Catholic University of America Press, 2018.

Williams, Anna N. *The Architecture of Theology*. Oxford: Oxford University Press, 2011.

Wippel, John. *Metaphysical Themes in Thomas Aquinas*. Washington, DC: The Catholic University of America Press, 1984.

_____. *Mediaeval Reactions to the Encounter between Faith and Reason*. Milwaukee: Marquette University Press, 1995.

_____. *Metaphysical Themes in Thomas Aquinas II*. Washington, DC: The Catholic University of America Press, 2007.

Yannaras, Christos. "Orthodoxy and the West." *Eastern Churches Review* 111, no. 3 (1971).

_____. *On the Absence and Unknowability of God*. Translated by Haralambos Ventis. London: T & T Clark, 2005.

_____. *Orthodoxy and the West*. Translated by Peter Chamberas and Norman Russell. Brookline, MA: Holy Cross Orthodox Press, 2006.

Yong, Amos. "What Evangelicals Can Learn from C. S. Peirce." *Christian Scholar's Review* 29, no. 3 (2000): 563–88.

Zabala, Santiago. *The Remains of Being*. New York: Columbia University Press, 2009.

Index

Absalon of Saint-Victor, 22

Academy of Athens, 21

Adorno, Theodore, 132, 137, 144n33, 166n76

Aeterni Patris, 47, 73, 81, 86n83, 90, 148

Alberigo, Giuseppe, 89

Albertus Magnus, 225

analogy: *analogia entis*, 3–4, 16, 27, 119, 157n58, 219, 220; Balthasar on, 222–23; Lateran IV statement on, 71n20, 159, 198, 203; predication of names to God, 3, 16, 156, 160

Anaximander, 6

Anselm: appeals to universal human rationality, 107–16, 118–19, 124; and experiential knowing, 104–9, 112–13, 119, 124–28; intends to persuade nonbelievers, 4, 98, 110; Kallenberg's critique of, 104–8; model for contemporary theology, 126–28; and relative autonomy of reason, 98–99, 109, 111, 115–16, 123–24

apophaticism: of Aquinas, 85n80, 158–59; in magisterial documents, 159; and postmodern theory of language, 155–61; of Pseudo-Dionysius, 25; of Vatican I, 68, 83, 159

Aquinas: accused of relying on philosophy alone, 28n32, 31; on analogy, 160, 220; apophaticism of, 85n80, 158–60; on being, 75–76; critique of Radical Aristotelianism, 14, 43–44, 123n53; *Fides et ratio* on, 71, 73–74, 81; and limitations of neo-scholasticism, 36, 48; on nature and grace, 214, 220; and philosophical pluralism, 51, 191; on relative autonomy of philosophy, 14, 43–44, 123n52, 224–25; on theology's use of philosophy, 13, 19–20, 34, 38, 204; on unity of faith and reason, 23, 68, 200; use of pagan philosophy, 35, 40, 43; on words used to express doctrine, 50

Aristotle and Aristotelian philosophy: *adaequatio rei et intellectus*, 84–85; conceptions of God, 13, 27; cosmology, 62; criticized by Luther and Melanchthon, 22, 24–26, 205; and doctrine of justification, 92, 207; and doctrine of the soul, 28–29, 204; and doctrine of the Trinity, 33; and doctrine of transubstantiation, 28–29, 48, 158; and modern scientific developments, 61–62; and neo-scholasticism, 36, 48; on practical and theoretical reason, 8, 140–41; on priority of truth over friendship, 184; Radical Aristotelianism, 14, 43–44, 106, 121, 123n53; used by Aquinas, 35, 40, 43; Western and Eastern receptions of, 29n37, 30. *See also* Aquinas; Hellenization thesis; neo-scholasticism

atheism, 181–82

Augustine: Azkoul's criticism of, 29; interest in interiority, 6, 53; on the "restless heart," 195, 222; on theology's use of philosophy, 33, 37, 69; use of Hellenistic philosophy, 23, 29, 33

autonomy. *See* relative autonomy of the natural order

Azkoul, Michael, 29

Balthasar, Hans Urs von: on Anselm's ontological argument, 98, 109n20, 112n29; on Catholicism's assimilation of new philosophies, 13, 35, 39; criticism of Aquinas, 31; dialogue with Barth on nature and grace, 3–4, 119–21, 157n58, 220–23; on Luther's critique of philosophy, 25n20; on Maréchal, 86n83; on relative autonomy of the natural order, 46, 120–21

Barth, Karl: critique of Anselm's ontological argument, 4, 98, 106n13, 115n36; fideism of, 3–4, 26–27, 130, 157n58; on nature and grace, 3–4, 119–20, 219–20; rejects "being" philosophy, 3, 13, 27, 31, 75, 119, 157n58, 219